Procedures and Policies of the

New York State Labor Relations Board

CORNELL STUDIES IN INDUSTRIAL
AND LABOR RELATIONS: *VOLUME XII*

*Cornell Studies in Industrial and Labor Relations are research
monographs developed by faculty and staff at
the New York State School of Industrial and Labor Relations.*

IN THIS SERIES

PUBLISHED BY

THE NEW YORK STATE SCHOOL OF
INDUSTRIAL AND LABOR RELATIONS

A Contract College of the State University · Cornell University, Ithaca, New York

PROCEDURES *and* POLICIES

OF THE

NEW YORK STATE LABOR

RELATIONS BOARD

By KURT L. HANSLOWE

Professor of Industrial and Labor
Relations and Professor of Law

CORNELL UNIVERSITY

Ithaca, New York

Preface

THIS volume was prepared because of the New York State Labor Relations Board's importance to many of the state's employers, employees, and unions, and because of the scarcity of work on state administrative tribunals. For many of New York's administrative agencies, Commissioner Robert M. Benjamin's exhaustive 1942 Report, *Administrative Adjudication in the State of New York* still represents the most intensive treatment.[1] The present book is mainly designed to bring the portion of Volume V of that Report, dealing with the Labor Relations Board, up to date, and also to highlight the more important substantive policies which the Board has evolved over the years. The hope is that this may prove useful for the practitioner and may also be of some interest to the student of public administration and administrative law.

Thus, the volume is intended to provide a systematic guide to the Board's procedures, as well as a somewhat more general survey of the substantive policies thus administered. The method used in its preparation was to start from Volume V of the Benjamin Report, especially on procedural matters, and to utilize the Board's decisions and annual analyses of decisions as the starting point on questions of substance. A grant from the Walter E. Meyer Research Institute of Law made possible visits to the offices of the Board for observation and discussion. These helped greatly to assure accuracy of description of the Board's *modus operandi*. The debt owed to Robert M. Benjamin and to his staff for their path-breaking earlier work is, in any event, enormous. It is difficult to undertake study of problems of public administration and administrative law in New York State, or indeed on a wider scale, without retracing many of their pioneering steps. Accordingly, it was

[1] A notable exception is Gellhorn and Lauer, "Administration of the New York Workmen's Compensation Law," 37 N.Y.U.L.Rev. 3, 204, 564 (1962).

discovered that many of their observations still hold true, despite numerous changes in detail. This is reflected in the fact that, especially in the procedural chapters of this book, much of the basic outline of their Report is adhered to.

An inordinate number of persons have helped to bring this exceedingly modest venture to its conclusion. They are so large in number that the author has a picture of himself as the recalcitrant ass, being dragged over the finish line by a horde of struggling minions. Among the latter are Richard Marks and George Rankey, research assistants, Theodora Bergen and Charlotte Gold, research associates, and Ronald Levine, student at the Cornell Law School. My thanks are due the members and staff of the Board, who bore up patiently under repeated professorial visitation. I am especially grateful to Board Chairman Jay Kramer for his generously cooperative attitude. He and Board General Counsel Philip Feldblum and Board Executive Secretary A. M. Goldberg were most helpful in reading and commenting on the study.

My thanks go to Miss Catherine Howard and to the Mrs. Marilyn Hickok and Joyce Martin who typed various versions and portions of the manuscript; also to Professor Leonard Adams, Director of Research and Publications at the New York State School of Industrial and Labor Relations, for providing research assistance. I am indebted also to Miss Frances Eagan of the School's editorial staff for polishing style and form. And I wish to thank my friend and colleague, Professor Donald E. Cullen, Acting Director of Research and Publications, whose deft editorial touch much improved this volume (thereby delaying its completion by several months). All of these people are responsible for whatever utility this volume may have. For its faults I am, of course, responsible.

Appreciation is also due the publishers of the *Labor Law Journal* and of the *New York University Law Review* for permission to use some passages appearing in articles of mine published there.

I can report, in conclusion, that I did *not* make my wife do any proofreading. I am grateful to her, however, for the reassuring confidence with which she received reports on progress of the book while being much preoccupied with interests and activities of her own.

Kurt L. Hanslowe

Ithaca, N. Y.
February 1964

vi

Contents

→ CHAPTER I ←

The New York State
Labor Relations Act

ON MAY 3, 1937, Governor Herbert H. Lehman sent a special message to the New York State Legislature urging the enactment of the Doyle-Newstein bill, so as to afford encouragement and protection of collective bargaining at the state level similar to that afforded by the National Labor Relations Act of 1935 (Wagner Act). Influenced by the decisions of the Supreme Court of the United States of April 12, 1937 in *Jones & Laughlin* and companion cases (upholding the constitutionality of the Wagner Act), the legislature passed the bill, and it was signed by Governor Lehman on May 20, 1937. The New York State Labor Relations Act went into effect on that day.

Section 700 of the act states in part:

When some employers deny the right of employees to full freedom of association and organization, and refuse to recognize the practice and procedure of collective bargaining, their actions lead to strikes, lockouts and other forms of industrial strife and unrest which are inimical to the public safety and welfare, and frequently endanger the public health.[1]

The act went on to declare that it was the public policy of the State of New York:

...to encourage the practice and procedure of collective bargaining and to protect the exercise by workers of full freedom of association, self-organization, and designation of representatives of their own choos-

[1]Labor Law §700. This paragraph was amended, L. 1940, c. 689, §1, eff. April 20, 1940, but there was no change in its substance. See L. 1937, c. 443, §1.

1

ing for the purposes of collective bargaining, or other mutual aid and protection, free from the interference, restraint or coercion of their employers.[2]

These purposes were to be implemented by methods substantially similar to those utilized in the Wagner Act. Thus, the state statute established an administrative agency in the form of the New York State Labor Relations Board and empowered it to resolve questions concerning the representation of employees by labor organizations and to prevent the commission of specified unfair labor practices on the part of employers. The procedures used in discharging these functions are described in subsequent chapters. In this chapter the substantive unfair labor practice provisions of the state act are summarized and a comparison is made with experience under the federal statute (both prior to, and following, the Taft-Hartley amendments of 1947).

Unfair Labor Practices

Section 704 of the state act lists the following activities which are declared to be unfair employer practices:

(1) To spy upon or keep under surveillance, whether directly or through agents or any other person, any activities of employees or their representatives in the exercise of the rights guaranteed by section seven hundred three.[3]

This unfair labor practice is illustrated in *Matter of Wags Transportation System, Inc.*[4] In this case three of the employer's management personnel were observed on two different occasions standing in front of the union meeting hall watching the entrance. The Board found that this activity was for the purpose of ascertaining the identities of employees associated with the union. The

---

[2]Labor Law §700.

[3]Section 703 provides: "Employees shall have the right of self-organization, to form, join, or assist labor organizations, to bargain collectively through representatives of their own choosing, and to engage in concerted activities, for the purpose of collective bargaining or other mutual aid or protection, free from interference, restraint, or coercion of employers, but nothing contained in this article shall be interpreted to prohibit employees from exercising the right to confer with their employer at any time, provided that during such conference there is no attempt by the employer, directly or indirectly, to interfere with, restrain or coerce employees in the exercise of the rights guaranteed by this section."

[4]Wags Transp. Sys., Inc., 16 S.L.R.B. 398 (1953).

Board ordered the employer to cease and desist from engaging in such surveillance.

(2) To prepare, maintain, distribute or circulate any blacklist of individuals for the purpose of preventing any of such individuals from obtaining or retaining employment because of the exercise by such individuals of any of the rights guaranteed by section seven hundred three.

There have been very few cases involving this unfair labor practice.

(3) To dominate or interfere with the formation, existence, or administration of any employee organization or association, agency or plan which exists in whole or in part for the purpose of dealing with employers concerning terms or conditions of employment, labor disputes or grievances, or to contribute financial or other support to any such organization, by any means, including but not limited to the following: (a) by participating or assisting in, supervising, controlling or dominating (1) the initiation or creation of any such employee organization or association, agency, or plan, or (2) the meetings, management, operation, elections, formulation or amendment of constitution, rules or policies, of any such employee organization or association, agency or plan; (b) by urging the employees to join any such employee organization or association, agency or plan for the purpose of encouraging membership in the same; (c) by compensating any employee or individual for services performed in behalf of any such employee organization or association, agency or plan, or by donating free services, equipment, materials, office or meeting space or anything else of value for the use of any such employee organization or association, agency or plan; provided that, an employer shall not be prohibited from permitting employees to confer with him during working hours without loss of time or pay.

This unfair labor practice refers, of course, to company unionism. An illustration is to be found in the case of *Magee Fuel Oils*.[5] In this case an association was formed and operated by the employer and the employees working under his direction. Its real purpose was to prevent employees from joining a legitimate labor union. After its initial organization, the association became defunct. The Board found that:

[5]Gerard H. Magee, dba Magee Fuel Oils, 19 S.L.R.B. 258 (1956).

3

...the Association was formed at the suggestion, with the participation, and under the control of Respondent and his representatives. It had, and has, no real existence of its own. It was established clearly, on this record, for the purpose of precluding legitimate organization by the employees and thus enabling Respondent to sit on both sides of the bargaining table simultaneously.[6]

As a remedy, the employer was directed to cease and desist from dominating or interfering with any employee association organized for the purpose of collective bargaining. Affirmatively, the employer was directed to withdraw recognition from the association as the collective bargaining representative of any of his employees.

(4) To require an employee or one seeking employment, as a condition of employment, to join any company union or to refrain from forming, or joining or assisting a labor organization of his own choosing.

(5) To encourage membership in any company union or discourage membership in any labor organization, by discrimination in regard to hire or tenure or in any term or condition of employment: Provided that nothing in this article shall preclude an employer from making an agreement with a labor organization requiring as a condition of employment membership therein, if such labor organization is the representative of employees as provided in section seven hundred five.

(Sections 4 and 5 are dealt with jointly because an unlawful discharge or refusal to reinstate ordinarily involves conduct prohibited by both of these sections.)

The position of the Board on discriminatory discharges—one of the most frequent violations of Sections 4 and 5—is illustrated in the case of *Siegel*.[7] In his Intermediate Report on a complaint of discriminatory discharge, the Trial Examiner stated that:

The Board has repeatedly made the point that the law permits the discharge of an employee for good or bad reasons or for no reason at all. But the law does not permit the discharge of an employee because he has joined a union.[8]

The comments of the Trial Examiner in this case reflect a Board policy of long standing. In cases of alleged discriminatory

[6]*Id.* at 270.
[7]Jacob Siegel, 21 S.L.R.B. 339 (1958). See also Max Katz, 21 S.L.R.B. 182 (1958). The principle was declared in Stork Club v. Boland, 282 N.Y. 256, 270, 26 N.E. 2d 247, 251 (1940).
[8]*Id.* at 346.

4

discharges, the Board is *not* concerned with whether or not the discharges are for "sufficient cause," such as excessive absenteeism. The sole concern of the Board is whether the discharges are for union activity or membership. Regardless of whether or not the discharges are justifiable by some other standard, if the Board finds that the discharges are not motivated by an intention to discriminate because of union activity or to discourage membership in a labor organization, the Board will dismiss the complaint.[9]

The second most frequent violation of Sections 4 and 5 is the refusal to reinstate strikers. The position of the Board on this matter is illustrated by the case of *Carlson Truck Service, Inc.*[10] In this case four employees picketed their employer in protest over the discriminatory discharges of three other employees. When these four employees sought to return to work, they were refused reinstatement on the grounds that they had quit their employment. The Board ordered reinstatement, holding that:

The right of employees to engage in a lawful strike is specifically preserved by the Act. . . .[11] Discrimination against employees for engaging in lawful concerted activities is an unfair labor practice within the meaning of Section 704, subdivisions 4 and 5 of the Act. . . .

Of course, an employer, itself guilty of no unfair labor practices, does not lose the right to protect and continue its business. Prior to a request for reinstatement, it may fill the positions left vacant by the striking employees with permanent replacements. . . . Here, however, we have found that the strike was not economic, but was caused by Respondent's unfair labor practices in unlawfully discharging [three employees], and in interfering with the rights of its employees. Under such circumstances, Respondent was under an affirmative duty to reinstate the strikers upon request, discharging, if necessary, any replacements hired during the strike.[12]

The affirmative remedy which the Board ordinarily orders the employer to take in cases of Sections 4 and 5 violations is reinstatement with or without back pay.[13]

(6) To refuse to bargain collectively with the representatives of employees, subject to the provision of section seven hundred five.

[9]See Celia Cambi, dba New Garden Theatre, 13 S.L.R.B. 242 (1950).
[10]Carlson Truck Service, Inc., 20 S.L.R.B. 41 (1957).
[11]See §§701 (3)(8); 703; 713.   [12]20 S.L.R.B. at 55.
[13]See Abe Spigner, dba Spigner & Sons Structural Steel Co., 15 S.L.R.B. 152 (1952).

The reference to Section 705 means that the union must be the exclusive bargaining representative of a majority of employees in an appropriate unit. In the case of *Sanford Box Repair Corp.*,[14] there was a question as to whether or not the union actually represented a majority of the employees. The Board pointed out that:

...in an unfair labor practice proceeding alleging a refusal to bargain, where no election by secret ballot has been conducted or Board certification otherwise issued, the proof of a Union's majority status must be clear.[15]

Furthermore, in the case of *Stanton & Ouderkirk, Inc.*,[16] the Board noted that where there is a question of representation in a refusal to bargain case, the Board has the authority and the obligation to settle that question of representation in conjunction with the unfair labor practice proceeding.

A frequent defense which the Board encounters in refusal to bargain cases is that the union no longer represents a majority of the employees. The two most common forms of loss of majority representation are loss after certification and loss as a result of unfair labor practices. The Board has established a policy to deal with both situations.

Board policy in regard to loss of majority representation after certification is illustrated in *Johnstown Milk Co.*[17] In this case, the Board had certified the union on January 28, 1954. On February 27th of the same year, some of the employees withdrew from the union. The employer concluded that, after February 27th, the union no longer represented a majority of the employees, and there was no longer an obligation to bargain with the union. The Board rejected this contention, holding that:

This letter [of withdrawal], however, did not terminate the Union's status as certified bargaining representative, or relieve Respondent of its obligation of dealing only with the Union which the Board had but recently certified on January 28, 1954, after an election by secret ballot, as the exclusive bargaining representative of the employees in the appropriate unit. One of the primary purposes of the Act is to stabilize

---

[14]Sanford Box Repair Corp., 21 S.L.R.B. 407 (1958).
[15]*Id.* at 410.
[16]Stanton & Ouderkirk, Inc., 19 S.L.R.B. 589 (1956).
[17]Johnstown Milk Co., 17 S.L.R.B. 634 (1954).

industrial relations. Hence, a bargaining relationship, once established, must be endowed with a longevity sufficient to accomplish its essential purpose.... The Act does not countenance employees to change bargaining representatives for any reason at any moment.[18]

The Board's position in this matter illustrates a point which is discussed in greater detail in Chapter VI: Once the Board certifies a union as the collective bargaining representative for a majority of employees in an appropriate unit, that certification remains in effect for at least one year, barring unusual or extraordinary circumstances. Change of mind with respect to the designated collective bargaining representative does not constitute such unusual or extraordinary circumstances. Furthermore, it is for the Board to decide, not the employer, when a union no longer represents a majority of the employees.

The policy of the Board in regard to loss of majority representation resulting from unfair labor practices is illustrated by *Moulders Motors, Inc.*[19] In this case the employer interfered with the rights of his employees and encouraged their withdrawal from the union. The Board rejected the employer's contention that he no longer had an obligation to deal with the union, holding that:

The Respondent cannot be permitted to successfully contend, in such circumstances, that the Union is disestablished as the bargaining representative of the employees who had previously, of their own free will, so designated the Union. To do so would permit the Respondent to profit by the results of its own wrongdoing.[20]

The remedial order in a refusal to bargain case ordinarily takes the form of a Board order directing the employer to cease and desist from refusing to bargain, and an affirmative order directing the employer to bargain with the union at the latter's request.

(7) To refuse to discuss grievances with representatives of employees, subject to the provisions of section seven hundred five.

The policy followed by the Board in a Section 704(7) violation is similar to the policy followed in a refusal to bargain case. In *Buffalo Cadet Cleaners Corporation,*[21] the employers refused to

---

[18]*Id.* at 639; Metropolitan Life Insurance Co. v. S.L.R.B., 280 N.Y. 194, 206, 20 N.E. 2d 390, 394 (1939).

[19]Moulders Motors, Inc., 21 S.L.R.B. 12 (1958).

[20]*Id.* at 24.

[21]Buffalo Cadet Cleaners Corp., 21 S.L.R.B. 444 (1958).

7

discuss layoffs and other matters with the union. The Board ordered the employers to cease and desist from refusing to discuss grievances and, affirmatively, to discuss grievances with the union upon request. The Board held that:

The Act mandates discussion of grievances. This contemplates and requires more than an employer's flat statement that he will not do anything about the matter. As with collective bargaining, the Act requires that the employer not only meet and talk with the Union, but that there be an endeavor in good faith to arrive at a mutually agreeable adjustment of the grievances.[22]

(8) To discharge or otherwise discriminate against an employee because he has signed or filed any affidavit, petition or complaint or given any information or testimony under this article.

This section is designed to protect employees against reprisals from their employers because of testimony or information given to the Board or its agents. The remedial orders issued by the Board in Section 704(8) proceedings are the same as those issued in 704(4) and (5) violations.[23]

(9) To distribute or circulate any black list of individuals exercising any right created or confirmed by this article or of members of a labor organization, or to inform any person of the exercise by any individual of such right, or of the membership of any individual in a labor organization for the purpose of preventing individuals so blacklisted or so named from obtaining or retaining employment.

(10) To do any acts, other than those already enumerated in this section, which interfere with, restrain or coerce employees in the exercise of the rights guaranteed by section seven hundred three.

This section quite obviously covers a multitude of sins. Among the employer activities prohibited by this section are the following:

(a) Coercive questioning of employees about their union membership or activities.[24]

(b) Threatening reprisals or offering inducements to employees.[25]

---

[22]*Id.* at 451.

[23]See William T. & George W. Mayer, dba Mayer's Parkway Restaurant, 17 S.L.R.B. 472 (1954).

[24]See Charlotte & Rudy Von DerWerth, dba Rudy's Pastry Shop, 17 S.L.R.B. 91 (1954).

[25]See William T. & George W. Mayer, dba Mayer's Parkway Restaurant, 17 S.L.R.B. 472 (1954).

8

(c) Signing contracts with non-representative unions.[26]

(d) Encouraging membership in a particular union.[27]

(e) Circulating anti-union petitions.[28]

In deciding whether a particular action is in violation of Section 704(10), the Board has continued to adhere to its 1941 *Columbia Valet* doctrine:[29] an act which violates another subdivision of Section 704 does not in and of itself constitute a violation of Section 704(10).

Some Comparisons with the National Act

We may begin our comparison of the State and National Labor Relations Acts by looking at the wording of Section 1 of the National Act. That section states in part that:

It is hereby declared to be the policy of the United States to eliminate the causes of certain substantial obstructions to the free flow of commerce and to mitigate and eliminate these obstructions when they have occurred by encouraging the practice and procedure of collective bargaining and by protecting the exercise by workers of full freedom of association, self organization, and designation of representatives of their own choosing, for the purpose of negotiating the terms and conditions of their employment or other mutual aid or protection.[30]

It will be noted by comparing Section 700 of the New York State Act and Section 1 of the National Labor Relations Act that the "Little Wagner Act" of New York was modeled rather closely after the original National Act. Indeed, closer examination shows that the substantive and procedural provisions of the two statutes were substantially similar in basic content.[31] There also were and are, however, significant differences, and these differences, of course, have become even more marked following the 1947 (Taft-Hartley) amendments and the 1959 (Landrum-Griffin) amendments of the National Labor Relations Act. Outlined below are the most important similar and dissimilar features.

[26]See Gerard H. Magee, dba Magee Fuel Oils, 19 S.L.R.B. 258 (1956).

[27]See Michael Sadallah, dba Towne House, 21 S.L.R.B. 466 (1958).

[28]See Moulders Motors, Inc., 21 S.L.R.B. 12 (1958).

[29]Columbia Valet Serv. Inc., 4 S.L.R.B. 512 (1941).

[30]29 U.S.C.A. §151. This portion of §1 remained unchanged.

[31]The similarity has been recognized by the New York Court of Appeals. Davega-City Radio, Inc. v. S.L.R.B., 281 N.Y. 13, 22, 22 N.E. 2d 145, 147 (1939); S.L.R.B. v. Holland Laundry, Inc., 294 N.Y. 480, 63 N.E. 2d 68 (1945).

Unfair Labor Practices. Both the New York Act and the National Labor Relations Act (prior to, as well as following, its amendment) list certain types of employer conduct which are considered to be unfair labor practices. The National Labor Relations Act contains five such unfair labor practices whereas, as we have seen, the New York Act contains ten. Furthermore, the unfair-labor practices listed in the New York Act, which have been described previously, are considerably more explicit and clearly defined than those listed in the National Act. The really significant difference between the New York Act and the National Labor Relations Act is, however, that the 1947 and 1959 amendments of the latter added, in Section 8(b), a list of certain labor union activities which are prohibited, such as coercion of employees, the closed shop, certain secondary boycotts, recognition picketing, and so forth. The New York State Act contains no such list of prohibited union activities. The activities prohibited by the New York Act are limited to employer conduct. It should be noted, however, that even though the New York State Act contains no parallel to Section 8(b) of the National Act, many of the activities prohibited by Section 8(b) are controlled in New York State by the courts. For example, assuming state jurisdiction, strikes for unlawful objectives and secondary boycotts may be enjoined by the New York courts. The significance of this circumstance is considered in Chapter IX, where proposals to amend the New York Act are evaluated.

Craft Units. Section 705(2) of the New York Act makes it *mandatory* upon the New York State Labor Relations Board:

...in any case where the majority of employees of a particular craft shall so decide the board shall designate such craft as a unit appropriate for the purpose of collective bargaining.

Thus, if a group of "true craft" employees indicate a preference for bargaining through a craft unit, the New York Board is *obliged* to hold an election among these craft employees to determine whether or not this preference represents the majority sentiment. If a majority of the craft employees vote to bargain through a separate craft unit, the Board then conducts an election to determine the specific union which the employees desire.

The Wagner Act contained no such mandatory craft unit provision. In the 1947 amendments, however, a proviso was added to Section 9(b) which stated:

That the Board shall not...decide that any craft unit is inappropriate for such purposes on the ground that a different unit has been established by a prior Board determination, unless a majority of the employees in the proposed craft vote against separate representation.[32]

In 1948, in *National Tube Company*,[33] the National Labor Relations Board was faced with a demand for an election under the amended Section 9(b). The Board held that Section 9(b) merely meant that the Board could not use a prior unit determination as the *sole* basis for denying a craft severance election. (The National Board had been using bargaining history as the major factor in determining whether or not to allow craft severance. It was because of this policy that Section 9(b) was amended.) The Board held that it was still at the Board's discretion whether or not to conduct an election. The position of the N.L.R.B. in this *National Tube* case was limited in 1954 in *American Potash & Chemical Corporation*.[34] In this case the Board stated that the right of separate representation would no longer be denied on the basis of prior bargaining history or integration of work. The N.L.R.B. cited the following rules to be followed in craft or departmental severance (the rules below represent the present policy of the N.L.R.B. on craft severance in all but four industries):

(a) Employees seeking separation must be true craftsmen or, in the case of departmentalization, functionally distinct and separate.

(b) The union seeking severance must be one that is specifically devoted to serving the special interests of the types of employees in question.

Thus, whereas the New York State Act has always made explicit provisions for craft severance, it was not until 1954 that the N.L.R.B. established a similarly definite policy on this matter.

Right of Strikers to Vote. Section 705(4) of the New York State

[32]29 U.S.C.A. §159.
[33]National Tube Co., 76 N.L.R.B. 1199 (1948).
[34]American Potash & Chemical Corp., 107 N.L.R.B. 1418 (1954). But see N.L.R.B. v. Pittsburgh Plate Glass Co., 270 F. 2d 167 (C.A. 4th cir. 1959), *cert. denied* 361 U.S. 943 (1960), holding the N.L.R.B.'s craft severance policy to be unreasonably discriminatory insofar as it exempted certain industries.

Act specifically excludes from voting in representation elections "...any individuals employed only for the duration of a strike or lockout...." Furthermore, the New York Board has consistently ruled since 1937 that persons who are on strike in connection with a *current* labor dispute are eligible to vote in a representation election, unless they have obtained substantially equivalent employment elsewhere. This procedure differs from the policy followed by the N.L.R.B.

The Wagner Act made no mention whatsoever of the right of strikers to vote in representation elections. It was the practice of the Board, however, to allow both strikers and strike replacements to vote. Section 9(c)(3) of Taft-Hartley was quite explicit about this problem: "Employees on strike who are not entitled to reinstatement shall not be eligible to vote." In simple terms this meant that permanently replaced economic strikers could not vote in representation elections. (Employees on strike in protest of an unfair labor practice could vote since they would generally be entitled to reinstatement.) In Section 702 of the Landrum-Griffin Act of 1959, Section 9(c)(3) of the National Act was again amended to read:

Employees engaged in an economic strike who are not entitled to reinstatement shall be eligible to vote under such regulations as the Board shall find are consistent with the purposes and provisions of this Act in any election conducted within twelve months after the commencement of the strike.[35]

Thus, while as of 1959 the Labor-Management Relations Act and the New York State Labor Relations Act were similar in the matter of allowing employees on strike in a current labor dispute to vote in a representation election, the state policy would still seem to be somewhat more generous insofar as the voting rights of strikers are concerned.

Runoff Elections. One of the significant differences in procedure between the New York State Board and the N.L.R.B. is the way in which the two agencies conduct runoff elections. In election cases where there is no majority for Union A, Union B, or "Neither," the New York State Board has consistently followed a policy of

[35]29 U.S.C.A. §159.

conducting a runoff election between the two unions. This policy is followed even if the vote for "Neither" is greater than the vote for either Union A or Union B. The Board reasons that so long as the employees do not cast a majority of votes for "Neither," this as least indicates a desire to be represented by *some* union. The Board then conducts the runoff election between the two unions to determine which one the employees desire.

Section 9(c)(3) of the Federal Act requires the N.L.R.B. to follow a different procedure. In cases where there is no majority for Union A, Union B, or "Neither," the N.L.R.B. conducts a runoff election between the two selections on the ballot which received the greatest number of votes. Thus, the runoff election may be conducted between the two unions or it may be conducted between one of the unions and "Neither."

Long-Term Contracts. At one point both the N.L.R.B. and the New York State Labor Relations Board followed similar policies in regard to long-term contracts as bars to representation elections. The pre-1958 position of the N.L.R.B. on long-term contracts was that contracts of a reasonable duration would bar representation elections if such contracts were similar in length to contracts covering a substantial part of the industry. Thus, prior to September 1958, the N.L.R.B. often found that contracts of three or even five years' duration would act as a bar to representation elections if a substantial part of the industry was covered by contracts of a similar duration. In September 1958, however, the N.L.R.B. changed its policy. The N.L.R.B. found that it was placing so much weight on maintaining stable labor relations that it was unduly limiting the rights of employees to select their bargaining representatives. The earlier policy was also found to be difficult of specific application because of its lack of definiteness. In order to bring the pendulum back to the middle, the N.L.R.B. adopted a policy of placing a maximum of two years on the amount of time in which a contract could be held as a bar to a representation election.[36] More recently this has been extended to a period of three years.[37]

The New York State Labor Relations Board has continued to

[36]See Pacific Coast Ass'n of Pulp & Paper Mfrs., 121 N.L.R.B. 990, 992 (1958).
[37]General Cable Corp., 139 N.L.R.B. No. 111 (1962).

13

follow a policy similar to that pursued by the N.L.R.B. prior to 1958. Thus, on the basis of bargaining history and practices in a substantial part of the particular industry, the New York State Labor Relations Board has frequently held three-year contracts, and in the harness race track industry has held five-year contracts, as bars to representation elections.

General Similarities. The five topics discussed thus far represent the major parallel features of the State and National Acts and of policy determinations of the two Boards. The following list contains a very brief description of some of the other similarities between the two acts and the two Boards.

(a) Both agencies rely very heavily on the solution of disputes through informal procedures. Both encourage the settlement of representation and unfair labor practice cases prior to the formal hearing stage. In representation proceedings, both agencies encourage consent election. Indeed, the State Board encourages settlement even after the formal stage has begun.

(b) Barring unusual circumstances, neither agency will conduct a representation election during the one-year period following Board certification of a labor union as the collective bargaining representative for a majority of the employees in a particular unit.

(c) The history of the two Boards has been marked by considerable similarity in administrative organization. Both agencies follow similar methods in the handling of representation and unfair labor practice cases. It should be noted, however, that there has been more complete separation of functions in the Federal Board since 1947, when the General Counsel was made an independent official, whereas the State Board has continued to use a system of internal separation of functions. Also, pursuant to a 1959 amendment of the Federal Act, wider authority has been delegated to N.L.R.B. regional offices in the disposition of representation cases.

(d) Both agencies have made provisions for separate bargaining units for supervisory and plant security personnel. (The N.L.R.B., since 1947, has been precluded by statute from dealing with problems of supervisory employees.)

(e) The findings of both Boards, if supported by substantial evidence on the entire record, are binding upon the reviewing courts. Thus, if any party is aggrieved by a final order of the Board, that party may seek appropriate relief in the courts. However, the courts may not overrule the findings of the Board if those findings are supported by substantial evidence.

(f) Certifications and Directions of Election issued by both Boards are not final orders and, as such, are generally not subject to judicial review, *except* in connection with the review of a final order in an unfair labor practice proceeding based upon the certification, or where the certification is in flagrant violation of an express statutory or constitutional right. Thus, for example, if the Board certified a particular union as the bargaining agent for a group of employees, the employer could refuse to bargain with the union, wait for the Board to issue an order directing him to bargain, appeal the Board's final order, and thus secure review of the Board certification in the unfair labor practice case.

This analysis and comparison could profitably go into much greater detail. Our purpose, however, is limited to giving the reader a brief survey of how the New York State Act fits into the general framework of the National Labor Relations Act, as amended.

The Problem of "Paper Locals"

One point on which the New York State Labor Relations Board's policy has been rather significantly different from that of the N.L.R.B., and which has received a considerable amount of attention, is the State Board's treatment of collusive or "sweetheart" contracts, especially those involving "paper locals" and racket-dominated or -infested labor organizations. Such organizations are usually independent and unaffiliated (that is, not part of a national or international union), and hence may be described as self-chartered. How widespread they are it is difficult to determine, but information disclosed by the New York State Labor Relations Board indicates that their number may be fairly sizeable.[38] It should be noted that such organizations are of particular significance to state labor relations policy because paper locals are apt either to be intrastate in character or at best at the margin of

[38]"The Record Shows that 'Racket' and 'Phantom Unions' Can Be Driven Out of Business," S.L.R.B. Press Release, March 2, 1962.

interstate commerce, which means that they are not likely to be subject to federal jurisdiction.

The paper local issue arises in at least the following four types of situations:[39]

1. The union and the employer enter into a collective bargaining agreement; the employment conditions set forth therein are extremely advantageous to the employer; the employer pays his employees' "union dues" out of his own pocket.

2. The same circumstances prevail, except that the employer withholds union dues from his employees' wages (sometimes without their authorization) and remits them to the union. A variation on this situation would be one where the employer withholds union dues but at the same time increases his employees' wages by the amount of the dues thus withheld, thereby in effect paying the dues out of his own pocket.

3. The employer "recognizes," but makes no agreement with, the union and hence remains essentially free to do as he pleases with respect to employment conditions. In return, the employer pays the union his employees' "dues" out of his own pocket.

4. There is no contract between the union and the employer, but the employer withholds union dues from his employees' wages and remits them to the union.

The New York Board took cognizance of these and other questionable agreements and organizations in 1959, and in June of that year called a conference of federal, state, and county prosecutors to discuss them and to formulate a program designed to deal with them. Board Chairman Kramer has written:

The board has made a fundamental policy determination in this regard. Indeed, in attempting to draw the line between paper locals and legitimate organizations, it has moved forward in a critical area with sureness and a devotion to the underlying concepts of our statute. Implicit in the statutory definition of "labor organization" as "any organization which exists and is constituted for the purpose, in whole or in part, of collective bargaining" is an intent, not only that the organization have the trappings and formalities of a body interested

[39]The term, "paper local," was originally applied to a labor organization without members, the purpose of which was to extort money from employers. In recent years, the meaning of the term has expanded to include the situations described here.

16

in collective bargaining, but also that it actually exist and be constituted for that purpose.

•   •   •

We have recognized that drawing the line is very difficult, but that
the effort to do so is exceedingly worthwhile. Thus, organizations
which have no devotion to genuine collective bargaining and which are
not interested in serving employees or actually bargaining with legitimate management are not, in fact, the labor organizations, within the
meaning of the statute, that the framers of our legislation were eager
to help. We have determined, therefore, that organizations which are
operated as rackets and are engaged in a pattern of collusive arrangements not only should be scrutinized closely at every stage but also,
wherever possible, should be proscribed.

•   •   •

...Thus, the board undertook to notify the various law enforcement
officers of all cases filed with it, and it improved its past method of
channeling information in particular cases to appropriate district
attorneys.[40]

Shortly after the June 1959 conference, the New York Board
considered the problem in the context of a representation proceeding brought before it.[41] The union involved had been organized as
an unaffiliated "independent," and had entered into relations with
a number of employers with one of which it had made a collective
bargaining contract. At the time of the hearing in the case, "there
were ten members in good standing, no executive board was 'in
operation,' and no trustees had been elected." The union had
approached the employer involved with the proposal that an
employee's wages be "raised" five dollars a month, that this same
amount be checked out of the employee's wages and be remitted
to the local as his dues, that it would not be necessary to sign the
contract or make any contributions to the union's welfare fund,
and that the employer contribute $300 to the local's treasury. The
State Board dismissed representation petitions filed by the union,
indicating that it would refuse to process any other petitions filed
by that union or to certify it, until the latter established that it was,

[40]Kramer, "Law and Policy in State Labor Relations Acts: The New York Board
as Innovator," 333 *Annals* of the American Academy of Political and Social Science
59, 67–68 (1961).
[41]Helsid Realty Corp., 22 S.L.R.B. 326 (1959).

17

in fact, a labor organization within the meaning of the statute. The Board elaborated its views as follows:

The Board does not make a qualitative judgment; it does not determine which "labor organization" is best qualified or most competent to fulfill that task. But the Act does require that an organization seeking to be certified as an exclusive bargaining representative of employees must in fact exist, in whole or in part, for the purposes of collective bargaining, both, according to its avowed purposes and in actual practice. . . .[42]

Board Chairman Kramer, in supplemental comments, highlighted the increasing problem being experienced by the agency with "independent" unaffiliated unions (self-chartered) in New York State. He indicated that, between 1956 and 1958, cases involving such locals had increased in volume from 19 percent to 25 percent of the Board's case load, and observed:

As in the case at bar, a great deal of the recently uncovered detail as to unlawful ends and illegal methods has related to unaffiliated, self-chartered locals and internationals. Our own files and decided cases convince that the problem, in its most acute form, concerns self-chartered locals, such as the one at bar, which are not bound by codes of ethics, which have no tradition of good faith collective bargaining with employers and no history of service to employees. We recognize, of course, that employees are not limited to joining unions affiliated with the major national organizations. They may join independent, unaffiliated labor organizations, and may also form their own organizations limited to the employees of a single employer. But in each of these instances, the organizations must meet the requirements of the Act—in fact as well as in form—before it may be certified by the Board as a "labor organization" designated and selected by employees as an exclusive bargaining representative.[43]

The approach announced in the *Helsid* decision above was refined by the Board's subsequently issuing a so-called "road map," setting forth five ways to challenge paper locals and sweetheart or collusive contracts. These are as follows:

1. The New York Board will investigate, in an election proceeding, whether a collective bargaining agreement has actually been made with a union representing a majority of the employees, or whether it has been illegally made with a union which actually did not represent the

[42]*Id.* at 329, 330.　　　　　　　　[43]*Id.* at 335.

majority of the employees. It will direct an election, in appropriate circumstances, to determine the desires of the employees, despite the existence of a non-representative contract.

2. A company union, outlawed under the statute, will be investigated in a representation proceeding and if found to be an illegal organization, will not be placed on the ballot in any election which may be ordered.

3. "Paper locals" or "dummy unions" will be found not to be labor organizations in a representation proceeding and they will be barred from the ballot in any election which may be ordered.

4. Deceptive and misleading names which may lead employees to believe that they are being represented by long-established unions will not be permitted on a ballot in any election conducted by the Board.

5. Challenges of "paper locals" may be made by legitimate organizations at Board hearings without proof that the legitimate organization actually does represent employees in the plant or facility. It will be sufficient for a legitimate organization, if it seeks to attack a collusive contract or "sweetheart" agreement or the "phony" status of another organization, to appear and present its proof without any further or additional evidence of interest.[44]

The Board, in accordance with its "road map," has implemented its five approaches in numerous decisions.[45]

The State Board's approach to this problem is in contrast to that of the N.L.R.B., which not only has consistently refused to decide the unfair labor practice issue of "company unionism" in representation proceedings[46] but has held that alleged corrupt practices in the administration of a petitioning union's internal affairs were not grounds for dismissal of the representation proceeding.[47]

Having given a survey of the statute it administers, we turn now to a description of the administrative organization of the New York State Labor Relations Board.

[44]"Five Ways to Challenge Paper Locals and Sweetheart or Collusive Contracts," S.L.R.B. Press Release, Dec. 22, 1959.

[45]Austin Gardens Garage Corp., 21 S.L.R.B. 115 (1958); West Farms Service Center, 23 S.L.R.B. 147 (1960); Rego Park Bowling Center, Inc., 23 S.L.R.B. 188 (1960); William Gold, Inc., 22 S.L.R.B. 503 (1959); Dunetz & Lovett, 25 S.L.R.B. 190 (1962); Klar, 25 S.L.R.B. 76 (1962).

[46]Contrast Marine Optical Mfg. Co., 92 N.L.R.B. 571 (1950); Times Square Stores Corp., 79 N.L.R.B. 361 (1948) with Aurora White Rock Laundry Corp., 24 S.L.R.B. 80 (1961).

[47]Alto Plastics Mfg. Corp., 136 N.L.R.B. 850 (1962).

CHAPTER II

The New York State Labor Relations Board: Organization and Personnel

AS INDICATED earlier, the New York State Labor Relations Act is administered and enforced by an administrative agency, created pursuant to Section 702 of the statute and entitled the New York State Labor Relations Board. The purpose of this chapter is to describe the organizational structure of the agency. Subsequent chapters focus on the procedures used by the agency in administering the statute and on the relationship of the New York Board to the courts and to the National Labor Relations Board.

The New York Board has powers both to enforce and to interpret and apply the law. Thus, as is true of many administrative agencies, it has functions of both an executive and a judicial nature. How these functions are distributed within the agency will become clearer as we detail its organizational structure and procedures.

Place of Board in Department of Labor

The New York State Labor Relations Board is a quasi-judicial administrative agency within the State Department of Labor. Moreso than any other agency in the Department, however, the Board is almost completely autonomous in carrying out its functions. Section 702(9) of the New York State Labor Relations Act states:

Notwithstanding the provision of any other law, neither the industrial commissioner nor any board or other agency of the department of labor shall in any way direct, review, modify or reverse any decision or finding of the board nor shall the industrial commissioner or any board or other agency of the department of labor supervise or control the board in the exercise of any powers or in the performance of any duties under this article.

Unlike other agencies in the Department of Labor, the Board also has the power to appoint its own subordinate personnel. Section 702(5) of the act provides that: "All employees of the board shall be appointed by the board in accordance with the provisions of the civil service law and rules."

Outside of the obvious control exercised over the Board by the courts and the legislature, the only other control upon the Board is exercised by the Industrial Commissioner. This control is found in Section 711 of the act which provides that:

Prior to the fifteenth day of November of each year, the industrial commissioner shall submit to the director of the budget for his approval an estimated budget of the administrative expenses of the New York state labor relations board for the ensuing fiscal year. All moneys appropriated to the department or the board, for the use of the board, shall be expended and audited in the manner provided for all other expenditures under the supervision of the industrial commissioner.

Thus, for all practical purposes, with the exception of budgetary matters, the New York State Labor Relations Board is an autonomous agency operating within the framework of the Department of Labor.

The Labor Relations Board and the Board of Mediation

The Labor Relations Board and the State Board of Mediation have always maintained a very close and informal working relationship. The two Boards frequently refer cases to one another. For example, an investigation by the Labor Relations Board of a charge or petition may indicate that the dispute centers in a disagreement about contract interpretation rather than on an unfair labor practice or a representation conflict. In such a case the Labor Relations Board would refer the matter to the State Board of Mediation.

21

The language of the acts setting up these two agencies is rather explicit as to the jurisdiction of the two Boards. For this reason, and because the Labor Relations Board is expressly forbidden under Section 702 (8) from engaging in any mediation activities except in connection with the investigation of a charge or petition, there appears to have been little jurisdictional trouble between the two.

The Board Members

The three Board members are appointed by the Governor by and with the consent of the Senate for terms of six years. (The initial appointments under the act were for terms of two, four, and six years, respectively.) With the exception of citizenship and New York State residency requirements, there are no specific qualifications for membership on the Board. It happens that at the present time all three Board members are attorneys. This, however, is not a statutory requirement.

Section 702(1) sets up the following procedure for the removal of Board members:

Any member of the board may be removed by the governor for inefficiency, neglect of duty, misconduct or malfeasance in office, and for no other cause, after being given a copy of the charges and an opportunity to be publicly heard in person or by counsel.

Subordinate Personnel

As previously mentioned, Section 702(5) of the act gives the Board power to appoint its subordinate personnel. The following list contains a brief description of the Board's staff organization:

Executive Secretary. The Executive Secretary's functions include responsibility for over-all administration and general supervision of the Board's staff. He prepares the Board's agendas, attends all Board meetings, and is responsible for carrying out Board policies and procedures. He handles budgetary and civil service matters, and represents the Board in dealing with other government agencies.

General Counsel. The General Counsel heads the Board's staff of attorneys. He is responsible for all litigation and represents the Board in the courts. He attends all Board meetings, advises the

Board on legal and policy questions, and examines the drafts of all decisions and orders before issuance. (The General Counsel originally supervised the work of the Litigation Attorneys; this responsibility was taken over by the Assistant, now Associate, General Counsel when that post was created in 1941.)

Associate General Counsel. As noted, the post of Assistant General Counsel was created in 1941. In 1943 this position was changed to Associate General Counsel with no change in duties. The Associate General Counsel supervises the activities of the Board's Litigation Division in connection with the prosecution of unfair labor practice cases. Thereby a fairly sharp *internal* separation of the prosecuting from the judging function is achieved. The Associate General Counsel also handles court litigation under the direction of the General Counsel.

Assistant General Counsel. This position was created in 1946 to take over the functions of Chief Review Attorney. The Assistant General Counsel supervises the activities of the Board's Review Division. He reviews and edits all draft decisions before submission to the General Counsel and the Board members.

Regional Attorneys. The Buffalo and Albany regions are headed by Regional Attorneys. The Regional Attorneys perform the work of Labor Relations Examiners in these two regions. They also act as Litigation Attorneys for the Board in the prosecution of unfair labor practice cases.

Division of Labor Relations Examiners. This division was originally composed of a Senior Examiner and seven Labor Relations Examiners. Another Senior Examiner was added in 1947 and the number of Labor Relations Examiners is now ten. The division is responsible for conducting the informal investigations in representation and unfair labor practice cases for the New York City office. (It will be recalled that this responsibility is carried on by the Regional Attorneys in Buffalo and Albany.)

Litigation Section. Under the supervision of the Associate General Counsel, the nine attorneys in the Litigation Section are responsible for the Board's preparation and prosecution of unfair labor practice cases. When the Board finds that a complaint should issue on a charge, a Litigation Attorney is assigned to draft the complaint and prepare the case for hearing. (It may again be noted that this responsibility is carried on by the Regional Attorneys in the Buffalo and Albany regions.) In view of the fact that the Board is the complainant when an unfair labor practice case reaches the formal hearing stage, the Litigation Attorney presents the affirmative case before the Trial Examiner on behalf of the Board.

Supervising Trial Examiner. The Supervising Trial Examiner is in charge of and supervises the Board's Trial Examiner Division. This responsibility includes the assigning of Trial Examiners. In addition, the Supervising Trial Examiner, himself, presides at formal hearings and performs all of the functions of the Trial Examiners.

Trial Examiners. Under the direction of the Supervising Trial Examiner, the six permanent Trial Examiners and a number of per diem Trial Examiners (originally there were four permanent Trial Examiners and twenty-five Examiners employed on a per diem basis) are responsible for presiding over the formal hearings in representation and unfair labor practice cases. When a complaint is issued in an unfair labor practice case or when the Board issues a notice of hearing in a representation case, a Trial Examiner is assigned to preside over the hearing. Once the hearing is concluded in an unfair labor practice proceeding, the Trial Examiner issues his Intermediate Report which is served upon all parties and filed with the Board. In a representation case, the Trial Examiner presents the Board with a confidential memorandum at the conclusion of the hearing.

Review Attorneys. Under the direction of the Assistant General Counsel, the eleven Review Attorneys are responsible for reviewing and analyzing the records of formal hearings, and assisting in the preparation of draft decisions in both unfair labor practice and representation proceedings. The Review Attorneys are, in effect, legal secretaries or assistants to the Board members. They may also assist with the preparation of briefs in court cases involving the Board.

Regional Offices. The Board has divided the state into three regions with an office in each region. Approximately 90 percent of the Board's cases come into the New York City office. With the exception of the two Regional Attorneys and their secretaries, all of the Board's personnel are located in the New York City office. Thus, although the act states that the principal office of the Board shall be in Albany, for all practical purposes the main office of the Board is in New York City. The three geographic regions are as follows:

Central Region—Office located in Albany, New York.

Western Office—Office located in Buffalo, New York.

Southern Office—Office located in New York City, New York.

Separation of Functions. As can be seen from the foregoing organizational description, the State Board has retained a "unitary command" structure throughout its history, although the investigatory and prosecuting function is kept *internally* separate from that of adjudication. In marked contrast, since 1947, one of the Taft-Hartley amendments has provided for an independent General Counsel to the N.L.R.B., with even more complete separation of the Board's administrative and judicial functions being suggested in 1960 by an Advisory Panel on Labor-Management Relations Law to the U.S. Senate Committee on Labor and Public Welfare.[1]

Indeed, one of the major recommendations of Commissioner Benjamin, in his 1942 study of administrative adjudication in the State of New York, was to similar effect that *two* boards be created, one the State Labor Relations Board, the other the State Labor Relations Authority.[2] The former was to discharge powers of adjudication in unfair labor practice and representation cases. The latter was to be given all powers of investigation and prosecution. This proposal, to which we shall return in the final chapter, was thought to be justified on grounds that no internal separation could be sufficiently complete, given the small size of the agency and ultimate responsibility in the hands of a single board. This recommendation was not adopted, although it has from time to

[1]S. Doc. No. 81, 86th Cong., 2d Sess. (1960). The panel was appointed pursuant to S. Res. 66 and S. Res. 141 of the 86th Congress.

[2]Benjamin, *Administrative Adjudication in the State of New York,* 47–66 (1942). See also, *id., V, Supplementary Report of the State Labor Relations Board,* 165–176 (1942).

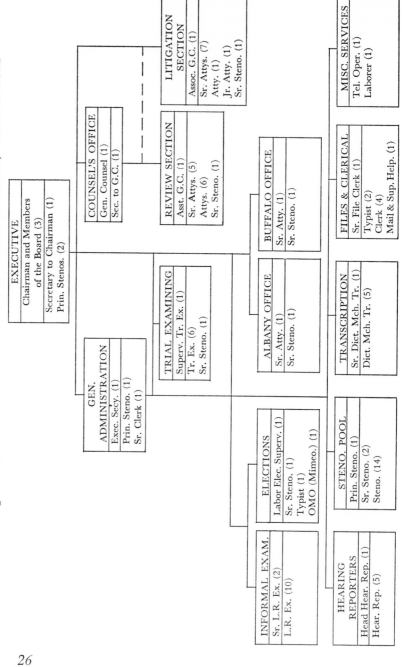

Chart 1. Organization of the New York State Labor Relations Board, December 1962.

EXECUTIVE
Chairman and Members of the Board (3)
Secretary to Chairman (1)
Prin. Stenos. (2)

GEN. ADMINISTRATION
Exec. Secy. (1)
Prin. Steno. (1)
Sr. Clerk (1)

COUNSEL'S OFFICE
Gen. Counsel (1)
Sec. to G.C. (1)

LITIGATION SECTION
Assoc. G.C. (1)
Sr. Attys. (7)
Atty. (1)
Jr. Atty. (1)
Sr. Steno. (1)

REVIEW SECTION
Asst. G.C. (1)
Sr. Attys. (5)
Attys. (6)
Sr. Steno. (1)

TRIAL EXAMINING
Superv. Tr. Ex. (1)
Tr. Ex. (6)
Sr. Steno. (1)

BUFFALO OFFICE
Sr. Atty. (1)
Sr. Steno. (1)

ALBANY OFFICE
Sr. Atty. (1)
Sr. Steno. (1)

MISC. SERVICES
Tel. Oper. (1)
Laborer (1)

FILES & CLERICAL
Sr. File Clerk (1)
Typist (2)
Clerk (4)
Mail & Sup. Help. (1)

TRANSCRIPTION
Sr. Dict. Mch. Tr. (1)
Dict. Mch. Tr. (5)

ELECTIONS
Labor Elec. Superv. (1)
Sr. Steno. (1)
Typist (1)
OMO (Mimeo.) (1)

STENO. POOL
Prin. Steno. (1)
Sr. Steno. (2)
Steno. (14)

INFORMAL EXAM.
Sr. L.R. Ex. (2)
L.R. Ex. (10)

HEARING REPORTERS
Head Hear. Rep. (1)
Hear. Rep. (5)

time been echoed in proposals to conform the New York statute to the amended Federal Act.[3]

This chapter has outlined briefly how the Board is organized and the principal functions of the various Board personnel. In the following chapters these functions of Board personnel are described in more detail, as we discuss the procedure followed by the Board in representation and unfair labor practice cases.

[3]See, for instance, the proposal made by the Chamber of Commerce in Report of the New York State Joint Legislative Committee on Industrial and Labor Conditions, 115–116 (1958).

CHAPTER III

The Unfair Labor Practice Case: Procedure Prior to Formal Hearing

THIS chapter and the next are concerned with the methods and procedures used by the New York State Labor Relations Board in the disposition of unfair labor practice cases, this being one of the two principal tasks with which it is charged (the other is the resolution of questions concerning the representation of employees). The procedures described here are those followed from the time an unfair labor practice "charge" has been filed to the issuance of a formal complaint or other disposition. This may be called the investigatory or informal stage.

First, however, we present a concise summary of the steps through which an unfair labor practice case moves.

Summary of Procedures

1. "A charge that any employer has engaged in or is engaging in any unfair labor practice may be made by any person or labor organization." Once a charge has been filed, the Board has authority to proceed with its investigation.

2. The charge is referred to one of the two Senior Labor Relations Examiners for assignment to a Labor Relations Examiner.

3. The Labor Relations Examiner's first step is to call the parties to the dispute together in an informal conference. The purpose of this informal investigation is twofold: (a) obtain the facts so as to provide the Board with sufficient information upon which to base

its decision concerning the disposition of the charge; (b) bring about a voluntary adjustment.

4. After the Labor Relations Examiner (or Regional Attorney in the Albany and Buffalo regions) completes his informal investigation, he submits a final report to the Board through a Senior Labor Relations Examiner.

5. If no adjustment has been reached by the parties in the course of the informal investigations, the Board must decide whether or not a complaint should issue on the charge. In making this determination, the Board studies the case file, the final report of the Labor Relations Examiner, and possible recommendations by the Senior Examiner.

6. If the Board decides that a complaint should issue on the charge, the case is referred to one of the Board's staff of Litigation Attorneys (Regional Attorney in the Albany and Buffalo regions). The Litigation Attorney drafts the complaint and prepares the case for hearing.

7. After the Litigation Attorney drafts the complaint, it is signed by the Associate General Counsel and served on all parties to the dispute in the form of a "complaint" and a "notice of hearing."

8. The complaint and notice of hearing contain the following items: (a) notification of availability of a copy of the Board's General Rules and Regulations; (b) copy of the final charge form; (c) the complaint, containing a concise statement of the alleged unfair labor practices; (d) notice of hearing before the Trial Examiner.

9. From seven to ten days after the complaint and notice of hearing are issued, a formal hearing is held before one of the Board's Trial Examiners. Since the Board, acting in the public interest, becomes the complainant in the case once a complaint is issued, the Board's Litigation Attorney presents the affirmative case for the Board. The person or labor organization making the charge is a party to the proceedings, but ordinarily plays a secondary role. The Respondent employer is usually represented by counsel.

10. At the conclusion of the formal hearing, the Trial Examiner examines the record and issues an Intermediate Report to all parties to the proceeding. The Intermediate Report contains a detailed statement of the facts and issues of the case, the conclu-

sions reached by the Trial Examiner, and his recommendation to the Board concerning the disposition of the complaint. The parties are then given an opportunity to file exceptions to the Intermediate Report and file briefs and present oral arguments before the Board.

11. Prior to issuing its "decision and order," the Board assigns the case to a Review Attorney. The first task of the Review Attorney is to review the entire record and to analyze the issues of the case as raised in the transcript of the hearing, the Trial Examiner's Intermediate Report, and the briefs and oral arguments presented to the Board, and to undertake necessary research.

12. On the basis of the Intermediate Report, exceptions thereto, various briefs and arguments, the Review Attorney's analysis, the Board makes its final determination in the case, and develops the rationale underlying the decision. The Review Attorney is once again utilized by the Board to draft a preliminary decision and order. Finally, and generally after considerable revision, the Board issues to all parties to the proceedings its decision and order.

13. The decision and order takes the following form: (a) a detailed opinion discussing the evidence and setting forth the reasons for the decision reached; (b) formal findings of facts and conclusions of law; (c) order directing the employer to cease and desist from engaging in such conduct as the Board has found to be unfair labor practices, and directing the employer to take certain affirmative actions to remedy the unfair labor practices. This usually includes a requirement that appropriate notices be posted concerning the unfair labor practices being remedied. (If the Board's final decision is that no unfair labor practices have been committed, the order takes the form of a dismissal of the complaint.)

14. Accompanying each decision and part of the order is a request that the Respondent notify the Board within a certain period of time concerning the steps taken to remedy the unfair labor practices and comply with the Board's order.

15. Any party aggrieved by the Board's final order may seek "judicial review" of that order in the appropriate court. The questions before the court in reviewing the Board's order are: (a) Are the Board's findings supported by substantial evidence? (b) Was the Board's order proper as a matter of law?

16. For all practical purposes, one of the most important aspects of the Board's procedure in unfair labor practice proceedings is the step of compliance. If the Respondent notifies the Board of a refusal to comply, and if the Board is unable to obtain compliance through informal means, the Board petitions the appropriate court for an enforcement order. Once the court has assumed jurisdiction and affirmed the Board's order, refusal to comply with the Board's order constitutes a refusal to obey the court order, subjecting the recalcitrant Respondent to the possibility of contempt of court.

These, then, are the major procedures followed by the Board in handling unfair labor practice cases. Each of these procedures will now be examined in detail, beginning with the filing of a charge.

The Charge

Section 706(2) of the New York State Labor Relations Act states in part that:

Whenever a charge has been made that any employer has engaged in or is engaging in any unfair labor practice, the board shall have power to issue and cause to be served upon such employer a complaint stating the charges in that respect and containing a notice of hearing before the board at a place therein fixed to be held not less than seven days after the serving of said complaint.

As this provision indicates, the New York State Labor Relations Board is *not* a self-starting agency. Before the Board can set its machinery in motion a charge must first be filed. Once the charge has been filed in its appropriate form, the Board has the power to proceed with its investigation.

Who May File Charge. Article III, Section 20 of the Board's General Rules and Regulations states that:

A charge that any employer has engaged in or is engaging in any unfair labor practice may be made by any person or labor organization.

Thus, the filing of a charge by "any person or labor organization" gives the Board its authority to proceed with its investigation and disposition of said charge.

Form of Charge. Article III, Section 21 of the General Rules and Regulations sets up the following form for the filing of charges (see Facsimile 1): *continued on p. 33*

Facsimile 1.

STATE OF NEW YORK
NEW YORK STATE LABOR RELATIONS BOARD

In the Matter of

               Employer

and

CASE NO............U............

1. Name of employer...Telephone No....................
2. Address of employer..
                                   (Include Post Office Zone Number)
3. Address at which alleged unfair practice occurred...
4. General nature of business...
5. Approximate total number of employees...
6. Number of employees involved in alleged unfair labor practice...................
7. Nature of work done by employees involved...

CHARGE

8. Pursuant to Section 706 of the New York State Labor Relations Act, the undersigned hereby charges that the above-named employer has engaged in and is engaging in unfair labor practices within the meaning of Section 704 of said Act, in that (*Specify* the particular alleged violation, with a brief statement of the facts supporting the charge.)

STATE OF NEW YORK
CITY OF   *ss.:*
COUNTY OF

.................being duly sworn, deposes and says that he has read the foregoing charge and knows the contents thereof; that the same is true to his own knowledge, except as to the matters therein stated to be alleged on information and belief, and as to those matters he believes it to be true.

....
(Signature)
Sworn to before me,
this   day of   19   .

....

Name of person or labor organization making the charge. (If made by a labor organization, give also the name and official position of the person acting for the organization.)

....

....
(Signature)

P. O. Address.....................................
     (Include Post Office Zone Number)

Telephone No. ....

(FILE ORIGINAL AND THREE COPIES OF THIS CHARGE)

A charge shall be in writing. The original shall be signed and verified before any person authorized to administer an oath. The original and three (3) copies of the charge shall be filed with the Board. Charge forms will be supplied by the Board upon request.

This section has been slightly amended from its original 1937 form, but the amendments have been in wording only and have had no effect upon Board procedure.

It should be noted here that, although the Board sets up a special form for the filing of charges, the Board has consistently held that objections will not be sustained because of any deficiencies in the form of the charge. The position of the Board in this matter, which will be elaborated upon in another place, applies to all of the Board's filing requirements. For example, in Section II of the Board's General Rules and Regulations dealing with petitions in representation cases, the rule states:

No petition in a proceeding under section 705 of the Act shall be dismissed for failure of the petitioner to set forth in the petition all the information required.

This is not to say that the Board will *never* sustain such objections, but rather that technical deficiencies in form are generally not grounds for objections. This is a matter of Board discretion.[1]

Contents of Charge. This is governed by Art. III, Section 22 of the General Rules and Regulations. Parts 3 and 4 of Section 22 have been slightly amended from the original 1937 Preliminary Rules and Regulations. Again, the amendments have been minor and without significant effect upon Board procedure. From an historical point of view, however, it is quite interesting to note the change in wording of Part 3.

Originally, among the information asked for in Part 3 was the "approximate percentage of sales made to points outside of New York State." The wording here was changed by the Board's 1951 amendments to the General Rules and Regulations, which added a request for additional information concerning the interstate character of the business of the employer or employers against whom the charge was being made. The practice now is to elicit this information by means of a separate commerce questionnaire which

---

[1] It has been held that such rulings by the Board with respect to formal adequacy of form (petition) do not raise a question of Board jurisdiction. See Hanley v. Boland, 177 Misc. 973, 33 N.Y.S. 2d 673 (Sup. Ct., Albany Co., 1939).

the employer is asked to complete whenever jurisdiction on commerce grounds is raised during the preliminary or informal stage (see Facsimile 2). The same procedure is followed in representation cases.

Facsimile 2.

PLEASE FILL IN BLANKS AND RETURN PROMPTLY
IF SPACE ALLOWED IS INSUFFICIENT USE BACK OF PAGE 2.

NEW YORK STATE LABOR RELATIONS BOARD
DATA RE INTERSTATE COMMERCE

I.   The enterprise is (1) a corporation .... (2) a partnership...............
(3) an individual business ....
(1) If corporation, the name as it appears on the certificate of incorporation is ....
The State and date of incorporation are ....
(2) If partnership, the name as it appears on partnership agreement and the full name of the partners are ....
....
....
The State, county and date of filing the partnership certificate are
....
(3) If individual business, the name as it appears on certificates of doing business is ....
The State, county and date of filing the certificate are ....
....

II.   General nature or type of business: (Check)
Manufacturer .... Wholesaler .... Retailer ....
Trucking .... Communications .... Transit System ....
Taxicab .... Service .... Public Utility .... News ....
Publisher .... Hotel-Motel .... Office or Industrial ....
Building .... Building and Construction ....
Other (please specify) ....

III.   The location of our principal office and branch offices are ....
....
....

IV.   The number and location by states, of our plants, warehouses, factories or stores are ....
....

FIGURES FURNISHED BELOW ARE FOR THE
12 MONTH PERIOD ENDING

	Month	Day	Year
V. Gross annual income $			

CASE NO. ....

VI.   Annual purchases of goods, supplies, commodities or services purchased
      a) directly from other firms outside the state $ ....
      b) from firms located inside the state but which originated outside the state $ ....

VII. Annual receipts from sales of goods, products or commodities delivered directly, or services rendered, outside the state $ ....

VIII. Annual receipts from goods, products or commodities sold, or services rendered, within the state to businesses subject to NLRB jurisdiction $ ....

IX.   Trucking industry only
      a) gross annual receipts from interstate operations $ ....
      b) gross annual receipts from interlining (deliveries, locally of goods which originated outside the state or are destined for shipment outside the state) $ ....

X.   National Defense
      Engaged in performance of contracts to provide goods or services related to national defense: Yes.................... No.....................
      If yes, the amount of such contracts during the past year totalled $ ....

XI.   Our company is a parent of, subsidiary of, or affiliated with the following business organizations. (Give names, addresses, relationship and business dealings) ....
....
....

XII. Additional facts relating to our business ....
....
....

XIII. Our company has been party to a proceeding before the National Labor Relations Board. (1) No................ (2) Yes .... (Give name, case number, regional office, date and disposition of case ....
....

XIV. The aforesaid answers are true to the best of my knowledge.

Dated: ....

               (Signed) ....
                                  (Name and Title)

(Detailed supporting data will be required, if necessary.)

CASE NO. ....

The reason for this change can be seen in the rather serious federal-state jurisdictional problems which became increasingly acute following the Taft-Hartley amendments to the National Labor Relations Act. The "no-man's land" created by Section 10(a) of Taft-Hartley brought about some perplexing problems of jurisdiction for the New York Board. From 1947 until 1959, when the Landrum-Griffin amendments were added to the Labor-Management Relations (Taft-Hartley) Act and the jurisdictional problem simplified, the Board found that it had to be particularly careful about exercising jurisdiction over cases in this "no-man's land." For this reason, the Board amended Part 3 of Section 22 to ask for the "approximate percentage and volume of sales to and purchases from, points outside New York State." With this additional information the Board had more on which to base its preliminary decision concerning jurisdiction and subsequent investigation.[2]

Withdrawal of Charge. It is a rule of the Board that charges may be withdrawn only with its consent and under such conditions as it may deem proper. In actual practice, the Board almost always gives approval to a request for withdrawal. If the Board believes, however, that the withdrawal of charges would violate the rights of employees, as in the case of discriminatory discharges, the Board may deny the request and proceed with the investigation. Again, this is a matter of Board discretion.

Amendment of Charge. At any time before the issuance of the Board's final decision and order, the charge may be amended in the discretion of the Board or the Trial Examiner. In order to understand the implications of this procedure, the following three points must be remembered:

1. Section 25(a) of the General Rules and Regulations states: "A charge shall not be part of the complaint." This provision was contained in the original 1937 Preliminary Rules and Regulations.

2. Section 24, dealing with the Board's or the Trial Examiner's power to amend the charge, was added to the Rules and Regula-

---

[2]The federal-state jurisdictional problem is discussed in detail in Chap. VIII. Also, it will be seen in Chap. VI that the same change in wording described above for the unfair practice charge is to be found in the petition for investigation and certification of representatives under Art. II, §9 of the General Rules and Regulations.

tions in 1940. This addition simply stated a procedure which had been followed since 1937.

3. In an unfair labor practice proceeding, when the Board decides that a formal complaint should issue on the basis of a charge, the Board becomes the complainant in the subsequent formal hearings before the Trial Examiner. Thus, it is the Board, acting in the public interest, rather than the person or labor organization filing the charge, which becomes the complainant in a formal hearing in an unfair labor practice case.

These three facts suggest the basis of the Board's power to permit amendment of a charge. When a charge is filed with the Board, the Board has the duty, not only to investigate that specific charge, but also to investigate all other unfair labor practices which come to its attention. Furthermore, since the charge is not a part of the complaint, when the Board issues a complaint it may include in it, not only the matters raised in the original charge, but any other unfair labor practices relating to the charge and uncovered in the course of its investigations.

The position of the Board in this matter is probably best illustrated by its decision in 1945, in *Taxi Transit Corporation*.[3] In this case an amended charge was filed with the Board as a result of evidence of a company union uncovered by the Board's investigations. The employers contended that the Board had initiated a part of the amended charge and thus had no jurisdiction over it. The Board rejected this contention, holding that:

...a charge constitutes neither pleading nor proof, but merely sets in motion the administrative machinery of inquiry; the Board's complaint is not limited to matters alleged in the charge and may be broader than the charge; the Board has not only the right but the duty, during the pendency of proceedings before it, to investigate all unfair labor practices related to those alleged in any charge filed with the Board or which grow out of the Board's investigation of the unfair labor practices charged, and this regardless of whether such practices were mentioned in the original charge or amendment thereof.[4]

The Board's policy and procedure in connection with the amending of charges continues to remain the same today.

[3]Taxi Transit Corp., 8 S.L.R.B. 136 (1945).
[4]*Id.* at 144.

Disposition of Charge

There are four possible dispositions of a charge that has been filed with the Board.

Adjusted. This applies to cases in which the parties reach an agreement between themselves before the issuance of a final decision and order. Once the parties reach an agreement, its details must be submitted to the Board for approval. If the Board approves, the charges are dropped and the case is closed. A case may be said to be "adjusted," if agreement is reached during the informal investigation or before or after the formal hearing, prior to decision.

Withdrawal by Complainant. As previously discussed, a charge may be withdrawn only with the consent of the Board. This applies to all cases in which the charges have been withdrawn for some reason other than an adjustment between the parties. Ordinarily, charges are withdrawn for lack of evidence or for lack of Board jurisdiction. A charging party may be urged to withdraw for these reasons, since the result would otherwise be dismissal by the Board.

Dismissed: Default of Party Filing. This applies to cases in which the complainant fails to press his charge. If a complainant abandons the charge, the Board notifies all parties concerned that the charge has been dismissed.

Dismissed on the Merits: or Complaint Authorized. This refers to Board action in those cases where the charges have neither been adjusted, withdrawn, or dismissed. Hence we are now in the post-investigatory stage of Board procedure, in which the Board must decide whether to dismiss the charges or authorize a complaint and proceed with the formal hearing. The Board may dismiss the entire charge, or it may dismiss only part of the charge and issue a complaint on the remaining part. Conversely, the Board may issue a complaint on the total charge or charges, or it may issue a complaint on a part of the charges. The charges are neither pleadings nor proof; they are simply allegations which the Board must investigate and weigh and then decide whether they merit the issuance of a complaint. The complaint as issued by the Board may state the original charge, or it may be broader than the charge. This is for the Board to decide.

The 1942 Benjamin Report noted that the Board, for administrative reasons, had delegated the authority to any *one* Board member to authorize complaints and dismiss charges. In 1943 the Board changed its administrative rule by requiring the concurrence of at least *two* Board members for the dismissal of an unfair labor practice charge.

(The reader's attention is directed to Table 4 in Appendix A, "Disposition of Closed Cases," for a statistical breakdown of cases closed in the various stages of investigation.)

The Informal Investigation

When a charge is filed in the New York City office, it is referred to one of the two Senior Labor Relations Examiners.[5] The Senior Examiner either retains the case himself or turns it over to a member of the Board's staff of Labor Relations Examiners for investigation.

The purpose of the investigation is twofold: (1) An attempt is made by the Labor Relations Examiner during the course of the informal investigations to bring about a voluntary adjustment between the parties. (2) During the investigation, the Examiner obtains information concerning the merits of the case. The decision of the Board as to whether or not a complaint should be issued will rest heavily upon the information supplied to it by the Labor Relations Examiner.

First Step in Investigation. Prior to assigning the case to one of the Examiners, the Senior Labor Relations Examiner studies the substance of the charge to determine whether or not any additional information is desired. If so, the Senior Examiner makes a note to that effect. At the request of the Senior Examiner, or upon his own initiative, the Labor Relations Examiner conducts a *preliminary inquiry* to obtain the needed additional information. This preliminary inquiry may take the form of an interview with the person making the charge, or it may be a request for affidavits giving the facts of the charge in more detail.

A second purpose of this preliminary inquiry is to determine

[5]Prior to 1947, there was only one Senior Labor Relations Examiner. The second post was created on Sept. 1, 1947.

whether or not the charges merit still further investigation. If in the preliminary inquiry the Examiner finds no merit in the charges, or if he finds that the Board lacks jurisdiction, the Examiner may either recommend that the complainant withdraw the charges or that the Board dismiss them. It should be emphasized that it is the Board, not the Labor Relations Examiner, that either dismisses the charge or approves the withdrawal. The Labor Relations Examiner may do no more than recommend.

Second Step: Initiation of Conferences. Following the preliminary inquiry (if one is conducted), the Labor Relations Examiner sends letters to all interested parties asking them to attend an informal conference. In many cases the employer and the charging party are represented by counsel. As previously mentioned, the purpose of the informal investigation is both to obtain the contentions and evidence of the parties and, if warranted, to attempt to bring about a voluntary adjustment of the dispute.

After the first informal conference is called, if no agreement is then reached, the Labor Relations Examiner may schedule another meeting of the parties. In addition, he may conduct personal interviews of parties and witnesses and/or request affidavits to substantiate allegations. In all that the Examiner does, he is attempting to maintain a liaison between the parties; he is attempting to direct the parties toward agreement. This quasi-mediation procedure followed by the Labor Relations Examiner has *always* been part of the Board's policy. In 1940 an amendment to Section 702(8) of the New York State Labor Relations Act added a proviso which made this procedure law:

...nothing contained in this subdivision shall be construed to prevent the board, its agents or employees, from engaging in any effort to obtain voluntary adjustments and compliance....

This proviso put the legislative stamp of approval on the Board's standard operating procedure.

One of the most important aspects of these informal conferences is that they are completely "off the record." From the very beginning, the Board has made it a policy not to allow statements and admissions made at informal conferences to be introduced as evidence in subsequent formal hearings.[6] This policy was made part of Section 59 of the 1940 General Rules and Regulations. The Board has consistently held that unless the parties expressly waive rule 59, no statements or communications made at the informal conferences will be admitted as evidence in the subsequent formal hearings. The position of the Board on this matter has been upheld by the courts.[7]

It is the Board's view that the off-the-record character of the informal hearings has contributed a great deal to the effectiveness of the act. And, in fact, when the very high percentage of both representation and unfair labor practice cases which have been disposed of at the stage of informal investigations is considered, one can see that this policy has proven itself by a history of success.[8]

This discussion of the off-the-record nature of informal investigations must be qualified in three ways:

1. The last sentence in Section 59 of the General Rules and Regulations adds the proviso that the rule does not apply to evidence concerning a consent card comparison pursuant to Section 16. (This is now of little significance, in view of the fact that the Board long ago abandoned the method of card comparisons to resolve representation questions. See Chapter V.)

2. When the Litigation Attorney is preparing the Board's case, he has access to the file of the informal investigation. Thus, although he may not introduce any of the facts divulged in the informal sessions as evidence in the formal hearings, he does use the file as the basic source for his case preparation. Furthermore, since various members of the Board and the Board's staff may have occasion to assist the Labor Relations Examiner in the conduct of the informal investigations, a knowledge of the facts of the case is likely to be shared by a number of persons. It is worth repeating,

[6]See Joseph L. Daly, Inc. 2 S.L.R.B. 332 (1939). See also Cosmopolitan House & Window Cleaning Co., 5 S.L.R.B. 249 (1942). At 262, the Board held that mere failure to object to the introduction of informal testimony as evidence is not sufficient; Rule 59 must be expressly waived.

[7]See S.L.R.B. v. Ralph W. Merians, Inc., 139 N.Y.L.J., Vol. I, No. 7, p. 5 (Sup. Ct. Jan. 10, 1958).

[8]Between July 1, 1937 and Dec. 31, 1962, of 12,769 unfair labor practice cases 10,609 were disposed of without having gone to the formal hearing stage. Board decisions needed to be rendered in 1,035 instances. See Table 4 in Appendix A.

however, that even though the proceedings of the informal investigations may be known to the Litigation Attorney and members of the Board and the Board staff, none of the statements or admissions made at the informal sessions may be admitted as evidence in the subsequent formal hearings.

3. As briefly mentioned before, Section 59 does not apply if all parties waive the rule.

(Because of differences in personnel in Buffalo and Albany, the informal investigatory procedure described above for the New York City office may differ in some respects from the procedure followed in Buffalo and Albany. For one thing, the investigations carried on in Buffalo and Albany are usually conducted by a Regional Attorney. But once the case reaches the formal hearing stage, the procedures become the same for all three offices.)

The Final Report. After the Labor Relations Examiner (or Regional Attorney) has concluded the informal investigations, a "final report" is submitted to one of the Senior Examiners. In cases where the charges have neither been adjusted nor withdrawn, this final report is quite detailed and analytical. It usually contains the full facts of the investigation together with the Examiner's opinion and recommendations. This report, together with the Examiner's complete file of the case, is sent to one of the Senior Examiners. The Senior Examiner studies the information contained in the file and the final report and, if further information is needed, refers the case back to the Labor Relations Examiner. Finally, the Labor Relations Examiner's Report, together with his and the Senior Examiner's recommendation are submitted to a Board member for action.

The Complaint. Once the final report with recommendations and the case file are submitted to a Board member, the next step is to decide whether or not a complaint (see Fac. 3, p. 44) should issue on the charge. In making this determination, the Board member may seek the advice of the General Counsel and other Board members, or he may even direct the Labor Relations Examiner or Regional Attorney to conduct further investigations. At times, though rarely, the final decision concerning the disposition of the case is made by the entire Board.

Before proceeding with a discussion of the procedure which is followed when the decision is made to issue a complaint, it is worth noting the situation which arises when the decision is made *not* to issue a complaint. As previously mentioned, the decision to dismiss a charge in an unfair labor practice case is made by at least two members of the Board. The interesting question which develops out of the decision to dismiss a charge is whether or not that decision is reviewable by the courts. In 1942, at the time of the writing of the Benjamin Report, no case had arisen in which the Board's determination not to issue a complaint was challenged. The Board noted then that there were three substantial reasons why a Board decision to dismiss a charge would not be reviewable: (1) There is nothing in the act which makes the issuance of a complaint mandatory upon the Board, nor is there anything which indicates any right of appeal from such a decision by the Board. (2) Section 25(b) of the General Rules and Regulations states quite specifically that if the Board in its discretion decides that no complaint should issue on the charge, the Board may make such other disposition of the charge as it deems proper. (3) A Board decision to dismiss a charge is not a final order and is not, therefore, subject to judicial review.[9]

The general rule has continued to be that refusal to issue a complaint is not judicially reviewable.

Complaint Authorization. Once a complaint has been authorized by the Board, the case file is referred to the Executive Secretary. The Executive Secretary transmits the file to the Associate General Counsel with a notation that a complaint has been authorized. The Associate General Counsel selects an attorney from the Litigation Division to draft the complaint and prepare the case for hearing. (In the Albany and Buffalo regions, as previously noted, the Regional Attorney acts as the Litigation Attorney.) In drafting the complaint and preparing the case for hearing, the Litigation Attorney may use the investigatory powers granted to him under Section 708 of the act in order to obtain all the information neces-

[9]Compare De Perno v. S.L.R.B. unreported (Sup. Ct. Feb. 28, 1953), wherein the court upheld the Board's dismissal of a complaint *following* a hearing. See also S.L.R.B. v. Babylon Cleaners, Inc., 130 N.Y.L.J. 916 (Sup. Ct. Oct. 28, 1953).

NEW YORK STATE LABOR RELATIONS BOARD

In the Matter of ABC BAKING CO. and Bakery and Confectionery Workers' International Union of America Local #30, Ind.	Case No. CU–0000

COMPLAINT

It having been charged by Bakery and Confectionery Workers' International Union of America, Local #30, Ind., herein called the Union, that ABC Baking Co., herein called the Respondent, has engaged in, and is engaging in, certain unfair labor practices as set forth and defined in the New York State Labor Relations Act, Article 20 of the Labor Law, herein called the Act, the New York State Labor Relations Board, after due consideration, hereby issues its complaint pursuant to Section 706 of the Act and alleges:

1. Respondent is, and at all times herein mentioned was, a domestic corporation, having its principal office and place of business at 112 Jones St. in the city of X, county of X, State of New York, where it owns and operates a bakery shop.

2. The Union is, and at all times herein mentioned was, a labor organization which exists and is constituted for the purpose, in whole or in part, of collective bargaining or of dealing with employers concerning grievances, terms or conditions of employment or other mutual aid or protection.

3. All employees employed by the Respondent in the bakery production unit, at the above address, constitute a unit appropriate for the purposes of collective bargaining.

4. Prior to March 2, 1960, a majority of the employees within the unit described in paragraph "3", above, designated and selected the Union as their representative for the purposes of collective bargaining with Respondent.

5. At all times since March 2, 1960, or thereabouts, the Union has been, and continues to be, the exclusive representative of the employees of the Respondent within the unit described in paragraph "3", above, for the purposes of collective bargaining in respect to rates of pay, wages, hours of employment, and other conditions of employment.

6. Commencing on or about March 2, 1960, and continuing to the date of this complaint, Respondent has failed and refused, and continues to fail and refuse, to meet, confer, discuss and negotiate, in good faith, with the Union for the purposes of collective bargaining concerning rates of pay, wages, hours of employment and other conditions of employment of Respondent's employees within the unit described in paragraph "3", above, although requested to do so by the Union.

7. Commencing on or about March 2, 1960, and continuing to the date of this complaint, Respondent sought to, and did, interfere with, restrain, and coerce its employees in the exercise of their rights to self-organization, to join or assist a labor organization of their own choosing, and to engage

in concerted activities for the purposes of collective bargaining and other mutual aid and protection, in that Respondent:

  (a) questioned its employees concerning membership in, and designation of, the Union, for the purposes of discouraging membership therein;

  (b) made statements to its employees disparaging the Union and its representatives, for the purpose of discouraging membership therein, designation thereof, and assistance thereto;

  (c) threatened to discharge any of its employees who joined, designated or assisted the Union;

  (d) offered benefits, rewards and other inducements to its employees to cause them to renounce their Union membership, their designation of, and their activity on behalf of the Union;

  (e) urged, directed, advised and warned its employees to refrain from joining, designating or assisting the Union and to refrain from engaging in concerted activities for the purposes of collective bargaining and other mutual aid and protection.

8. On or about March 8, 1960 Respondent discharged John Doe heretofore employed by it.

9. At all times since March 8, 1960, or thereabouts, Respondent failed and refused, and continues to fail and refuse, to reinstate the said John Doe to its employ.

10. Respondent discharged and failed and refused, and continues to fail and refuse, to reinstate John Doe, as heretofore alleged, for the reason that he joined or assisted the Union and engaged in concerted activities for the purposes of collective bargaining and other mutual aid and protection.

11. By reason of the facts hereinabove set forth, Respondent has required, and continues to require, its employees, as a condition of employment, to refrain from forming, joining or assisting a labor organization of their own choosing and has thereby engaged in, and is engaging in, unfair labor practices within the meaning of Section 704, subdivision 4, of the Act.

12. By reason of the facts hereinabove set forth, Respondent has discouraged, and continues to discourage, membership in a labor organization by discriminating in regard to hire and tenure and other terms and conditions of employment of its employees and has thereby engaged in, and is engaging in, unfair labor practices within the meaning of Section 704, subdivision 5, of the Act.

13. By reason of the facts hereinabove set forth, Respondent has refused, and continues to refuse, to bargain collectively with the Union as the exclusive bargaining representative of its employees within the unit appropriate for the purposes of collective bargaining and has thereby engaged in, and is engaging in, unfair labor practices within the meaning of Section 704, subdivision 6 of the Act.

14. By reason of the facts hereinabove set forth, Respondent has interfered with, restrained and coerced, and continues to interfere with, restrain, and coerce, its employees in the exercise of the rights guaranteed them by Section 703 of the Act and has thereby engaged in, and is engaging in, unfair labor practices within the meaning of Section 704, subdivision 10, of the Act.

WHEREFORE, the New York State Labor Relations Board on the—— day of May, 1960, issues its complaint against ABC Baking Co.

Board Litigation Attorney   Associate General Counsel

sary to process the case. As well as studying the case file, the Litigation Attorney interviews the witnesses concerned.

In preparing the complaint the Litigation Attorney may find it necessary to have the charge amended to conform with the complaint. (It is not necessary under the law for the complaint to be the same as the charge, but it is the policy of the Board to have uniformity between the allegations of the charge and those of the complaint.) The amendment may be for the purpose of clarifying the original charge or it may be for the purpose of adding supplemental allegations on the basis of the Board's investigations.

Once the complaint has been drawn by the Litigation Attorney, it is submitted to the Associate General Counsel for his approval and signature. The complaint is then served on the parties together with a notice of hearing (see Facsimile 4).

Notice of Hearing. Section 26 of the Board's General Rules and Regulations states that:

After a charge has been filed, if it appears to the Board that formal proceedings should be instituted, the Board may issue and cause to be served upon the parties a complaint in the name of the Board, containing a concise statement as to the alleged violations of the Act and a notice of hearing before the Trial Examiner at a place fixed therein, and at a time not less than seven (7) days after the service of the complaint.[10]

The complaint and notice of hearing, sent to the Respondent(s) and the person or labor organization making the charge and to all other parties having a possible interest in the proceedings, contain the following items: (a) notice that the Board's General Rules and Regulations are available upon request; (b) copy of the final charge form; (c) the complaint, containing a concise statement of the alleged unfair labor practices; (d) a notice of hearing before the Trial Examiner.

Amendment of Complaint. As in the case of the amendment of a charge, a complaint may be amended or a supplemental complaint added in the discretion of the Board or the Trial Examiner at any time before the issuance of the final decision and order. The complaint may be amended or supplemented upon motion of the

[10]The Board's policy is to give at least ten days' notice of hearing instead of the seven days required in this section.

Facsimile 4.

NOTICE OF HEARING

PLEASE TAKE NOTICE, that on the   day of   , 196 , at
      o'clock in the   noon, at 270 Broadway, Borough of Manhattan, City, County and State of New York, a hearing will be conducted before the New York State Labor Relations Board on the allegations set forth in the Complaint attached hereto, at which time and place you will have the right to appear, in person or otherwise, and to give testimony.

You are further notified that, pursuant to the Board's Rules and Regulations, you have the right to file with the New York State Labor Relations Board a verified answer to the Complaint. The original answer and two (2) copies thereof must be filed with the Board within five (5) days, together with proof of service of a copy thereof on each party and the Board's Litigation Attorney.

IN WITNESS WHEREOF, the New York State Labor Relations Board has caused this Notice of Hearing to be signed by its Associate General Counsel on the   day of   , 196 .

_____
Associate General Counsel

_____
Board Litigation Attorney

TO:

APPLICATION FOR ADJOURNMENT WILL BE CONSIDERED ONLY UPON SUBMISSION OF AN AFFIDAVIT BASED UPON A LEGAL EXCUSE. THE HEARING WILL PROCEED FROM DAY TO DAY UNTIL CONCLUDED.

A COPY OF THE RULES AND REGULATIONS WILL BE FURNISHED UPON REQUEST.

Litigation Attorney or upon the Board's own motion. In effect, this provision gives the Board power to amend the complaint so as to include additional information or allegations uncovered in the course of the formal hearings before the Trial Examiner.[11]

Withdrawal of Complaint. On motion of the Board or the Litigation Attorney, the Board may withdraw its complaint, in whole or in part, at any time prior to the issuance of a final decision and order. A case may be discontinued by the Board where the parties reach a compromise prior to the issuance of a decision and order

[11]The reader will note in §27 of the General Rules and Regulations that the original Preliminary Rules and Regulations (1937) contained a provision dealing with the amendment of complaints. The 1951 amendments added to §27 the proviso dealing with supplemental complaints. Again, this addition to the section simply codified an established Board procedure.

or in cases where the evidence introduced at the formal hearing indicates that the allegations were without foundation. It is worth emphasizing that the Board, acting through its Attorney, is the party which initiates the complaint withdrawal, since the Board is the complainant at this stage of the proceedings. In the withdrawal of a charge, on the other hand, it is ordinarily the person or labor organization which is the moving party.

Answer to Complaint. Section 29 of the General Rules and Regulations provides in part that:

The party or parties against whom the complaint is issued shall have the right to file an answer [see Facsimile 5] within five (5) days after the service of the complaint.[12]

[12]The Board frequently allows more than five days.

Facsimile 5.

NEW YORK STATE LABOR RELATIONS BOARD

In the Matter of ABC BAKING CO. and Bakery and Confectionery Workers International Union of America, Local #30, Inc.	Case No. CU–000

ANSWER

ABC Baking Co., (referred to as the Respondent), through its Attorney, hereby makes Answer, duly verified, to the complaint issued by the New York State Labor Relations Board:

1—Admits the allegations set forth in Paragraphs numbered 1, 2, 8, and 9 of the said complaint.

2—Denies the allegations set forth in Paragraphs 3, 4, 5, 6, 7, 10, 11, 12, 13, and 14.

WHEREFORE, this Respondent demands that the Complaint be dismissed.

DATED: 17 May 60

Richard Roe, Pres.
ABC BAKING CO.
Richard Roe, Pres.

The Rules and Regulations go on to state that the answer is to contain a specific admission or denial of each allegation in the complaint. If the Respondent claims that he is without knowledge of the allegation or allegations, this statement is considered a denial. Any allegation not specifically denied in the answer, unless Respondent claims he is without knowledge, may be deemed admitted and true.

In very few cases do Respondents fail to file answers to the complaints. Section 34 of the General Rules and Regulations contains a provision, however, dealing with those cases in which Respondents do not file an answer. This section states:

If the party or parties against whom the complaint is issued fails to file an answer in the manner and within the time herein provided, it may be limited to cross-examination of witnesses called by the Board's Attorney or Trial Examiner and shall have such rights as the Trial Examiner may deem proper.

The 1937 Preliminary Rules and Regulations placed no specific restrictions on the right of Respondents failing to file answers to the complaint. In the 1940 amendments to the Rules and Regulations, a provision was added stating in part that persons failing to answer "shall not have the right to interpose or seek to establish any affirmative defenses." The section was again amended in 1943 to read as the present Section 34. As it reads now, Section 34 gives the Trial Examiner rather complete discretion as to what the defaulting respondent may do at the hearings. In actual practice, however, Respondents who fail or refuse to file answers are seldom penalized to any serious extent in the formal hearings. This, however, is left to the Trial Examiner's discretion.

CHAPTER IV

The Unfair Labor Practice Case: The Formal Stage

A RELATIVELY small number of cases goes beyond the procedural steps described in Chapter III. Thus, of 12,769 unfair practice cases closed between the time of the Board's establishment and the end of 1962, 10,609 were disposed of prior to authorization of a hearing (see Appendix A). This chapter is concerned with that smaller number of cases which are not thus informally concluded. Such cases will proceed to a formal hearing conducted by a Trial Examiner, following which an Intermediate Report will be issued by the Examiner and a final decision and order by the Board.

The Formal Hearing

As previously noted, it is the policy of the Board to schedule hearings from seven to ten days after issuance of notice of hearings. Frequently, this period is extended beyond ten days upon application for temporary adjournment. The Board seems to be exceedingly liberal in this matter.

The Trial Examiner. In the early days of the act's administration there was no special group of Trial Examiners. If the Board members themselves could not handle a case, outside attorneys or attorneys from the Board's staff were appointed to act as Trial Examiners. This practice was challenged in the case of *Metropolitan Life Insurance Company* v. *Boland*,[1] on the grounds that these Trial Examiners were not being appointed in accordance with the rules

[1]Metropolitan Life Ins. Co. v. Boland, 281 N. Y. 357, 23 N. E. 2d 532 (1939).

of the Civil Service Commission. This contention was upheld by the Court of Appeals, and Section 702(5) was subsequently amended to provide that: "All employees of the board shall be appointed by the board in accordance with the provisions of the civil service law and rules."

As a result of this decision, early in 1940 the Board adopted its present system of Trial Examiners. Four permanent Trial Examiners and a staff of twenty-five per diem Trial Examiners were designated by the Board to assume the responsibility of presiding over the formal hearings. As previously noted, the number of permanent Trial Examiners is now six, under the direction of a supervising Trial Examiner.

Although the Trial Examiner may be selected from among the Board members, the permanent Trial Examiners, or the per diem Examiners, in actual practice the Trial Examiner is almost always selected from the permanent staff. Beginning in 1940, the Board members appeared less and less frequently in the capacity of Trial Examiners. At the present time it is extremely rare for a Board member to preside as Trial Examiner.

Section 49 of the General Rules and Regulations sets forth the duties and powers of the Trial Examiner:

During the course of any hearing, the Trial Examiner, in addition to the other powers specifically conferred upon him, and subject to the limitations imposed upon him by these Rules and Regulations, shall have full authority to control the conduct and procedure of the hearing and the record thereof, to admit or exclude testimony or other evidence, and to rule upon all motions and objections. It shall be the duty of the Trial Examiner to see that a full inquiry is made into all the facts in issue and to obtain a complete record of all facts necessary for a fair determination of the issues. The Trial Examiner shall have the right to call and examine witnesses, to direct the production of papers or other matter present in the hearing room, and to introduce documentary or other evidence, except as may otherwise be limited herein.

As can be seen from this description of duties and powers, the Trial Examiner performs a function somewhat similar to that of a judge in a non-jury court action, but the Trial Examiner performs additional functions as well. He has the power and the responsibility, where he deems it necessary, to do everything within the limits of the Rules and Regulations to get the parties to reach an agreement and to obtain all the necessary facts of the case. Thus, in many cases, the Trial Examiner actively participates in the hearings, questioning witnesses and calling for written documents and other evidence.

In an unfair labor practice proceeding, the Trial Examiner has no access to the file on the case. (In a representation proceeding, the Trial Examiner would have the case file, since there would usually be no Board Litigation Attorney present at the hearings.) The Board's attorneys are instructed not to discuss the case with any of the Trial Examiners. Furthermore, once the hearing begins, the Trial Examiner is free from any direction by members of the Board or the Board's staff (with the one exception of the Supervising Trial Examiner). The reason for thus insulating the Trial Examiner in unfair labor practice proceedings is, of course, to secure separation of prosecution and judging functions and to assure the parties the greatest degree of impartiality by the Examiner. The Trial Examiner has no prior information concerning the case other than the final charge form, the complaint, and answer. He has, therefore, no preconceived notions about the validity of the allegations. All of this is designed to assure that the parties to the unfair labor practice proceedings receive fair and impartial treatment. This policy of the Board has done a great deal to eliminate possible posthearing objections to the conduct of the hearings and the Trial Examiner.

Conduct of Hearing. Hearings in unfair labor practice cases are, by their nature, adversary proceedings. There is often a strong feeling of animosity between the parties. This is particularly so when the cases involve discriminatory discharges. Feelings and emotions are apt to run high; it is up to the Trial Examiner to control the conduct of the hearings and bring something positive out of them. The duty of the Trial Examiner is well illustrated in the following statement from the Benjamin Report:

One of the original Board members...regularly impressed upon the Board's personnel that it was one of their primary functions "to get the poison out of the situation"....[2]

[2] *V. Administrative Adjudication in the State of New York* 80 (1942).

The actual conduct of the hearings is similar to the conduct of trials in non-jury court actions. Although the State Labor Relations Act provides that the Board or its agent are not bound by the technical rules of evidence prevailing in the courts, in fact the Trial Examiners follow the rules of evidence quite closely. This is not to say that there is no flexibility in the conduct of the hearings. For example, opinion evidence and hearsay are occasionally permitted by the Trial Examiner. In order, however, to facilitate the fair conduct of the hearings and eliminate possible posthearing objections, the Trial Examiner usually insists on applying the common law rules concerning the introduction of evidence and the conduct of the proceedings. (It will be noted in the next chapters that the conduct of hearings in representation cases, which are not treated as adversary proceedings, is more flexible than the conduct of unfair labor practice cases.)

The Litigation Attorney. As has previously been pointed out, the Board's Litigation Attorney is responsible for presenting the case on behalf of the Board, which is the complainant in the proceeding. The work of the Litigation Attorney is supervised by the Associate General Counsel. Ordinarily, however, the Litigation Attorney operates independently in the preparation and presentation of the case before the Trial Examiner.

The Union's Attorney. The person or labor organization filing the charge is a party to the proceedings and usually arranges to be represented by counsel. However, since the Board's Litigation Attorney is responsible for presenting the case, the union's attorney generally plays a secondary role in the proceedings. There are a few exceptions to this in unfair labor practice cases, when the union's attorney is especially knowledgeable of the facts. And in representation cases involving a claim of company domination of another union, the Board may permit the union making the claim to present the case rather than the Board's Litigation Attorney.

The Respondent's Attorney. We have already indicated that the hearings in unfair labor practice cases are adversary in character. In the early period of the act, the Board found that the actions of the Respondents' attorneys frequently contributed greatly to this contentious atmosphere. The Board found that many attorneys would purposely stir up trouble and "bait" the Trial Examiner in the hope of using the resultant confusion as a posthearing objection. In the 1940 General Rules and Regulations, Section 53, the Board attempted to deal with this problem in the following way:

Any person who engages in contemptuous conduct before a Trial Examiner may, in the discretion of the Trial Examiner, be excluded from the hearing room or further participation in the proceedings. Any attorney who engages in contemptuous or unprofessional conduct before a Trial Examiner or the Board may, in the discretion of the Trial Examiner or the Board, be excluded from further participation in the proceeding, and a reasonable adjournment shall be granted to afford the client of such attorney opportunity to obtain other counsel. Any attorney excluded from a proceeding by a Trial Examiner may appeal such exclusion to the Board.

The 1941 amendments to the General Rules and Regulations deleted all but the first sentence of this section. As one might suppose, the reason for the 1941 amendment was that the New York Bar Association did not look at all favorably upon the singling out of attorneys in the wording of the 1940 Rules, nor the power of the Board to exclude attorneys from the proceedings. Although Section 53 now contains no mention of any specific party, the power to exclude attorneys from the hearings has not been taken from the Trial Examiner.

Although the friction has not been completely eliminated, over the years the Board has experienced less and less difficulty along these lines. This is not to say that all relations among the parties are amicable. Unfair labor practice cases are adversary proceedings and still tend to generate some ill feeling. But that the amount of open acrimony during such proceedings has greatly diminished over the years is a tribute to the hearing procedure which the New York State Labor Relations Board has developed and followed.

Oral Arguments and Briefs. At the close of a hearing in an unfair labor practice proceeding, the Trial Examiner may, at his discretion, permit the parties to file briefs and other written statements with him, and/or argue orally before him. In most cases a request to file briefs or present argument is granted by the Trial Examiner.

Posthearing Procedure

At the conclusion of the formal hearing in an unfair labor practice proceeding, the Trial Examiner prepares an Intermediate Report for service on the parties and submission to the Board.

Intermediate Report (see Appendix B for an example). During the early period of the act, there was no provision in the Board's procedure which called for an intermediate step between the conclusion of the hearings and the issuance of a final decision and order. Soon, however, the Board decided that it would be fairer to serve the parties with a proposed decision and then give them an opportunity to file exceptions and present additional argument before the Board. The procedure arrived at by the Board, called "Proposed Findings of Fact, Conclusions of Law and Order," was as follows:

1. At the close of the hearing, a Review Attorney was assigned to prepare a report on the case for the Board. (In cases where a Board member acted as Trial Examiner, the Board member would make an oral report directly to the two other Board members, and the services of the Review Attorney would be largely eliminated.) The report of the Review Attorney was based entirely on the transcripts and exhibits of the case; the Review Attorney had no access to the general file nor to the Trial Examiner or other members of the Board's staff who might supply him with additional information.

2. When the Review Attorney concluded his study, the Executive Secretary was notified and the matter was put on the agenda for the next Board meeting. The Review Attorney appeared at the meeting and gave an oral report of the facts of the case.

3. After considering the report of the Review Attorney and other pertinent facts, the Board members decided upon their proposed "findings of fact, proposed conclusions of law and proposed order." The Review Attorney was then assigned the task of preparing a preliminary draft of the Board's intermediate determination. After additional revision, the Board's intermediate determination was served on the parties to the proceedings.

4. The parties were then given an opportunity to file exceptions and present oral arguments before the Board.

The significant omission in the above procedure was, of course, that the firsthand knowledge of the Trial Examiner (particularly in the appraisal of witnesses' demeanor and credibility) was not utilized in the Board's intermediate determination. The report was written from a secondary source rather than from the primary source which the Trial Examiner could have supplied.

Late in 1939, the Board recognized the deficiencies in the proposed findings of fact, conclusions of law and order procedure, and adopted the present Intermediate Report procedure, which is as follows:[3]

1. At the conclusion of the hearing, the Trial Examiner prepares a report for issuance to the parties, containing a detailed statement of the facts and issues of the case, the conclusions reached by the Trial Examiner, and a recommendation to the Board concerning the dispositions of the case.

2. The parties, upon receiving the Intermediate Report, may then file exceptions and present oral arguments before the Board.

Oral Arguments before the Board. Section 60(c) of the General Rules and Regulations states in part:

A request for oral argument may be filed with the exceptions. Upon such request or upon its own motion, the Board shall issue a notice to all parties and to Board's attorney, informing them of the time and place set for oral argument.

This procedure differs from that followed in representation cases. In unfair labor practice cases, posthearing oral arguments before the Board are a matter of *right* for the parties. In representation cases, on the other hand, posthearing oral arguments before the Board are a matter of Board discretion.[4] This difference stems from the fact that an unfair labor practice case is an adversary proceeding, often full of conflicting and contradictory contentions, resulting in a final and judicially enforceable order which nearly always affects one party or the other in a legally significant manner. Thus, because of the very nature of the proceedings and of the Board's final decision, the parties, from the very beginning of the

[3]For a more complete description of the Intermediate Report procedure, see §60 of the General Rules and Regulations.
[4]*Ibid.*, §55.

act's administration, were allowed to argue orally before the Board at the conclusion of the hearings as a matter of right.

Representation proceedings, on the other hand, are viewed as basically investigatory in nature. Not that serious conflicts and bad feelings never arise in representation proceedings; they do. The course of the proceedings in representation cases, however, ordinarily revolves around a question of fact: Does a particular group of employees desire to be represented by a union, or not? Thus, because of the relatively trouble-free nature of representation proceedings, and in order to avoid purely dilatory tactics, the Board has deemed it advisable to make posthearing oral arguments a matter of Board discretion. In actual practice, however, the Board will seldom deny a request for such oral arguments.

Procedure Prior to Decision and Order. Upon issuance of the Intermediate Report, or sometimes earlier, a Review Attorney is assigned to the case. The functions of the Review Attorney are much the same here as under the earlier proposed findings of fact, conclusions of law and order procedure, except that now the Review Attorney has access to the Intermediate Report (and exceptions thereto), as well as the transcript of the hearings. After exceptions and briefs have been filed, and oral arguments heard, the Review Attorney prepares an analysis of the case for presentation to the Board. The Review Attorney usually presents this report orally (see Facsimile 6).

On the basis of the Intermediate Report, the exceptions, the briefs and arguments, and the Review Attorney's review and analysis, the Board prepares its final determination of the case. In making this determination, the Board may be able to arrive at a decision on the basis of the information presented, or it may have to request the Review Attorney to make a further analysis on some portion or portions of the record, or engage in additional research on difficult points of law. The Board has well described its decisional process at pages 5 and 6 of its Thirteenth Annual Report (1950):

Before a case comes up at a Board meeting for decision, the Board members have read the Intermediate Report, the exceptions thereto,

continued on pps. 59–60

Facsimile 6.

MEMORANDUM TO REVIEW ATTORNEYS:

Re: *Presentation of Reviews*

The following revised memorandum concerning the presentation of reviews is being reissued at the direction of the Board.

A rigid pattern for the presentation of case reviews manifestly is both undesirable and impracticable. Nevertheless certain basic rules should be followed.

The reviewer's full knowledge of the evidence manifestly is necessary, but it is not sufficient unless the information can be conveyed to the Board. Careful consideration should be given, therefore, to the manner and form of presentation which will most clearly and concisely detail the issues, the evidence, and the law.

Review Attorneys frequently read their notes or a prepared statement. The difficulty of remembering all the details of a case is fully appreciated. But nothing is more trying to attention and receptivity than to listen to the reading of a written report delivered in a monotone. It should be the reviewer's goal to make the presentation interesting as well as objective, accurate and complete.

Oral presentation can be absorbed more readily if the course to be followed is outlined in advance. Visual presentation will often save time and make for greater understanding and accuracy. For example, in cases involving disputed units, a chart showing the categories of employees and the contentions of the parties frequently will be most helpful. Where comparisons are necessary, the use of parallel columns will be of great assistance. In many cases, a written chronological outline will serve to highlight and give form to the presentation.

The review of an unfair labor practice case should begin with a statement of the substance of the complaint and the contents of the answer. All too often, the pleadings are ignored, although they frame, and frequently narrow, the issues. The Trial Examiner's recommendations and the exceptions thereto should follow. The reviewer is then in a position to outline the basic issues, the contentions of the parties, and to announce the order in which they will be discussed. If disposition of one issue may eliminate others, it should be so stated. This may also be a propitious point to acquaint the Board with any loose ends, such as undecided motions, etc.

In a representation proceeding, the review should begin with the names of the employer and the unions involved, their status in the proceeding (petitioner, intervenor, etc.), and the nature of the employer's business. The issues should then be outlined, specifying the unit contentions of the parties, contract bar claims, jurisdictional questions, etc. The Trial Examiner's recommendation, if any, should be stated and the order of discussion outlined.

For intelligible and interesting presentation of the evidence proper organization is of prime importance. Merely paginating the Intermediate Report is not adequate. In some cases, a chronological development may be best. In others, it may be necessary to disregard chronology and discuss the evidence in terms of related issues and patterns. The proper method of development depends upon the facts, issues and the nature of the particular case, and requires analysis and thought. Care should be exercised that discussion of the evidence is related to the issues. *All* the evidence on each issue should be noted and correlated *in advance,* so that it does not become necessary to hunt through the pagination for specific evidence on a particular issue. Any conflicts in testimony, and the Trial Examiner's credibility findings, should be mentioned. Undisputed or documentary evidence supporting the credibility of one witness as against another should be called to the attention of the Board.

It is important that a current check be made of the Board's records, and any pending case involving the same employer brought to the Board's attention.

In addition to the presentation of the factual evidence, the reviewer should be thoroughly familiar with, and ready to cite and discuss, prior Board and court decisions on the same and related issues. Distinctions between cases, and inaccuracies in briefs submitted by the parties, should be pointed out. Where any substantial question of law or policy is involved, a written memorandum should be prepared and submitted at least two working days prior to the review. Merely stringing along a number of quotations *is not sufficient.* The memorandum should first analyze and define the question, and then discuss the cases in point, summarizing their factual backgrounds and true holdings, as well as quoting therefrom.

The reviewer, who has read, analyzed and paginated the record, and done research on legal questions presented, manifestly is the person most familiar with the testimony, exhibits, and precedents. It is his duty to give an objective, accurate and *complete* report. If there are matters which the Board has not considered during the discussion of the case, the reviewer should, *and must,* bring them to the attention of the Board.

Compliance with the foregoing will not only make for better presentation to the Board, but will do much to expedite the preparation and submission of the draft decision. Once the complete groundwork is done, the actual drafting of a decision should approach the routine in most cases. The attorney should not first begin to think about a case *after* it is decided at the Board meeting. Adequate preparation to report is, at the same time, a preparation of the bulk of the material for the final decision.

General Counsel

all briefs that have been submitted, and they have heard the oral argument on the exceptions. At the meeting the Board members, and the Review Attorney assigned to the case, are present, as well as the General Counsel and the Executive Secretary, neither of whom participate in the prosecution of cases before the Board.

The review attorney commences with a resumé of the pleadings and a statement of the issues presented. Before the Board are the pleadings, the minutes of the hearing, the exhibits, and all other pertinent papers, including the briefs. Also at hand are digests of the evidence, both witness by witness, and topic by topic, with special emphasis upon the points as to which there is conflict. Each of these contain references to the precise pages of the transcript of the testimony and to the exhibits. These digests are prepared by the review attorney and are accompanied by a memorandum on such points of law as are involved.

The review attorney then summarizes such matters as are admitted or are not in dispute. He follows this by recounting the evidence both pro and con on all disputed matters, referring the Board to particular pages of testimony or particular exhibits relevant thereto. The Board members read, or have read to them by the review attorney, all specific portions of the record deemed of significance on doubtful points.

A review attorney makes no findings for the Board. After discussion and deliberation on the question as to how conflicting testimony is to be resolved, what inferences are to be drawn from the evidence, and of any legal questions which are involved, the Board reaches its decision.

The review attorney is then advised in considerable detail as to the particular bases of the Board's decision and the manner in which it is to be treated. The review attorney then drafts a decision consisting of a full discussion of the evidence, findings of fact, conclusions of law and order. A copy of this draft goes to each Board member. The draft is first checked by the Assistant General Counsel in charge of review, and then gone over by the General Counsel who was present at the Board meeting at which the case was decided.

The draft is then submitted to the members of the Board who themselves make corrections, amendments, additions and deletions. When the draft has been finally approved by the Board members, it is put in final form for their signatures.

In making its final determination, the Board considers the report and recommendations of the Trial Examiner. The Board is, however, under no obligation to abide by the determinations of the Trial Examiner. The final decision concerning the disposition of the case rests entirely with the Board.

The position of the Board is well illustrated by the case of *New York State Labor Relations Board* v. *Clarence Jernigan.*[5] In this case, the Trial Examiner recommended that the complaint of

---

[5]Clarence Jernigan, 11 S.L.R.B. 526 (1948), *enforcement denied,* 121 N.Y.L.J. 788 (Sup. Ct. March 3, 1949), *aff'd,* 275 App. Div. 834 (1st Dept. 1949), *rev'd,* 300 N.Y. 482, 88 N.E. 2d 720 (1949). Cf. Kilgus v. Board of Estimate of City of New York, 308 N.Y. 620, 127 N.E. 2d 705 (1955).

discriminatory charges be dismissed. The Board rejected the Trial Examiner's recommendations and issued a cease and desist order. The Board's position, made known at Special Term of the Supreme Court, was as follows: (1) a Trial Examiner's report is merely a recommendation and is not binding upon the Board; (2) final decision concerning the disposition of the case rests solely with the Board; (3) where there is substantial evidence to support the Board's decision, the courts may not overrule that decision on the basis that it conflicts with that of the Trial Examiner. Special Term of the Supreme Court, affirmed by the Appellate Division, vacated the Board's order. The Court of Appeals, however, found that the Board's decision was supported by substantial evidence and reversed the two lower courts.

Decision and Order

The Intermediate Report has been filed with the Board by the Trial Examiner; exceptions, briefs, and oral arguments have been properly filed and duly considered; the Review Attorney has analyzed the case and presented his report to the Board; the Board has studied the information relating to the case. We have now arrived at that step in the procedure in which the Board has reached its final decision concerning the disposition of the unfair labor practice complaint, and is prepared to issue its "decision and order."

Preparation of Decision and Order. After making a determination, the first step in the Board's procedure for issuing a decision and order is to have the Review Attorney prepare a preliminary draft of the decision and order. This draft is submitted to the Assistant General Counsel, the General Counsel, and the Board members, who may revise it several times. When the decision and order is in its final form, it must then be passed upon by all three Board members.

Form and Content. The decision and order is divided into three parts (see Appendix B for sample):

1. The first (or decision) part contains a rather detailed opinion. The opinion contains a discussion of the evidence, findings of fact and conclusions of law, and notes any deviations from the Trial Examiner's Intermediate Report and the reasons for such devia-

tions. This, then, is the decision portion of the decision and order.

2. The second portion of the decision and order includes findings and conclusions setting down precisely what unfair labor practices the employer or employers must cease committing.

3. The third part contains the Board's order which may include a cease and desist provision, as well as directing the employer or employers to take certain affirmative actions to remedy the unfair labor practice or practices. (If the Board's final decision is that no unfair labor practices have been committed, the order takes the form of a dismissal of the complaint.)

The Board gets its power to order the employer to take affirmative action from Section 706(3) of the act. Among specific actions which the Board may require the employer to take are: (1) Cease recognizing and bargaining with an employer-dominated union; (2) Award back pay; (3) Reinstatement with or without back pay of employees unlawfully discriminated against under Section 704 of the act; (4) Reinstatement with or without back pay of all employees out of work as a result of unfair labor practices; (5) Maintenance of a preferential hiring list for employees out of work in connection with an unfair labor practice dispute.

In actual practice, the Board adheres quite closely to the affirmative orders noted above. (The one significant addition to the above actions is the Board's general practice of ordering the employer(s) to post notices stating that the employer(s) will subsequently not engage in the activities from which he has been ordered to cease and desist.)

The Board's policy regarding reinstatement and back pay for employees out of work in connection with an unfair labor practice dispute must be considered in some detail. As concerns reinstatement, the policy followed by the New York State Board is substantially similar to that followed by the N.L.R.B. Both Boards have followed the policy that employees out of work in connection with an *economic strike* may be permanently replaced prior to applying for reinstatement at the conclusion of the strike. The only qualification is that, if employees are offered reinstatement, that offer must be unconditional and non-discriminatory.

In regard to unfair labor practice strikes, both Boards have followed the policy that employees out of work in connection with such a strike must be reinstated upon request, even if this entails discharge of replacements. If no opening is available for the employees, the employer must put them on a preferential hiring list, to be hired as soon as positions open up.

The policy of the New York State Labor Relations Board in cases of discriminatory discharges is to issue an affirmative order directing reinstatement and back pay. The Board calculates the back pay due in one of two ways: (1) the employer is ordered to compensate the employee in full for earnings lost from the date of the discharge or other discrimination to the date of the offer of reinstatement in accordance with the Board's order; or (2) to compensate in full from the date of the discharge or other discrimination to the date when the employee receives other regular employment paying wages at least equal to those paid by his employer. From the amount due in either (1) or (2) may be subtracted any amounts received in other employment.

The first alternative formula is used if the offer of reinstatement precedes the employee's receiving other employment. The Board has explained this approach as follows:

Formerly the Board, in the absence of special circumstances, ordered the payment of back wages from the date of a discriminatory discharge to the date of an employer's offer of reinstatement in accordance with the Board's order, less any amounts earned during that intervening period.... [The new alternative formula] was deemed necessary in order to discourage employers from deliberately postponing offers of reinstatement, by allowing unlawfully discharged employees to work as long as possible in higher positions elsewhere, then decreasing the back pay due from the employer and also serving to nullify the effect of the order.[6]

On the other hand, the Board also insists that employees seeking back pay should have made reasonable efforts to obtain other equivalent employment. Thus, in the case of *Glow Service Garage*[7]

[6]Seventh Annual Report of the New York State Labor Relations Board, 20 (1944). See, for example, Abe Spigner, dba Spigner & Sons Structural Steel Co., 15 S.L.R.B. 152 (1952).

[7]Ralph & Harold Glotzer, dba Glow Serv. Garage, 19 S.L.R.B. 295, 302 (1956). See also Harmony Tea Shoppe, 15 S.L.R.B. 91 (1952).

the Board pointed out, in discussing the requirement that employees seek equivalent employment, that:

We make this requirement because "an employee who has been discriminatorily discharged cannot wilfully incur losses by refraining to seek other employment after his discharge"....

Many cases have arisen in which employers have requested the Board to subtract from the amount of back wages due certain payments received by employees during the period. The Board has consistently held that only wages received in the course of employment may be deducted from the amount due. Thus, in the case of *A. M. Sea Tree Corporation, et al.,*[8] the Board held that money received from the union strike fund did not constitute earnings in other employment and could not be deducted from the amount due the employee. Likewise, in the case of *Drha, et al.,*[9] the Board held that unemployment insurance benefits would not serve to reduce the amount of back pay due for lost earnings.

Compliance with Decision and Order

The duties and powers of the Board do not cease with the issuance of the decision and order. In fact, the issuance of the decision and order marks the beginning of the most vital step in the proceedings—securing compliance.

Accompanying each decision and order is a requirement that the Respondent notify the Board within ten days of what steps have been taken to remedy the unfair labor practice(s) and comply with the Board's order.[10] The responses may take any one of the following forms:

Notification of Compliance or Intention to Comply. If the parties have reached an agreement on compliance, this must be approved by the Board. (This approval is nearly always granted, although the Board is not bound by postdecision settlement.) In many cases the Board is requested by one of the parties to assist in arranging compliance. And the Board in any case checks compliance on its own initiative.

[8]A. M. Sea Tree Corp., 16 S.L.R.B. 567 (1953).
[9]Frank Drha, 19 S.L.R.B. 371 (1956). See also Paragon Oil Co., 8 S.L.R.B. 676, 681 (1945).
[10]The period is usually a week to ten days.

No Response. In cases where the Board does not receive some sort of notification, the usual procedure is to write or telephone the Respondent and inquire directly into the steps taken to comply with the Board's order.

Notification of a Request for Reargument or Reopening of the Hearings. The Board set up the following policy for the reopening of hearings in the 1940 General Rules and Regulations:

No motion for leave to reopen a hearing because of newly discovered evidence shall be entertained unless it is shown that such additional evidence is material; that the motion has been timely made, and that there were reasonable grounds for the failure to adduce such evidence at the hearings. Nothing contained in this section shall be deemed or considered to limit the right and power of the Board, in its discretion and on its own motion, to reopen a hearing, and take further testimony.

This section has subsequently been changed to delete much of the wording of the 1940 version. The present wording conveys the same meaning as the 1940 wording, but simply leaves the matter up to the discretion of the Board.[11]

Notification of Noncompliance or Intent to Seek Court Review. When the Board discovers that its order is not being complied with, or when it is notified of an intention to seek court review of its order, the next step in the procedure, judicial review, is initiated.[12]

There remain a few additional aspects to the hearing procedure, common to both representation and unfair labor practice cases, which have been purposely left until now, so as to maintain a clear line of thought in our discussion of unfair labor practice procedure. The picture will now be completed by fitting in these remaining fragments.

Hearings: Motions

The Board's General Rules and Regulations set up two separate procedures for dealing with motions made during the hearing and with motions made before or after the hearing.

Motions during Hearing. Section 38 of the General Rules and Regulations states:

[11]See §58 of the General Rules and Regulations.
[12]Judicial review is treated in detail in Chapter VII.

All motions made during a hearing, except as otherwise provided, shall be made orally at the hearing and shall be decided by the Trial Examiner. All such motions and the rulings and orders thereon shall be part of the record of the proceeding.

This section, in conjunction with Section 49, gives the Trial Examiner rather complete control over the conduct of hearings. There are, however, two major qualifications to the Trial Examiner's authority.

First, any decision or ruling of the Trial Examiner may be made the subject of a posthearing exception, to be ruled upon by the Board. Second, one motion which the Trial Examiner may *not* rule on is a motion to dismiss the complaint. In the *Matter of Max Davidoff, et al.,*[13] the Board clarified the authority of the Trial Examiner in regard to dismissing complaints. The Board noted that Rules 38 and 49 applied to matters such as the order of proof and the introduction of evidence. As to the matter of complaints, however, the Board pointed out that Section 706(3) vested the Board, and the Board alone, with the ultimate disposition of the proceedings. This authority rests with the Board under the law, and cannot and will not be delegated to the Trial Examiner.

Motions before and after Hearing. Section 39 of the General Rules and Regulations sets up fairly detailed procedure for the filing of motions before or after hearings. In essence, this section states that motions must indicate in detail the relief sought. Motions must be filed with the Board with supporting affidavits. The Board, in its discretion, may grant the motion on the materials submitted or it may schedule oral argument or hearing before ruling on the motion.

Whether or not to grant such motions is within the Board's discretion. Furthermore, the Board's decision in this matter is not subject to judicial review. The courts have held that the Board's ruling on motions are intermediate orders, over which the courts have no jurisdiction.[14] Intermediate orders may be reviewed only in connection with an appeal from a final Board order.

The most common type of motion before the hearing in an

[13]Max Davidoff, 14 S.L.R.B. 450 (1951).
[14]Bank of Yorktown v. Boland, 172 Misc. 885, 16 N.Y.S. 2d 756 (Sup. Ct. 1940), *aff'd,* 259 App. Div. 1073, 21 N.Y.S. 2d 612, *aff'd,* 284 N.Y. 749, 31 N.E. 2d 510 (1940).

unfair labor practice case is the motion for a "bill of particulars." Even this type of motion is filed rather infrequently now. The fact that the Board does not receive many applications for bills of particulars is a tribute to the conscious efforts of the Board to include in the complaint a detailed statement of the allegations. This particularization obviates, to a large extent, the need for any supplemental statements.

There has similarly been little need for Board review of Trial Examiners' rulings on requests for adjournments.

The most common types of posthearing proceedings are requests in the form of objections and motions to argue orally before the Board. As noted earlier, oral arguments before the Board are a matter of right in unfair labor practice cases, whereas the granting of such motions is a matter of Board discretion in representation cases.

Application to Intervene. Section 41 of the General Rules and Regulations sets forth the procedure to be followed in filing an application to intervene.[15] This section specifies that the application is to be filed with the Board at least two days before the commencement of hearing.[16] The Trial Examiner has the duty of ruling on such applications.[17] The Trial Examiner may permit intervention under such terms as he determines will best effectuate the policies of the act. In both representation and unfair labor practice cases, the Board attempts to eliminate the need for intervention applications by inviting all interested parties to attend the proceedings. Applications for intervention occur most frequently in connection with representation cases.[18]

[15]Intervention occurs when a person or organization seeks to participate in a proceeding as a party interested in the outcome.

[16]Trial Examiners have been quite lenient about this two-day rule and other formal requisites for intervention, even to the point of allowing intervention on the basis of an oral request made at the beginning of the hearing.

[17]The 1937 Preliminary Rules and Regulations provided for the Board to pass on such applications. This was changed in 1940.

[18]The Board has held that parties seeking to intervene in representation cases must first demonstrate a sufficient interest in the proceedings by way of a claim of representative interest, before being included on the ballot; J. I. M. Cab Corp., 15 S.L.R.B. 683 (1952). One major exception to this rule occurs in cases where the intervening union appears for the sole purpose of questioning the status of the petitioning union as a labor organization within the meaning of the act; Vincenze Aceto. dba Charcoal Center, 20 S.L.R.B. 233 (1957). The Board holds in

Continuation of Hearing. Section 52 of the General Rules and Regulations states:

Subject to the Board's approval, the Trial Examiner may continue a hearing from day to day or adjourn it to a later date or to a different place by announcement thereof at the hearing or by other appropriate notice.[19]

Hearing; Variance between Pleading and Proof. Section 56 of the General Rules and Regulations states:

A variance between an allegation in a petition under Section 705 of a pleading in a proceeding under Section 706, and the proof, is not material unless it is so substantial as prejudicially to mislead the Board or any party or Board's Attorney. If the variance is not material, the Trial Examiner may admit such proof and the facts may be found accordingly.

Since, as has been discussed previously, it is Board policy to permit amendment of the charge and, if necessary, the complaint to conform with the evidence uncovered in the course of its investigations, controversies over variances between the pleading and the proof are relatively infrequent.[20] Because of this Board policy, variances between the pleading and the proof, when they do occur, ordinarily occur in such incidental matters as names, dates, times, and the like.[21]

Witnesses and Subpoenas

As noted earlier, the conduct of hearings in unfair labor practice and representation proceedings resembles the conduct of trials in non-jury court actions. This similarity extends to the examination of witnesses. Section 43 of the General Rules and Regulations states that: "Witnesses at all hearings shall be examined orally

---

such cases, which have grown in significance and number since the Helsid decision of 1959 (*supra* Chap. I, n. 41), that the intervening union is not required to demonstrate a representative interest, but may be allowed by the Trial Examiner to intervene for the limited purpose of challenging the petitioning union's status as a labor organization. In such cases the union would be allowed to intervene but would not be placed on the ballot.

[19]The 1937 Preliminary Rules and Regulations left the matter of the continuation of hearings up to the discretion of the Trial Examiner. This was made subject to Board Approval in 1940.

[20]As will be noted in the next chapter, the Board follows the same policy in regard to the amendment of petitions in representation cases.

[21]F & F Serv. Stations, Inc., 13 S.L.R.B. 650 (1950).

under oath or affirmation, and a record of the proceeding shall be made and kept by the Board."

Application for Subpoena. Section 44 of the General Rules and Regulations states in part:

A party or Board's Attorney may apply to a Member of the Board for the issuance of subpoenas or subpoenas duces tecum. Such application shall be timely. It shall specify the name of the witness or the documents or things the production of which is desired, with such particularity as will enable such documents to be identified for purposes of production, the return date desired, and the general nature of the facts to be proved by the witness or the documents or things sought to be produced.

The Board derives its power to issue subpoenas from Section 708(1) of the act, which states:

Any member of the Board shall have power to issue subpoenas requiring the attendance and testimony of witnesses and the production of any evidence that relates to any matter under investigation or in question before the Board, its member, agent, or agency conducting the hearing or investigation.

It should be noted that only Board members have the power to issue subpoenas and subpoenas duces tecum. This power apparently may not be delegated.

It has been the policy of the Board to be liberal in granting subpoenas requiring the attendance and testimony of witnesses. In regard to subpoenas requiring that books and documents be produced, the Board has been strict. It must be demonstrated that the information requested relates specifically to pertinent facts of the case. The Board will not issue a subpoena if the information requested is so vague and general as to indicate an "exploratory expedition" by the party applying for the subpoena.

Enforcement of Subpoenas. There are two methods by which the Board can enforce its subpoenas. It can apply to the court for enforcement or it can employ the procedure set forth in Section 46 of the General Rules and Regulations.

Section 708(3) of the New York State Labor Relations Act sets up the following procedure for the enforcement of subpoenas:

In case of contumacy or refusal to obey a subpoena issued to any person the supreme court...upon application by the board shall have jurisdiction to issue to such person an order requiring such person to appear before the board, its member, agent, or agency, there to produce evidence if so ordered, or there to give testimony touching the matter under investigation or in question; and any failure to obey such order of the court may be punished by said court as a contempt thereof.

Thus, in order to secure enforcement of its subpoena, the Board must work through a court. The power of enforcement and punishment for noncompliance rests with the court, not with the Board.[22]

Although the Board does not have the power of enforcement it does, nevertheless, have at its disposal a very powerful sanction. Section 46 of the General Rules and Regulations states:

If a party refuses or fails, without reasonable excuse (a) to obey any subpoena or subpoenas duces tecum, or (b) to answer any question which has been ruled pertinent or proper, the Trial Examiner may strike from the record the pleading and/or all testimony offered in behalf of such party at the hearing, or may strike those portions of the testimony which are related to the question which the party has refused to answer, or to the matter called for in the subpoena. When the party so refusing or failing to obey a subpoena, or to answer any question which has been ruled pertinent and proper, is the person or labor organization making the charge, then the Trial Examiner shall have the same power to strike all or part of the evidence presented by the Board's Attorney at the hearing. The Trial Examiner may preclude the reintroduction of any testimony so stricken.

If a party fails or refuses, without reasonable excuse, to obey any subpoena duces tecum, the Trial Examiner may preclude such party from introducing any proof concerning such documents or things, or from introducing them in evidence.

If a party is a corporation or a labor organization, this section shall apply to failures and refusals of its officers and agents.[23]

Thus, the Board has recourse to two methods whereby recalcitrant parties may be required to appear as witnesses and produce pertinent documents. In practice the Board is generally able to obtain compliance with its subpoena through informal procedures.

[22]See Boland v. Busch Jewelry Co., 102 N.Y.L.J. 1159 (Sup. Ct. Oct 17, 1939).

[23]This rule was criticized by Benjamin who suggested that it may be beyond the Board's authority to adopt and enforce. *V, Administrative Adjudication in the State of New York* 181–182 (1942).

If a party refuses to obey the Board's subpoena, the Board first contacts that party to inform him of the seriousness of noncompliance. In most cases this is all that is necessary to obtain compliance. Realization by the party or parties refusing to comply of the two sanctions available to the Board is usually sufficient.

This concludes consideration of Board procedures in unfair labor practice cases. The procedures would seem, on the whole, to be adequate to their purpose which is, on the one hand, to achieve compliance with the declared policies of the statute concerning unfair labor practices and, on the other, to assure procedurally fair treatment through quasi-judicial means of those charged with violation of the act.

CHAPTER V

Board Procedure in Representation Cases: The Informal Stage

THE resolution of questions concerning the representation of employees is the second principal responsibility of the New York State Labor Relations Board. The present and following chapters analyze the manner in which the Board deals with this type of case.

Summary of Procedures

1. A representation petition may be filed with the Board "by an employee or his representative, or by an employer or his representative." The filing of the petition vests the Board with authority to investigate the question or controversy concerning representation.

2. The petition is referred to one of the two Senior Labor Relations Examiners who either retains the case himself or assigns it to a Labor Relations Examiner. (The case is assigned to a Regional Attorney if the petition comes from the Albany or Buffalo regions.)

3. The Labor Relations Examiner calls the parties together in an attempt to settle the controversy without resorting to a formal hearing. Settlement at this informal stage in the proceeding may occur through a private adjustment between the parties or through a Board-conducted consent election.

4. If the petition is neither adjusted nor withdrawn in the informal conferences, the Labor Relations Examiner submits a final report with recommendation to the Board.

5. If a hearing is authorized, the case is referred to the Supervising Trial Examiner to arrange a date for the hearing. The notice of hearing, along with a copy of the original petition, is sent to the employer(s) and the interested union(s).

6. Approximately one week after the notice of hearing has been issued, a formal hearing is held before the Board's Trial Examiner. In almost all situations, the responsibility for presenting the case before the Trial Examiner belongs exclusively to the parties to the proceedings. The Trial Examiner is, however, responsible for the development of a full and complete record. On a few occasions a Board attorney from the Litigation Section may be assigned to participate in the hearing.

7. At the conclusion of the formal hearing, the Trial Examiner submits a report to the Board. The report contains a summary of the issues and the contentions of the parties, together with the Trial Examiner's opinion and recommendations. The parties to the proceedings are given an opportunity to file briefs with the Trial Examiner and with the Board and, at the discretion of the Board, to argue orally. As soon as the record has been transcribed, a Review Attorney is assigned to analyze the case and present the Board with an analysis of the record of the case.

8. On the basis of the briefs, arguments, and reports by the Trial Examiner and the Review Attorney, the Board issues its decision on the merits of the case. The Board's decision contains a reasoned opinion, findings of fact and conclusions of law. The Board's decision and order ordinarily takes the form of either a dismissal of the petition or the direction of an election.

9. If the Board directs that a representation election be held, a notice of election is sent out to all parties to the proceedings. The notice of election, which is posted at the employer's place of business and distributed among eligible voters, contains the following information: (a) The time and place of the election, along with the choices to be placed on the ballot; (b) The employees eligible to vote in the election; (c) The voting procedure employed by the

Board; (d) The number of election observers each of the parties may have at the polling place.

10. The representation election is then conducted by secret ballot under the supervision of an agent or agents from the Labor Relations Board. The ballots are counted and a "Report upon Secret Ballot" is issued to all parties. The parties are given five days to file objections to the election. If any ballots are challenged during the election, they are placed in a sealed envelope and retained by the Board. If the number of challenged ballots is insufficient to affect the results of the election, they are not opened or counted. If, however, the number of ballots is large enough to change the election results, a hearing is held before a Board's Trial Examiner to determine the voting eligibility of the employees whose ballots were challenged.

11. In cases involving two or more unions (and a "no union" choice) if, after the election has been conducted, none of the choices receives a majority of the votes, the Board conducts a runoff election between the two unions receiving the greatest number of votes.

12. On the basis of the final results of the representation election, the Board either dismisses the petition for lack of majority or issues a certification of representatives. Unless there are unusual or extraordinary circumstances, the Board's certification bars a representation investigation for a period of one year.

We turn now to a detailed description of these representation case procedures. The triggering mechanism in this type of case is the petition.

The Petition

Section 705(3) of the New York State Act states in part:

Whenever it is alleged by an employee or his representative or by an employer or his representative, that there is a question or controversy concerning the representation of employees, the board shall investigate such question or controversy and certify in writing to all persons concerned the name or names of the representatives who have been designated or selected.

The procedure followed by the Board in representation cases parallels its procedure in unfair labor practice proceedings at the preliminary stage. Thus, the Board may not investigate on its own initiative a question or controversy concerning representation, but only after a "petition for investigation and certification of representatives" has been filed (see Facsimile 7). Once a petition has been filed by an employee or an employer or their representative, the Board's authority to proceed with its investigation begins.

Who May File Petition. According to Section 705(3) of the act, a petition may be filed by either employees, employers, or their representatives (see Facsimile 8). As originally enacted, however, Section 705(3) made only the investigation of employee petitions mandatory upon the Board; the investigation of employer petitions was left up to the Board's discretion. Although the Board made it a practice of almost always investigating employer petitions anyway, Section 705(3) was, nevertheless, amended in 1940 to make the investigation of both employer and employee petitions mandatory upon the Board.

As indicated, the Board has a statutory obligation to proceed with an investigation once a petition has been filed. This obligation is qualified in one major respect by the circumstance that the purpose of the Board's investigatory machinery is to resolve questions concerning representation. Hence there must first be a determination of the *existence* of such a question or controversy. A question or controversy ordinarily exists under the following circumstances: (1) The employer refuses to recognize a labor union as the exclusive bargaining representative for a particular group of employees; (2) Doubts of good faith arise concerning the current representative status of a previously recognized labor organization; (3) Two or more rival labor organizations make conflicting claims to exclusive representation.

Thus, if the Board finds that a question or controversy concerning representation does not exist, it may dismiss the petition and refuse to conduct an investigation. Section 705(4) of the act specifically provides in part that:

...no election need be directed by the Board solely because of the request of an employer or of employees prompted thereto by their employer....

In other words, the Board has a statutory obligation to investi-

STATE OF NEW YORK
Before the NEW YORK STATE LABOR RELATIONS BOARD

In the matter of—

                               Employer } CASE NO. ....E............

        and

                               Petitioner

PETITION FOR INVESTIGATION AND CERTIFICATION OF REPRESENTATIVES PURSUANT TO SECTION 705 OF THE NEW YORK STATE LABOR RELATIONS ACT

1. Name of employer ....Telephone No. ....

2. Address of employer ....
   (Include Post Office Zone Number)

3. General nature of business ....

4. Approximate total number of employees ....

5. The types, classifications or groups of employees which the petitioner claims constitute the appropriate bargaining unit or units ....
   ....

6. Number of employees within such unit or units ....

7. Address at which employees in such unit or units are employed ....

8. Names and addresses of any other known individuals or labor organizations who claim or may claim to represent any of the employees in such bargaining unit or units ....
   ....

9. Does the petitioner request certification as the collective bargaining representative of the employees within the bargaining unit or units claimed to be appropriate? ....

10. The undersigned hereby alleges that a question or controversy has arisen concerning the representation of the employees in the above bargaining unit or units, in that:

[IF ADDITIONAL SPACE IS NECESSARY, ADD RIDER]

The undersigned requests that pursuant to section 705 of the New York State Labor Relations Act, the New York State Labor Relations Board investigate such controversy and certify to the parties the name or names of the representatives designated or selected by said employees.

STATE OF NEW YORK ⎫
CITY OF ⎬ ss.:
COUNTY OF ⎭

.................being duly sworn, deposes and says that he is.......... of the petitioner herein; that he has read the foregoing petition and knows the contents thereof; that the same is true to his own knowledge, except as to the matters therein stated to be alleged on information and belief, and as to those matters he believes it to be true.

....
(Signature of Petitioner's
Representative)

Sworn to before me
this   day of   19   .
....

Name of employees or representatives filing this petition. (If a labor organization, give also name and official position of person acting for the organization.)

....

By: ....
(Signature and Title of Petitioner's
Representative)

Address ....
(Include the Post Office Zone Number)

Telephone No. ....

(FILE ORIGINAL AND THREE COPIES OF THIS PETITION)

---

gate a petition only when a genuine question or controversy concerning representation exists. The presence of that question or controversy is for the Board to determine. The following cases illustrate some of the more common situations in which the Board may dismiss a petition and refuse to proceed with an investigation.

In the *Matter of Lucullus Cake Shop*[1] the Board dismissed the employer's petition on the following grounds:

We have frequently processed such petitions, conducted elections, and issued "Certificates of Representation," when it appeared, or was undisputed that a question or controversy concerning representation actually existed. At the same time, we have made it clear that we will not allow an employer to "jump the gun" by petitioning the Board as soon as a union appears on the scene, and forestalling attempts at organization by a premature election.

In this case, two AFL unions had established picket lines for the purpose of organizing the employees. Neither of the unions represented or claimed to represent any of the employees, nor had either of the unions demanded that the employers sign a contract. On the

[1]George & Hannah Schaller, dba Lucullus Cake Shop, 13 S.L.R.B. 540, 545 (1950).

Facsimile 8.

Before the NEW YORK STATE LABOR RELATIONS BOARD

In the matter of—

CASE NO. ....EE..........

Petitioner

PETITION BY EMPLOYER FOR INVESTIGATION PURSUANT TO SECTION 705 OF THE NEW YORK STATE LABOR RELATIONS ACT

1. Name of petitioning employer ....

2. General nature of business ....

3. Approximate number of employees ....

4. The types, classifications or groups of employees which the petitioner claims constitute the appropriate bargaining unit or units ....
   ....

5. Number of employees within such unit or units ....

6. Names and addresses of known individuals or labor organizations who claim or may claim to represent any of the employees in such bargaining unit or units ....
   ....
   ....

7. Any other facts which petitioner considers relevant ....
   ....

8. The undersigned hereby alleges that a question or controversy has arisen concerning the representation of the employees in the above bargaining unit or units, in that:

The undersigned requests that pursuant to section 705 of the New York State Labor Relations Act, the New York State Labor Relations Board investigate such question or controversy.

STATE OF NEW YORK ⎫
CITY OF ⎬ ss.:
COUNTY OF ⎭

Name of petitioner. (If a corporation, the name and official position
of the person signing this petition.)

.................being duly sworn,
deposes and says, that he is..........
of the petitioner herein; that he has
read the foregoing petition and knows
the contents thereof; that the same is
true to his own knowledge, except as to
the matters therein stated to be
alleged on information and belief, and
as to those matters he believes it to be
true.

....

....
(Signature and title)

....
(Signature)

Address ....
(Include Post Office Zone Number)

Sworn to before me
this   day of   19   .

....

Telephone No. ....

(FILE ORIGINAL AND THREE COPIES OF THIS PETITION)

---

basis of these facts, the Board found that no question or controversy concerning representation existed.

In the *Matter of G.&L. Luncheonette*,[2] the Board changed its position on employer petitions filed in situations where the union demands a contract but does not make a claim to representation. Prior to 1950, in a case such as this, the Board would have dismissed the employer's petition on the grounds that no question or controversy existed. This left the union free in some situations to use economic pressure against the employer despite the union's lack of majority status. In this instance the Board refused to grant the union's motion to dismiss the employer's petition, holding that:

No matter how much a union, in terms, may disclaim representation, a demand for a contract is tantamount to such a claim, for a condition precedent to a Union's right to act as the bargaining representative of the employees and demand a contract, is the designation of the union by a majority of the employees as their collective bargaining agent.[3]

[2]James Lombardi & Walter Goldstein, dba G. & L. Luncheonette, 14 S.L.R.B. 472 (1951).
[3]*Id.* at 473.

79

Matter of Bell Diner[4] involved a procedural aspect of this problem. The employer had filed a petition and requested the Board to investigate the representation status of the union. The union, during the hearing, admitted *on the record* that it did not represent any of the employees in the unit in question. The Board thereupon terminated its investigation, holding that:

...but where, as here, the Union, on the record, formally and unequivocally concedes its lack of representation status, the purpose of the proceeding has been fulfilled. Where such formal admission has been made, any doubts as to the Union's status have been resolved.[5]

Thus far, in discussing the various situations in which the Board might or might not dismiss a petition or terminate an investigation, we have been referring to situations in which the Board's decisions have been discretionary. Prior to 1957, however, there was one type of petition which the Board, by statute, could not investigate; this restriction was on petitions involving two unions affiliated with the same parent labor organization.

Before 1957, Section 705(3) stated in part that the Board:

...shall not have authority to investigate any question or controversy between individuals or groups within the same labor organization or between labor organizations affiliated with the same parent labor organization.

In 1957 the words "concerning the internal affairs of any labor organization" were added to the above quoted section of 705(3). In addition a proviso was added which stated that:

...Nothing contained in this proviso shall be deemed to preclude the board from investigating and determining which, if any, of affiliated groups or labor organizations have been designated or selected by employees as their representatives for the purposes of collective bargaining within the meaning of this article.

One of the major reasons for this amendment can be observed in

[4]Michael E. Asimas, dba Bell Diner, 17 S.L.R.B. 256 (1954).
[5]*Id.* at 257. In Fleetwood Acres, Inc., 19 S.L.R.B. 110 (1956), the Board pointed out the difference between a Board order terminating a proceeding and an order dismissing a petition. The termination of an investigation, as in the above case, means that a question of controversy *does* exist, "but the Board is able to determine the Union's lack of representative status upon the basis of the information already in the record, so that continued investigation is unnecessary," *id.* at 113. See also Bannison Mfg. Co. 18 S.L.R.B. 231 (1955).

the *Matter of Hotel Pierrepont Affiliates, et al.*[6] In this case, both the petitioning and the intervening unions claimed to represent the employees in question. While the Board's investigation of this case was pending, the AFL and the CIO completed their merger. This merger made the petitioning and intervening unions affiliates of the same parent labor organization—the AFL-CIO—and the Board was required by the statute to dismiss the petition.

This illustrates what could have repeatedly happened following the AFL-CIO merger if Section 705(3) had not been amended. The basic purpose of the original Section 705(3) apparently was to keep the state's "hands off" jurisdictional disputes among affiliated unions and to allow such unions themselves to settle their differences. With the merger, however, the legislature saw that a continuation of the original Section 705(3) would greatly reduce the ability of the Board to deal with representational questions. The amendment probably also reflects a more sophisticated appreciation of the distinction between jurisdictional disputes over which union is to perform certain work and organizational disputes over which union is to represent certain workers.

Form of Petition. Section 8 of the General Rules and Regulations states that:

A petition for certification pursuant to Section 705 of the Act may be filed with the Board by employees, employers or their representatives. The petition shall be in writing. The original shall be signed and verified before any person authorized to administer an oath. The original and two copies of the petition shall be filed with the Board.

As was briefly pointed out in Chapter III, Section 11 of the General Rules and Regulations states that:

No petition in a proceeding under Section 705 of the Act shall be dismissed for failure of the petitioner to set forth in the petition all the information required.

Thus, for example, in the *Matter of Saks & Co.,*[7] the Board refused to sustain the employer's objection that the union's peti-

---

[6]Hotel Pierrepont Affiliates, 19 S.L.R.B. 586 (1956).

[7]Saks & Co., 2 S.L.R.B. 554 (1939). See also H. F. McChesney, as owner of Adelphi Hosp., 2 S.L.R.B. 266 (1939). In the Saks case the employer claimed unsuccessfully that the petition was insufficient because it failed to allege the facts giving rise to the controversy and improperly alleged the number of employees involved.

tion was insufficient because it failed to state the complete facts of the alleged question or controversy. The decision in this case illustrates a procedure of long standing. The Board has been consistently lenient with regard to the formal adequacy of petitions. This is not to say that the Board never sustains objections to the adequacy of petitions, but simply that it does not sustain objections based on purely technical deficiencies in form.

Contents of Petitions. These are governed by Section 9 of the General Rules and Regulations and are illustrated by Facsimiles 7 and 8.[8]

Notice of Pending Petitions. Section 12 of the General Rules and Regulations sets up the following procedure for notifying parties of pending petitions:

Upon the filing of a petition under Section 705 of the Act, notice thereof, including the date when such petition was filed, the name and address of the employer affected and the nature of his business, the unit claimed to be appropriate and the name of the person or organization filing the same, shall be posted on the public docket maintained by the Board.

This section is of importance because it represents a rather significant practical change in Board procedure.

Prior to 1940, upon receiving a petition the Board's practice was to notify all potentially interested parties that a petition had been filed. Although this procedure worked reasonably well, there were, nevertheless, situations in which the Board found itself entertaining requests for intervention, filed by unions which had not been notified of the original petition for the investigation and certification of representatives. Thus, in 1940 the Board began the procedure of posting petitions on the public docket so as to assure that all interested parties would have an opportunity to make their representation claims known. This procedure was formally incor-

---

[8]These regulations were amended in 1951 to require more detailed information concerning the interstate commerce character of the employer's business. Prior to 1951, the section asked for "the approximate percentage of sales made to points outside New York State, or the approximate amount of business transacted outside New York State, and any other facts concerning interstate commerce, if any." The 1951 change in this section illustrates the federal-state jurisdictional problem created by §10 (a) of Taft-Hartley. (The reader will recall a similar charge concerning unfair labor practice proceedings.)

porated in the General Rules and Regulations in 1943. At the present time the Board uses both the public docket and individual correspondence (based on Board records) to notify parties of pending petitions. Copies of notices are also routinely mailed to the state AFL-CIO.

The Informal Investigation

Once a petition is filed, the investigating procedure followed by the Board resembles that followed in the investigation of unfair labor practice charges. A Senior Examiner either retains the case himself or assigns it to a member of the Board's staff of Labor Relations Examiners for investigation.[9]

Purpose of Investigation. The purposes of the investigation in a representation case are similar to those in an unfair labor practice proceeding: (a) The Labor Relations Examiner attempts to effect a voluntary adjustment between the parties; (b) The Labor Relations Examiner obtains the necessary information upon which the Board bases its decision concerning the determination of the petition.

First Step in Investigation. The first step in the Board's investigation is, of course, to determine whether a question or controversy concerning representation exists. If the preliminary investigation shows that such a question or controversy may exist, the Examiner must focus on the following issues:

1. What is the appropriate unit of employees for purposes of collective bargaining?

2. What employees are eligible to vote and should be included in the collective bargaining unit?

3. What labor organizations have a substantial interest in the representation proceedings?

4. Is an election by secret ballot necessary to settle the controversy?

5. Are the unions involved bona fide labor organizations within the meaning of the statute?

6. Is there a contract or certification bar to an election?

[9]It will be recalled that the Regional Attorneys for the Buffalo and Albany regions conduct the informal investigations for their regions.

Since each one of the above issues is vital to representation proceedings, some of their substantive aspects must be explored.

Section 705(2) of the New York State Labor Relations Act states:
The Board shall decide in each case whether, in order to insure to employees the full benefit of their right to self-organization, to collective bargaining and otherwise to effectuate the policies of this article, the unit appropriate for purposes of collective bargaining shall be the employer unit, multiple employer unit, craft unit, plant unit, or any other unit; provided, however, *that in any case where the majority of employees of a particular craft shall so decide the board shall designate such craft as a unit appropriate for the purpose of collective bargaining.*[10]

As the wording of Section 705(2) indicates, the Board has a statutory obligation to designate separate craft units where a majority of craft employees so decide. As was indicated in Chapter I, this differs somewhat from the approach followed by the National Labor Relations Board under the federal statute. In the New York Board's procedure, in cases of craft unit determination, the employees of the proposed craft unit are given a ballot with a "yes" and "no" choice as to separate craft unit representation. If the vote is for separate representation as a craft, a second election is held to determine choice of bargaining representative, if any.[11] It may be noted that the craft proviso has not been frequently invoked.[12]

The procedure of determining what employees should be included in the bargaining units has involved some interesting problems. One of the most interesting of these relates to the minimum size of the bargaining unit.

Prior to 1939, the Board had decided to dismiss all representation petitions where the bargaining unit embraced only a single employee. It changed its rule on this in the *Matter of 117-14 Union Turnpike, Inc.,*[13] and held:
Nor should the fact that a superintendent is the only such employee in a building deprive him of the privileges and protection guaranteed by the Act. Certainly a single employee may designate a representative to

---

[10]Italics added.
[11]See Great Atlantic & Pacific Tea Company, 3 S.L.R.B. 933 (1940).
[12]The probable explanation for this is that most large industrial bargaining units where craft severance is apt to be a problem are under N.L.R.B. jurisdiction.
[13]117-14 Union Turnpike, Inc., 2 S.L.R.B. 866, 872 (1939).

act for him. Reading the statute as a whole, in the light of practical experience concerning the purposes of collective bargaining, we find no reason to believe that the Legislature intended to deny the Board the power to find appropriate a unit composed of a single employee, where, as here, the circumstances warrant.

The Board has continued, since 1940, to adhere to its single employee unit policy, illustrated in the above case.

A second interesting, though somewhat minor, Board rule relating to unit determination involves the personal relationship of employees to employer. The Board has followed a policy of excluding from the bargaining unit close relatives of the employer. Thus, in the *Matter of J. H. Thomas Manufacturing Corporation*,[14] the union contended that the brothers-in-law of the employer's president should be excluded from the bargaining unit. The Board agreed with the union's contention stating that:

We have consistently held that a close family relationship materially differentiates the interests of such relatives from those of other employees and warrants their exclusion from the unit of other employees.[15]

Another element in the area of unit determination has to do with the propriety, in the eyes of the Board, of an agreement between the parties concerning the appropriate bargaining unit. In the *Matter of W. T. Grant Company*,[16] the parties made an agreement on the appropriate bargaining unit. The Board pointed out in this case that:

A private agreement cannot relieve this Board from discharging the duty imposed upon it by the Legislature to determine from *all* the facts what unit is appropriate for the purposes of collective bargaining.[17]

In other words, such an agreement concerning the bargaining unit is subject to Board approval and, therefore, to possible Board change.

A fourth, and extremely important, Board rule on units concerns units of supervisory employees. We shall, however, postpone our

---

[14]J. H. Thomas Mfg. Corp. 16 S.L.R.B. 449 (1953). See also James Stephan, dba Queens Diner, 16 S.L.R.B. 630 (1953); S.L.R.B. v. Post Pharmacy, Inc., 208 Misc. 78, 142 N.Y.S. 2d 669 (1955).

[15]J. H. Thomas Mfg. Corp. 16 S.L.R.B. 449 (1953).

[16]W. T. Grant Co., 6 S.L.R.B. 11 (1943).

[17]*Id.* at 14.

discussion of this group of employees until we deal with the question of federal-state jurisdictional problems.

The question of what labor unions have a sufficient interest in the proceedings has not presented the Board with many serious problems. The Board's position on this matter of demonstrating a sufficient interest in the proceedings has remained the same since the beginning of the act, and is well illustrated in the *Matter of John Hancock Mutual Life Insurance Company*.[18] The Board held in this case that in order to establish interest:

...a union need not prove that it represents a majority of employees in the appropriate unit. However, evidence must be presented indicating a reasonable probability that the petitioning union is the current choice of sufficient employees to warrant the continuation of the investigation by directing the holding of an election.

Although this decision relates to a petitioning union, the same general rule applies to the interests of intervening unions.

There is one major exception to the Board's ruling that an intervening union must show sufficient interest in order to become a party to the proceedings. In the *Matter of Mayer's Parkway Restaurant*,[19] a labor union moved to intervene on the grounds that the petitioning union was employer-dominated. The employers urged that the application be denied since the intervening union had not demonstrated sufficient interest. The Trial Examiner, affirmed by the Board, allowed the intervening union to participate for the limited purpose of establishing its claim of employer-domination. The Board held that:

It is not necessary for a union seeking to intervene for the purpose of questioning a petitioner's status as a labor organization to show interest by way of representation....[20]

The question of determining the means by which a representation dispute is to be settled brings to light some interesting and effective Board procedures. Section 705(3) of the act states that the Board:

[18]John Hancock Mutual Life Ins., Co., 8 S.L.R.B. 24, 27 (1945).
[19]William T. & George W. Mayer, dba Mayer's Parkway Restaurant, 17 S.L.R.B. 472 (1954).
[20]*Id.* at 473. This rule has, of course, been greatly developed in connection with the paper local problem discussed in Chap. I.

...may conduct an election by secret ballot of employees, or use any other suitable method to ascertain such representatives....

Election by secret ballot procedure is discussed later. Here we are interested in the "other suitable method(s)" referred to in Section 705(3).

The most informal method used to ascertain the appropriate bargaining unit and exclusive bargaining agent is an adjustment between the parties through informal conferences. The Board's role in this kind of situation is to supervise the conferences and approve of the adjustments. In such cases of informal adjustment through conferences, the employer and the union may execute a recognition agreement in which the unit is agreed upon and the employer concedes that the union represents a majority, and agrees to recognize and bargain with the union. This particular method of adjustment is no longer favored by the Board which prefers the device of the consent election.

Informal adjustments occur most easily when only one union is involved. Where two unions indicate an "interest" in the proceedings, there is less chance of reaching an adjustment without recourse to formal action. Where, however, investigation of a two-union case clearly indicates that only one of the unions has a real interest in the proceedings, the Labor Relations Examiner may be able to induce the second union to withdraw. A two-union election by consent of the parties is another possible disposition. In other cases, however, the second union may continue to assert a claim of interest and thus force a formal hearing.

More common is an agreement to have the Board conduct a consent election (see Facsimile 9). This situation ordinarily occurs after the parties have reached agreement on the appropriate unit, but cannot agree on whether or not the union does in fact represent a majority of the employees in the particular unit. At this point the Examiner suggests that the parties settle the controversy without resorting to a formal hearing, by means of a secret ballot election.[21]

[21]The device of a "comparison" of the union's membership cards with the employer's payroll list is no longer used as a means of resolving the majority status issue.

NEW YORK STATE LABOR RELATIONS BOARD

	CASE NO.

AGREEMENT FOR CONSENT ELECTION

The undersigned Employer and the labor organization, herein called the Union, subject to the approval of the New York State Labor Relations Board, herein called the Board, hereby mutually stipulate and agree as follows:

1. The Union, or each Union, is a labor organization which exists and is constituted for the purpose, in whole or in part, of collective bargaining and of dealing with employees concerning grievances, terms and conditions of employment and other mutual aid and protection.

2. A question or controversy has arisen concerning the representation for purposes of collective bargaining, of the employees of the Employer within the unit or units defined in paragraph "4", below.

3. An election by secret ballot shall be conducted under the supervision of the Board, among the employees, in the unit or units defined in paragraph "4", below, to determine whether or not the said employees desire to be represented by the undersigned Union, or one of the undersigned Unions. The election shall be conducted at a time and place to be fixed by the Board, and in accordance with the customary procedures and policies of the Board.

4. The unit or units appropriate for the purposes of collective bargaining in which said election shall be held is, or are:

5. The eligible voters shall be those employees included within the unit or units defined in paragraph "4", above, who were in the employ of the Employer

and who are so employed on the date of the election, including employees who did not work during said period because they were ill, on vacation or temporarily laid off, but excluding employees who have quit or been discharged for cause and have not been rehired or reinstated prior to the date of this election.

6. The Employer will furnish to the Board, at least   days prior to the election, an accurate list of all eligible voters, together with payroll receipts or other documents containing the signatures of the said employees and their social security numbers, and such other records as may be necessary to the proper conduct of the election.

7. At least twenty-four hours before the election, the Employer will post in a conspicuous place in his premises copies of the Board's Notice of Election and the said eligibility list.

8. The sole question to be voted on at the election shall be: "Do you desire to be represented for the purpose of collective bargaining by:

9. Each party hereto may station one observer at each polling place during the election for the purpose of challenging the eligibility of voters and to witness and certify the count. Observers shall be designated by the respective parties, subject to the approval of the Board.

10. Challenges of the eligibility of voters, objection to the conduct of the election, and all other questions arising out of the election shall be determined by the Board and the decision of the Board shall be final and binding upon the parties.

11. The Employer will not interfere, directly or indirectly, with the employees' free choice of a collective bargaining representative.

12. If a majority of the eligible employees in the unit, or in any of the units, voting in the election, indicate their desire to be represented by the undersigned Union, or any of the underground Unions, the Board may certify that such Union has been duly designated by the employees in said unit, or units, as their representative for purposes of collective bargaining. The Employer agrees that it will recognize and negotiate in good faith with the Union or Unions, so certified by the Board as the exclusive representative, or representatives, of the employees in the said unit or units.

13. If two unions appear on the ballot and neither receives a majority of the valid votes cast at the election in the unit, or if there be more than one unit, in any unit, but the total number of valid votes cast in said unit for the two unions constitutes a majority of the valid votes cast, the Board may conduct a second or run-off election in such unit, or units, in which the employees may choose between the two unions as their representative for purposes of collective bargaining.

14. In the event the Board conducts a second or run-off election or directs a new election, the Board may fix a new eligibility date.

15. To the best knowledge and belief of the undersigned, no other labor organization, group or individual claims or asserts an interest in representing the employees in the said unit or units.

IN WITNESS WHEREOF, the parties hereto have caused this instrument to be duly executed this   day of   , 196 .

WITNESSETH: EMPLOYER ....

                                     by ....

.... UNION ....

                                     by ....

.... UNION ....

.... by ....

As noted, the consent election procedure becomes somewhat more difficult when more than one union is involved. It is possible, of course, that the unions and the employer might reach agreement on the unit and then request the Examiner, or agree to the Examiner's request, to determine the exclusive bargaining representative without using the formal hearing procedure. In such a situation the Examiner arranges for a secret ballot election among the employees to determine the bargaining representative.[22] Where two unions are involved, and where one of the unions will not agree to a consent election, the policy is to send the case to formal hearing.

After conducting a consent election, the Board's dismissal or certification of representatives is the same as its dismissal or certification after a formal hearing. Once the parties sign a consent election agreement, they are bound by the results of that election. The consent procedure, then, is as binding on the parties as is a representation election following a formal hearing before a Trial Examiner, and is subject to the same postelection rules.

Second Step: Initiation of Conferences. The second step in the informal representation investigation—the initiation of conferences—is really an extension of the first step. It is at this second step, and through the conference procedure, that the Labor Relations Examiner attempts to get the parties to come to an agreement without recourse to a formal hearing.[23] As was previously discussed, consent at this stage of the proceeding may result from complete agreement between the parties through informal conferences or, as is more likely, through consent elections. If settlement is not reached at this point, and if the petition has not been dismissed or withdrawn by the petitioner, the second stage of the Board's machinery is set in motion—the formal representation hearing before a Trial Examiner.

Disposition of Petitions

Before moving on to a discussion of the formal hearing pro-

---

[22]We specify a consent election here because for all practical purposes the Labor Relations Examiner will always use the election rather than the card comparison in multiple union cases.

[23]The same rule applies here as applies to informal conferences in unfair labor practice cases—the information received is "off the record" and is not admissible in a subsequent formal hearing.

cedure, it may be well to recall the various ways in which the representation petitions are disposed of. The disposition of petitions follows the same general pattern as the disposition of charges in unfair labor practice cases. In general, petitions may be disposed of as follows:

Adjustment. At any point prior to the end of the formal hearings, the representation petition may be adjusted. Generally, a petition is said to be adjusted when the parties reach a voluntary agreement or after a consent election the union is, or is not, certified as the exclusive bargaining agent for a particular unit of employees.

Withdrawal by Petitioner. At any time before or after the notice of hearing, the Board may permit the withdrawal of the petition. Withdrawal ordinarily occurs when the union, as the petitioner, realizes that its organizing efforts have failed or when the petitioner clearly sees that its petition will ultimately be dismissed by the Board for lack of jurisdiction or for "no representation question or controversy." Ascertainment that the unit sought is inappropriate, that the Board is without jurisdiction, that there is a contract bar to an election, or that employee interest in the union has dwindled may be among reasons for withdrawal. It should be noted that, as in the case of unfair labor practice charges, the petition may not be withdrawn without the Board's consent.

Petition Dismissed.[24] When investigation clearly indicates that no question or controversy exists, the Board may dismiss the petition on its merits. A petition may also be dismissed when the party filing it defaults by not following through and pressing the claim. Third, the Board may dismiss a petition on grounds that it is within the N.L.R.B.'s jurisdiction.

Formal Hearing Authorized. If a petition has neither been adjusted, withdrawn, nor dismissed, a formal hearing is authorized to settle the question or controversy.

This concludes the informal phase of the Board's work in representation proceedings. It is noteworthy that of 26,046 representation cases filed with the Board prior to the end of 1962, 22,082 were closed before authorization of a formal hearing (see Appendix A).

[24]As is the case in the dismissal of charges in unfair labor practice proceedings, the Board's decision to dismiss a petition is not subject to judicial review. Inappropriateness of the unit sought, lack of status as a labor organization, and contract bar are typical grounds for dismissal.

CHAPTER VI

The Formal Stage of the Representation Case

WITH the authorization of a formal hearing, we move to the second major phase of the Board's procedure in representation cases.

Procedure Prior to Hearing

Once the Labor Relations Examiner or Regional Attorney decides that no adjustment is forthcoming (and there is neither withdrawal nor default), he submits a final report with recommendations to the Board. It is important to note here that the Board does not have the same discretion in deciding whether to authorize a hearing as it does in deciding whether or not to issue a complaint in an unfair labor practice proceeding. The statutory language of Section 706(2) relating to unfair labor practice is that "the Board *shall have power* to issue...a complaint."[1] The discretion indicated in Section 706(2) is not to be found in the language of Section 705 relating to petitions filed in representation proceedings. This section states that "the board *shall* investigate such question or controversy" and *"shall* provide for an appropriate hearing...."[2] Although, as previously indicated, there are situations in which the Board may dismiss petitions, these situations are the exception rather than the rule. In general, therefore, where the parties have not themselves disposed of the petition, the formal hearing is automatic.

[1]Italics added. [2]Italics added.

92

Notice of Hearing. When a hearing is authorized by the Board, the case is referred to the Supervising Trial Examiner to arrange a date for the hearing (see Facsimiles 10 and 11). Ordinarily the hearing is set for seven days from the time of the issuance of the notice of hearing. The notice of hearing is sent to the employer(s) and the interested union(s).

It is interesting to compare the form of the notice of hearing with the form of the complaint. It will be recalled that when issuing a complaint and notice of hearing in an unfair labor practice proceeding, the Board takes great care to attach to the notice of hearing a detailed statement of the alleged unfair labor practice(s). Such specificity is generally not true of a notice of hearing in a representation proceeding. The only document attached to the notice of hearing is a copy of the petition filed with the Board. No attempt is made by the Board to specify the issues other than the limited specification in the petition. Furthermore, no provisions are made, as are made in unfair labor practice proceedings, for the filing of answers and other pleadings. The reasons for the difference in form and procedure between unfair labor practice and representation proceedings are fairly plain. In representation cases there is no particular reason to specify the issues, since the points of agreement and disagreement are generally well known to all parties concerned and are, in any event, to some extent clarified by the allegations in the petition. In unfair labor practice cases, however, the proceeding is viewed as adversary in character, and the issues are more complex than the relatively simple factual question of whether or not a particular union represents a group of employees in an appropriate unit.

Parties to the Proceedings. As in unfair labor practice cases, the Board's Trial Examiner supervises the hearing in representation proceedings. The Trial Examiner is selected from among the six permanent Examiners or from the Board's panel of private per diem Examiners.

Usually, the only parties to the representation proceeding are the representatives of the employer(s) and the union(s). The responsibility for presenting the case before the Trial Examiner generally

continued on p. 95

NEW YORK STATE LABOR RELATIONS BOARD

In the Matter of

⎫
⎬ CASE NO.
⎭

NOTICE OF HEARING

There has heretofore been filed a petition with the New York State Labor Relations Board by

alleging that a question or controversy has arisen concerning the representation of certain employees of

and requesting that, pursuant to authority granted in Section 705, subdivision 3, of the New York State Labor Relations Act, the New York State Labor Relations Board investigate such question or controversy and certify the name or names of the representatives that have been designated or selected by said employees. Copy of said petition is attached hereto. It appearing to the New York State Labor Relations Board that a question or controversy has arisen concerning the representation of the employees of

YOU ARE HEREBY NOTIFIED, that, pursuant to Section 705, subdivision 3, of the said Act, on the day of   , 196 , at   o'clock in the   noon, at 270 Broadway, Borough of Manhattan, City, County and State of New York, a hearing will be conducted before the New York State Labor Relations Board upon the question or controversy concerning representation, at which time and place you shall have the right to appear, in person or otherwise, and to give testimony.

IN WITNESS WHEREOF, the New York State Labor Relations Board has caused this, its Notice of Hearing, to be signed by the Executive Secretary. Dated: New York, N. Y.

_____
Executive Secretary

APPLICATION FOR ADJOURNMENT WILL BE CONSIDERED ONLY UPON SUBMISSION OF AN AFFIDAVIT BASED UPON A LEGAL EXCUSE. THE HEARING WILL PROCEED FROM DAY TO DAY UNTIL CONCLUDED.

A COPY OF THE BOARD'S RULES AND REGULATIONS WILL BE FURNISHED UPON REQUEST.

NEW YORK STATE LABOR RELATIONS BOARD

In the Matter of

CASE NO.

INTERVENTION NOTICE OF HEARING

PLEASE TAKE NOTICE, that, on the   day of   , 196
at   o'clock in the   noon, at the offices of the Board, 270 Broadway, Borough of Manhattan, City of New York, a hearing will be conducted upon the matters raised by the annexed petition.

If you claim any interest in this proceeding you may move for leave to intervene in accordance with Section 41 of the General Rules and Regulations of the Board, a copy of which is attached. Failure to move for leave to intervene will be deemed an admission of lack of interest.

IN WITNESS WHEREOF, the New York State Labor Relations Board has caused this, its Intervention Notice of Hearing, to be signed by its Executive Secretary on

_____
Executive Secretary

TO:

APPLICATION FOR ADJOURNMENT WILL BE CONSIDERED ONLY UPON SUBMISSION OF AN AFFIDAVIT BASED UPON A LEGAL EXCUSE.

---

belongs to the parties to the proceedings. Only rarely is a Board attorney from the Litigation Section assigned to participate in the hearing.[3] Even when a Litigation Attorney is assigned, his role is secondary to that of the parties, and his primary job is to make certain that an accurate record is kept. The Trial Examiner, however, has the principal responsibility for seeing to the adequacy of the record.

Consolidation of Proceedings. Section 705(3) of the Labor Rela-

---

[3]The reader will note the difference between this procedure and the procedure followed in unfair labor practice cases, in which the Board is the complainant and the Litigation Attorney presents the case before the Trial Examiner on behalf of the Board.

tions Act specifically gives the Board the power to consolidate unfair labor practice and representation proceedings. Consolidation occurs frequently in cases where an election petition has been filed by a union or employer and, at the same time, the union charges that another union interested in the proceedings is employer-dominated. Other employer unfair practices, such as discrimination or interference and coercion, may also be involved in consolidated proceedings. In a consolidated case of this nature, the Board will assign a Litigation Attorney to present the case before the Trial Examiner. The Trial Examiner may also give the union's attorney an opportunity to participate in proving the allegation in the course of the representation hearing.

A significant difference in procedure between the New York State Labor Relations Board and the National Labor Relations Board should be noted. As a general rule it can be stated that the N.L.R.B. has made it a policy not to proceed with a representation proceeding in the light of a pending unfair labor practice charge and rarely consolidates the two types of cases. Although the New York Board may follow the N.L.R.B.'s procedure, it may also consolidate the proceedings or (but less frequently) it may dispose of the representation case before deciding the unfair labor practice charge. The New York Board will pursue the latter course only if the unfair practice charged is waived as a possible postelection objection in the representation proceeding. The Board has followed this consolidation procedure because of its efficacy in more expeditious disposition of related problems.

The Hearing

One of the most noticeable differences between representation and unfair labor practice proceedings is the character of the respective hearings. As mentioned previously, unfair labor practice hearings are often characterized by a tense, bellicose atmosphere. This is not so apt to be the case in representation hearings which, by their nature, tend to be fact-finding investigations and thus less adversary in character. In fact, where only one union is involved in the representation proceeding, the parties frequently appear in person without the assistance of legal counsel.

Purpose of Hearing. The purpose of the representation hearing is, of course, for the Trial Examiner to obtain sufficient information concerning those issues upon which the parties themselves could not agree, to allow the Board to reach a decision on the disposition of the petition. In order to simplify factual issues and to make as complete a record as possible, a procedure was initiated in 1941 whereby the parties were requested to stipulate all agreed facts. This procedure has had the effect of expediting the hearing by focusing attention on disputed issues.

In the early days of the Board's operations, one of the purposes of the hearing was to determine whether the evidence warranted a representation election, or whether the question of representation could be decided by means of a card comparison. If the Board decided that the representation question could be settled by a simple card comparison, the necessary documents were subpoenaed and, if a majority of the employees indicated a desire to be represented by the particular union, the Board issued a certification of representatives. As early as 1939, however, the Board began to shift its policy in the direction of avoiding the card comparison as a method of determining representation status at the formal hearing stage of the proceedings. It can be stated as a general rule that at the present time the Board will almost always use the election procedure to determine the question of representation.[4]

Rules of Evidence. As in unfair labor practice cases, the Trial Examiner conducts the hearings in representation proceedings in a manner similar to that of a judge in a non-jury court action. One difference between the two types of cases is that in the formal hearing in a representation proceeding the Trial Examiner frequently allows a relaxation of the rules of evidence. Another is that the Trial Examiner is apt to participate somewhat more actively in developing the record made in a representation proceeding than is true of unfair labor practice cases.

[4]The Board does on occasion utilize a prehearing election procedure. See § 705 (3) of the act; Guardian Vault Company, 23 S.L.R.B. 183 (1960) overruling Queensbury Hotel Company, 21 S.L.R.B. 108, 161 (1958). This has been useful in securing speedy hearings. A party, intent upon delay, when informed of the possibility of a prehearing election, is more likely to assume a cooperative attitude. The procedure is likewise useful in situations involving large numbers of separate but similar or identical representation cases, issues, and/or units.

97

Posthearing Procedure

The posthearing procedure in representation cases, which in many respects is considerably different from that in unfair labor practice cases, consists of the following steps:

Report of Trial Examiner. Prior to June 1941, the Trial Examiner submitted no posthearing report to the Board. The transcript of each hearing simply was sent to the Board without any opinion or recommendation by the Trial Examiner. On June 2, 1941, the Board modified its posthearing procedure by requiring the Trial Examiner to fill out a questionnaire at the conclusion of the hearing. The questionnaire requested factual information on the case as well as the Trial Examiner's opinions and recommendations. This questionnaire form, which was really only a checklist for the benefit of the Trial Examiner, was not used for long.

At the present time, the Trial Examiners have no specific form to follow in presenting their report to the Board. In general, however, the present-day reports by the Trial Examiners contain the same information as the reports contained in the 1941 questionnaires. The Examiner files a report on the factual merits of the case, together with an opinion and recommendation for Board action. It is important to note at this point that the Trial Examiner's posthearing report in a representation case is filed only with the Board. It is not served upon the parties with an opportunity to file exceptions. The reader will recall that this is significantly different from the posthearing procedure in an unfair labor practice case, in which the Trial Examiner serves his Intermediate Report on all parties to the proceedings, and gives the parties an opportunity to file exceptions to the Report.

Briefs and Arguments. Section 55 of the Board's General Rules and Regulations states:

At the close of hearings in a proceeding under Section 705, the Trial Examiner shall permit the parties to file briefs or written statements, which shall be addressed and submitted to the Board. . . . Requests for oral argument before the Board must be submitted to the Trial Examiner at the close of the hearing. The granting or denial of *permission to argue orally before the Board shall be within the discretion of the Board.*[5]

[5] Italics added.

As indicated previously, the request for oral argument before the Board is a matter of right in unfair labor practice proceedings, whereas the granting of oral argument in representation proceedings is a matter of Board discretion in order to eliminate the possibility of time-consuming, dilatory tactics by one party or another. As a practical matter, the number of requests for oral arguments in representation cases is much smaller than the number of requests for such arguments in unfair labor practice cases. Furthermore, the Board will ordinarily permit oral arguments in representation cases, even though the authority exists to deny such requests.

Review Attorney. After briefs and arguments have been presented to the Board, a Review Attorney is assigned to analyze the case and to present the Board with a report on the record of the case. The Review Attorney is also utilized by the Board to prepare a draft decision and order in accordance with the Board's final determination of the issues in dispute.

Board's Decision. On the basis of the briefs, arguments, and reports by the Trial Examiner and by the Review Attorney, the Board prepares to render its decision on the case (see Appendix B for an illustrative decision). The Board's decision and order in a representation case is very much like the decision and order in an unfair labor practice case, in that it contains an opinion, findings of fact and conclusions of law, and an affirmative order. The Board's order may take any one of three forms:

1. A Dismissal of the Petition on the Merits. The Board will issue an order of this nature when, for example, the facts indicate either that the Board lacks jurisdiction or that no question or controversy concerning representation exists (because of inappropriateness of unit, or contract bar, or because the petitioner is not a bona fide labor organization).

2. Certification of Representatives without an Election. As we have indicated, a certification of representatives without an election in the postformal hearing stage of the procedure is now a rarity.

3. Direction of Election. If a petition is neither dismissed nor withdrawn, an election is ordered to determine which, if any, union is the appropriate collective bargaining representative for a particular unit of employees.

STATE OF NEW YORK
NEW YORK STATE LABOR RELATIONS BOARD

NOTICE OF ELECTION

To Determine the Representative for Collective Bargaining Desired by Employees of

HARLEM EMBERS, INC.

On Wednesday, December 12, 1962, an election by SECRET BALLOT will be held in the Main Dining Room, Ground Floor, Theresa Hotel, 2090 7th Avenue, New York City, pursuant to an Agreement dated December 3, 1962. The polls will be open from 3:30 P.M. to 5:00 P.M.

This election will be conducted by the State Labor Relations Board for the purpose of determining if the employees described below desire to be represented for purposes of collective bargaining by Cafeteria Employees Union, Local 302, AFL-CIO, or by Retail, Wholesale & Chain Store Food Employees Union, Local 338, AFL-CIO, or by Harlem Labor Union, Inc., or by None of these Unions. The decision of the majority of those actually voting will be determinative. A union so chosen becomes the exclusive bargaining representative of all employees in the unit.

ELIGIBILITY OF VOTERS

Those eligible to vote shall be all employees, excluding executives of Harlem Embers, Inc., employed on Wednesday, November 28, 1962, and who are still employed at the time of the election.

A list of eligible employees will be posted conspicuously on the employer's premises in advance of the election. A duplicate will be used at the election. Names erroneously omitted or erroneously included may be added or struck from before or during the election, if proof of an error is submitted to the Board agent in charge of the election.

Voters are requested to bring their SOCIAL SECURITY CARDS for identification.

INSTRUCTIONS TO VOTERS

This is an election by *SECRET BALLOT*. A sample ballot is attached hereto. Official ballots will be distributed at the polling place. VOTE BY MARKING ONLY X IN ONE SQUARE. *ANY OTHER MARK WILL VOID YOUR BALLOT*. If you make any mistake in marking your ballot, return it to the Board's agent, who will destroy it immediately and give you another ballot. Fold your ballot and deposit it personally in the ballot box.

USE BLACK LEAD PENCIL ONLY

MARK ONLY X ON YOUR BALLOT INSIDE ONE SQUARE

DO NOT SIGN YOUR NAME

100

AUTHORIZED OBSERVERS

The employer and the union may each designate 1 observer, who will be appointed by the Board. These observers will act as watchers at the polling place and assist the Board's agent in identifying voters.

COUNTING OF BALLOTS

Ballots will be counted by the Board's agent after closing of the polls. Authorized observers may be present.

INTERFERENCE, COERCION AND ELECTIONEERING

Voters shall be allowed to vote without interference or coercion. Electioneering will not be permitted at or within 50 feet of any entrance to the building in which the election is being held. The Board expects voluntary compliance with this regulation; otherwise it will be strictly enforced.

STATE LABOR RELATIONS BOARD

................................, Chairman

New York, N.Y.   ...., Member

12/5/62   ...., Member

THIS IS THE ONLY OFFICIAL NOTICE OF THIS ELECTION

A Board order directing a representation election sets in motion another part of the Board's machinery. We now turn to an examination of the procedures used by the Board in conducting elections.

Representation Elections

The Board's "direction of election" ordinarily orders a secret ballot election to be conducted among specific eligible voters within twenty days of the date of the Board's decision. Under the terms of Section 705(1) of the Labor Relations Act, the result is determined by the majority of eligible employees voting rather than by a majority of employees eligible to vote.

101

Conduct of Elections. One of the first steps in conducting a representation election is to send out a notice of election, to be posted and distributed at the employer's place of business (see Facsimile 12).[6] A listing of eligible voters is then prepared.

Prior to 1940, § 705(4) of the act stated that no election could be "conducted on the employer's property, during working hours, or with his participation, assistance or supervision." This section was amended in 1944 to allow the Board, if it deemed it necessary, to conduct elections on the employer's property, during working hours, with the employer's participation and assistance.

If only one union is involved in the representation election, the employees are given a choice between that union and "no union." If more than one union is involved, however, the employees are given a choice on the ballot among the several unions and "neither union" (see Facsimile 13). Up until October of 1939, in a multiple union representation election the Board did not provide a space on the ballot for "neither union," unless it received a specific request to do so or unless evidence indicated that a majority of the employees might not desire to be represented by any union. In the *Matter of Hotel St. George Corporation,* the Board announced its new policy on the form of ballots in multiple union elections as follows:

While the Act endows workers with complete freedom to exercise the right of self-organization and to designate representatives for the purposes of collective bargaining, if they desire to do so, it is an obvious corollary that the Act likewise endows workers with equally complete freedom to refrain from such self-organization and to declare that such is the desire or preference of the majority. The Act enunciates a right. It does not impose an obligation.... Therefore, unless we arrange the ballot so that employees may vote against representation by either of the contesting unions as well as for representation by one or the other, it is entirely possible that the election will not express the true desires of the employees and a bargaining representative may be imposed upon a majority which does not desire such a representative.[7]

---

[6]Although the notice of election in Facsimile 12 only calls for one observer, the number allowed by the Board will vary with the number of employees voting. The Board will not appoint observers whose positions in the union or company would allow them to create an impression of undue influence at the polling place.

[7]Hotel St. George Corp., 2 S.L.R.B. 585, 586–587 (1939).

The actual balloting is very closely supervised by the Board to assure a fair and secret election. Each employee wishing to vote must identify himself (the notice of election requests the voters to bring their social security cards for identification) and sign an election register. The signatures on the register are then compared with authenticated signatures previously filed with the Board. As each employee presents himself to vote, his name is checked off the eligibility list by the observers and by the Board's agent. The employee then casts his ballot in secret and deposits it in a sealed ballot box.[8]

Report upon Secret Ballot. After the balloting has been concluded, the Board's agent requests the observers to attest to the fairness of the election as part of the "report upon secret ballot," which also sets forth the numerical results of the vote (see Facsimile 14, p. 106).

The next step is the service upon all parties of this report. This lists all of the pertinent information on the balloting. The report concludes with a statement, similar to Section 17 of the General Rules and Regulations, informing the parties that if no objection is filed to the report within five days the ballots will be destroyed and the Board will either issue a certification of representatives or dismiss the petition for lack of majority.

Challenged Ballots. In the course of the election, the Board's agent or the observers of either party may challenge the ballot of any employee. An employee whose ballot is challenged is allowed to vote, and his ballot is then put into a sealed envelope. If the number of challenged ballots is such that it could not change the election results, the ballots remain sealed. If, however, the number of

---

[8]It is of historical interest to note that in 1941 the Board permitted employees inducted into the armed forces to cast absentee ballots, while withholding the right to vote from the replacements of these employees. For practical reasons, this policy was changed in Horn & Hardart Co., 6 S.L.R.B. 628 (1943). The absentee ballot was no longer extended to servicemen, and their replacements were allowed to vote. The Board provided at that time: "The period of certification in such circumstances shall be limited not only by the terms of Section 19, but also by the duration of the war. Any certification hereafter issued during the war will be subject to the right of any union or employer to commence a new representation proceeding after the end of the war. A petition may then be filed by or on behalf of the employees who exercise the right to return to the employ of the Employer from the armed services of the United States," 6 S.L.R.B. at 635.

103

SAMPLE
BALLOT

STATE OF NEW YORK

SAMPLE
BALLOT

STATE LABOR RELATIONS BOARD

OFFICIAL BALLOT

Secret Poll of Employees of
HARLEM EMBERS, INC.

Mark an X on this ballot in ONE square only. Make no other mark.

If you desire to be represented by	If you desire to be represented by	If you desire to be represented by	If you desire to be represented by
CAFETERIA EMPLOYEES UNION, LOCAL 302 AFL-CIO	HARLEM LABOR UNION, INC.	NO UNION ON THIS BALLOT	RETAIL, WHOLESALE & CHAIN STORE FOOD EMPLOYEES UNION LOCAL 338, AFL-CIO
Mark an "X" in Square below	Mark an "X" in Square below	Mark an "X" in Square below	Mark an "X" in Square below
☐	☐	☐	☐

This is a SECRET BALLOT and must NOT be signed.

challenged ballots is large enough to have a possible effect upon the outcome, a hearing is scheduled before a Trial Examiner. At the hearing, the parties are given an opportunity to present evidence concerning the voting eligibility of the employees whose ballots were challenged. On the basis of the evidence presented in the hearing, the Board makes a decision as to which employees are eligible. The ballots of the eligible employees are then opened, counted, and added to the original election returns. The parties are given an opportunity to be present on such occasions.

Runoff Elections. As noted in Chapter I, one of the truly significant differences between the procedures of the State and National Boards lies in the conduct of runoff elections. In New York State, if the employees are given a choice between "Union A," "Union B," and "Neither Union," and if none of the three choices receives a majority, a runoff election is conducted between the two *unions.*[9] It is the Board's view that if a majority of employees do not vote for "Neither Union," this indicates a desire by the majority to be represented by *some* union. The Board then conducts a second election to determine which of the two unions the employees want to have as their collective bargaining representative. It might be argued, particularly in light of the Board's decision in the *Matter of Hotel St. George Corporation,*[10] that the Board's runoff election procedure does not fully guarantee to employees the freedom to refrain from self-organization, since a no-union vote of less than a majority in the first instance does not *necessarily* mean that a majority of employees want to be represented by either Union A or Union B in the second instance. This has, nevertheless, been the policy consistently followed by the Board.

Postelection Objections. Section 17 of the General Rules and Regulations establishes the following procedure for determining postelection objections:

Upon the conclusion of any election or elections, the Board, its Labor Elections Supervisor or other agent shall prepare a report as to the result of the election or elections. The Board shall cause this report to be served upon the parties. Within five (5) days thereafter, any party may serve upon all other parties, and file with the Board (with proof of service) an original and three (3) copies of objections to the election or elections or to the report thereon. The objections shall contain a concise statement of the facts constituting the grounds of objection. The Board may direct oral argument to be heard before it, or direct that hearings be held before a Trial Examiner, or otherwise investigate

[9]Section 705 (5) of the act also states that if there are three or more unions on the ballot and none of them receives a majority, a runoff election will be conducted between the two unions receiving the greatest number of votes on the first ballot.

[10]See *supra* n. 7.

NEW YORK STATE LABOR RELATIONS BOARD

CASE NO.
DATE OF ELECTION
PLACE OF ELECTION
NOTICE OF ELECTION DATED
CODE NO.

REPORT UPON SECRET BALLOT

The undersigned agent of the Board certifies that the ballots cast at this election were fairly and accurately counted and tabulated and that the secrecy of the balloting was maintained. The results of said count and tabulation follow:

APPROXIMATE NUMBER OF ELIGIBLE VOTERS   _____

TOTAL NUMBER OF BALLOTS DEPOSITED IN THE
    BALLOT BOX   _____

    1. Number of votes for   _____

    2. Number of votes against   _____

TOTAL NUMBER OF VALID BALLOTS COUNTED
    _____

    3. Number of blank ballots   _____

    4. Number of void ballots   _____

    5. Number of challenged ballots   _____

GRAND TOTAL OF BALLOTS TABULATED
    _____

DATED:

           _____
           For the State Labor Relations Board

The undersigned acted as party observers in the conduct of this election. We hereby certify that the ballots cast at this election were fairly and accurately counted and tabulated by us. We further certify that the ballot box was sealed and protected in the interests of a fair and secret vote, and the secrecy of the balloting was maintained throughout the election, and that the results were as indicated above.

    For the Employer   For the Union

    _____   _____

                                 Petitioner

    _____   _____

    _____   _____

Unless objections to this Report Upon Secret Ballot, together with a concise statement of the facts constituting the grounds of objections, are filed within five (5) days, and as prescribed by Section 17 of the Board's General Rules and Regulations (see below) the Board may constitute such failure as a waiver of objections.

Dated: New York, N. Y.

_____

LABOR ELECTIONS SUPERVISOR

> Section 17 of the Board's General Rules and Regulations:
> "Procedure Following Elections; Objections: Upon the con-
> clusion of any election or elections, the Board, its Labor
> Elections Supervisor or other agent shall prepare a report
> as to the result of the election or elections. The Board shall
> cause this report to be served upon the parties. Within five
> (5) days thereafter, any party may serve upon all other
> parties, and file with the Board (with proof of service) an
> original and three (3) copies of objections to the election or
> elections or to the report thereon. The objections shall
> contain a concise statement of the facts constituting the
> grounds of objections. The Board may direct oral argument
> to be heard before it, or direct that hearings be held before
> a Trial Examiner, or otherwise investigate or make its
> determination with respect to the objections or to any
> challenged ballots."

THE UNDERSIGNED HEREBY WAIVES THE RIGHT TO FILE OBJECTIONS TO THE ELECTION AND HEREBY CONSENTS TO THE FORTHWITH ISSUANCE BY THE BOARD OF A CERTIFICA-TION OF REPRESENTATIVES. AN ORDER OF DISMISSAL.

_____   _____
       Employer   Petitioner

                                       _____

_____

or make its determination with respect to the objections or to any challenged ballots.

The usual procedure followed by the Board in the case of post-election objections is to consider the facts of the objections at a regular Board meeting. If the facts presented fail to sustain the objections, the Board overrules them and makes the appropriate order on the results of the election. If, however, a prima facie case is made to support the objections, the Board (in some cases following an investigation by a labor relations examiner) notifies all parties of the time set for oral arguments before the Board. On the basis of the oral arguments the Board may direct a formal hearing before a Trial Examiner. If the facts presented in the hearing sustain the objections, a new election may be ordered by the Board.

A common ground for a postelection objection is a complaint by the union that the employer has influenced and interfered with the results of the election. Thus, in the case of *Grippo Manufacturing Company*,[11] the union filed a postelection objection in which it claimed that the employer had interfered with the election by telling employees that they would "feel sorry" if the union won the election. The Board found that this comment, in conjunction with other actions by the employer, constituted interference with the employees' right to a free choice of a collective bargaining representative. The Board sustained the union's objection, vacated the election, withdrew its "report upon secret ballot," and directed that a new election be held if the union so requested within twenty days of the Board's decision. This case typifies the Board's procedure when it sustains postelection objections.

With this discussion of the Board's postelection objections procedure the main body of this chapter ends. At this point the parties have used the Board's machinery to settle the question of representation, and the Board has either issued a certification of representatives or dismissed the petition for lack of majority (see Facsimiles 15 and 16). Let us carry the discussion one step further, however, and analyze the policy of the New York State Labor Relations Board with regard to the life of a Board certification and to contract-bar rules. A brief analysis and description of the Board's policy on these two subjects are essential to our discussion of the procedure followed in representation proceedings, since the Board's decision to dismiss a petition or order an election in a particular case may depend upon the present state of a prior Board certification, or upon the Board's contract-bar rules.

[11]Joseph Steinbrunner & Peter Manzari, dba Grippo Mfg. Co., 21 S.L.R.B. 291 (1958).

NEW YORK STATE LABOR RELATIONS BOARD

In the Matter of

NAME OF EMPLOYER(S)
-and-
NAME OF UNION(S)

DECISION NO.

CASE NO.

DISMISSAL OF PETITION

On   (Date of Election) , an election was conducted in the above matter pursuant to the (agreement of the parties of date) or (Board's Direction of date).

It appears from the Report Upon Secret Ballot that no collective bargaining representative has been selected, since of the approximately 20 eligible voters, 19 cast valid ballots of which 8 were for (Name of Union) and 11 against.

No objections have been filed by any of the parties within the time provided therefor.

By virtue of and pursuant to the power vested in the Board by the New York State Labor Relations Act, it is hereby

ORDERED, that the (amended) petition filed herein on (date of filing) by (Name of Union)

be, and the same hereby is, dismissed.

Dated: New York, N. Y.
        June   , 1963

_____
Chairman

_____
Member

_____
Member

Duration of Certification and Contract Bar

Section 702(7) of the act empowers the Board to make rules concerning the "life of the selected representatives." Accordingly, Section 11 of Article III of the Preliminary Rules and Regulations established the rule of certifying a collective bargaining representa-

NEW YORK STATE LABOR RELATIONS BOARD

In the Matter of	DECISION NO.
NAME OF EMPLOYER(S)	
-and-	CASE NO.
NAME OF UNION(S)	

CERTIFICATION OF REPRESENTATIVE

An election having been conducted in the above matter on (Date of Election)   , pursuant to the (agreement of the parties of date) or (Board's Direction of date) and it appearing from the Report Upon Secret Ballot that a collective bargaining representative has been selected, and no objections having been filed by any of the parties within the time provided therefor,

NOW, THEREFORE, pursuant to the provisions of Section 705 of the New York State Labor Relations Act, it is hereby

CERTIFIED, that (Name of Union)

having been designated and selected as their representative for the purposes of collective bargaining by a majority of the employees casting valid ballots in the election said (Name of Union)

is the exclusive representative for the purposes of collective bargaining of all (Description of bargaining unit, e.g.—: Production and maintenance employees (excluding salesmen, office-clerical employees and supervisors) employed by XYZ Company, Inc.)

Dated: New York, N. Y.
        June   , 1963

_____
                    Chairman

_____
                    Member

_____
                    Member

tive for a period of one year, with the proviso that the Board might extend the certification or, in the event of unusual or extraordinary circumstances, shorten the period. The wording of this section was changed in the 1940 Rules and Regulations to read that a certification shall remain in effect for a period of one year "and thereafter until such time as it shall be made to appear to the Board that the certified representative does not represent a majority of the employees within an appropriate unit."[12] Under the present wording of this section, the burden of proving that the life of a certification should be shortened rests upon the party seeking to shorten it, rather than upon the party seeking to extend it. The effective starting time for a certification will be deemed postponed for as long as there is an unlawful refusal to bargain.

The Board has consistently followed the policy of refusing to investigate a representation petition filed during the one-year period following the Board certification. Thus, in the *Matter of Tony's Restaurant*,[13] the Board reiterated that: "...A Board certification, *absent extraordinary circumstances*, remains in effect for at least one year."[14] In the *Matter of Twentieth Century Barber Shop*,[15] the Board observed that the following situations are not "extraordinary circumstances" in the sense of Section 19, and, therefore, do not qualify as reasons for shortening the life of a Board certification:

1. A change of mind by the employees with respect to the designated collective bargaining representative.[16]

2. Voluntary quitting on the part of employees in the bargaining unit.[17]

3. Change of personnel due to turnover.[18]

In the above *Twentieth Century Barber Shop* case, the employer petitioned to shorten the life of the Board's prior certification on the grounds that because of high turnover the union no longer represented a majority of the employees. In rejecting the petition, the Board explicated its policy, stating:

This policy of the Board has been adopted to promote stability in labor relations. A bargaining relationship, once rightfully established, must

---

[12]§19 of the present General Rules and Regulations.
[13]Anthony Carbone, dba Tony's Restaurant, 10 S.L.R.B. 734, 735 (1947).
[14]Italics added.
[15]Anthony Rossi, dba Twentieth Century Barber Shop, 18 S.L.R.B. 92 (1955).
[16]See Stamford Bakeries, Inc., 18 S.L.R.B. 77 (1955).
[17]See Frank Santini, dba San Remo Café, 18 S.L.R.B. 18 (1955).
[18]See L. Morales & Sons, 12 S.L.R.B. 328, 335 (1949), *enforced,* 123 N.Y.L.J. 535 (Sup. Ct., Kings Co., 1950).

be permitted to exist and function for a reasonable time. To give effect to every short term change in circumstances would result in chaos and upset the stability of industrial relations which the Act contemplates. Moreover, employers are more likely to bargain in good faith, as required by the Act, if they know that an apparent change in the union's status will not terminate their obligation to bargain.... These considerations of policy here outweigh the desire to give effect to the immediate, and possibly fluctuating, wishes of the affected employees....[19]

It should be noted that the Board's certification policy applies only to situations in which a certification has actually been issued by the Board. Thus, in the *Matter of National Transportation Company*,[20] the employer sought to have the union's representation petition dismissed because less than a year had elapsed since the same union had lost a representation election. The Board refused to dismiss the petition, pointing out that Section 19 of the General Rules and Regulations refers only to the life of a certification, and does not apply to elections not resulting in certification.[21]

Following the same reasoning, the Board has continued to make a distinction between a recognition agreement and a Board certification. In the *East Nassau Medical Group*[22] case, a union filed a representation petition with the Board. Another union intervened and contended that a recognition agreement between it and the employer, entered into that same year, constituted a bar to the Board's investigation of the petition. The Board rejected the intervening union's contention, pointing out again that Section 19 applies only to a formal Board certification. Section 19 does not apply to a recognition agreement.

There are a number of other special circumstances involving this matter of the Board's policy on formal certifications as bars to

[19]18 S.L.R.B. 93. In Fort Hamilton Constr. Corp., 14 S.L.R.B. 83, 87 (1951), *enforced*, 128 N.Y.L.J. 229 (Sup. Ct. August 9, 1951), the Board reiterated that a union's loss of majority after certification does not relieve the employer of his duty to bargain with that union. It is for the Board, not the employer, to decide when a union no longer represents a majority of the employees.

[20]Nat'l Transp. Co., 8 S.L.R.B. 9 (1945).

[21]The reader will note the significant difference in policy as between the New York State Labor Relations Act and the Labor-Management Relations Act. Section 9 (c) (3) of the Labor-Management Relations Act states that "No election shall be directed in any bargaining unit or any subdivision within which, in the preceding twelve-month period, a valid election shall have been held."

[22]Dr. Robert K. March, dba East Nassau Medical Group, 21 S.L.R.B. 491 (1958).

representation investigations. As a general rule, however, we can say that, absent unusual or extraordinary circumstances, a formal Board certification will bar a representation investigation and election for a one-year period.

The preceding discussion has dealt with the duration of certification in the absence of a collective bargaining contract. We now turn to the situation where a contract is in effect.

For all practical purposes, the New York State Labor Relations Board first announced its contract-bar rules in January of 1938 in the *Matter of Crystal Cab Corporation, et al.*,[23] stating what has come to be known as the *Crystal Cab* doctrine. In this case, two months after a consent election had been held and a contract entered into, a second union filed a representation petition with the Board. The Board dismissed the petition on the ground that no question or controversy concerning representation existed. In dismissing the petition the Board pointed out that it had a dual responsibility in administering the act both to protect the employees' right of self-organization and collective bargaining and to promote stable labor-management relations. The Board noted that use of its machinery to disrupt a collective bargaining relationship entered into in good faith would be contrary to the Board's obligation to promote stability of labor relations. The contract-bar rule which emerged from the Board's decision in this case, and which the Board has consistently applied since 1937, is as follows:

In the absence of unusual circumstances, the designation of the collective bargaining agency must be found to continue for the reasonable period of one year from the date of the execution of the contract. So long as that designation can be said to continue, the claims of any alternative organization to act as the representative for the same employees cannot be entertained....[24]

There are, of course, a number of exceptions and refinements to the Board's one-year, contract-bar rule. The most important of these exceptions arise out of the following situations:

1. A contract made with a union "not shown to have been the freely selected representative of a majority of the employees in the appropriate bargaining unit" does not bar a Board representation

[23]Crystal Cab Corp., 1 S.L.R.B. 207 (1938).
[24]New York Rapid Transit Corp., 1 S.L.R.B. 214, 218 (1938).

113

investigation and election.[25] The same is true of contracts made prematurely before a representative group of workers is employed and of bare recognition agreements.

2. Oral agreements do not bar the Board from investigating a representation petition.[26]

3. A contract with an automatic renewal clause does not bar a Board investigation if a petition is filed within a reasonable time period before the date of the automatic renewal.[27]

4. The execution of an extension of a contract prior to the renewal or expiration date of the original contract is considered to be a "premature extension." If a petition is filed prior to the expiration or automatic renewal date of the earlier contract, the second contract does not bar an investigation.[28]

5. Contracts of indefinite duration do not preclude the Board's investigation of representation petition.[29]

6. Long-term contracts do not bar representation proceedings beyond a reasonable period of time. The reasonableness of the contract period is determined by the Board from a study of collective bargaining agreements in the industry.[30]

This concludes our consideration of Board procedures in representation proceedings. It can be said, concerning them, that they are adequately designed for, and have served well, the purpose of providing a fair and effective means of dealing with the question of the representation of employees for purposes of collective bargaining. In discharging this aspect of its responsibility, the Board has had the task of balancing the freedom of employee choice with that of providing a degree of stability in union-employer relations, and the principles of certification and contract bar have been developed to that end. A further problem of the judicial reviewability of Board action in representation cases is discussed in the following chapter.

[25]See Pre-Vue Television Serv., 14 S.L.R.B. 162 (1951).
[26]See Absenal Realty Corp., 14 S.L.R.B. 648 (1951).
[27]See Broad-Smith Co., 18 S.L.R.B. 156 (1955). For a discussion of the N.L.R.B.'s policy on automatic renewal clauses, see Deluxe Metal Furniture Co., 121 N.L.R.B. 995 (1958).
[28]See Auto Apartments, Inc., 14 S.L.R.B. 436 (1951).
[29]See Maxwell Apartments, Inc., 18 S.L.R.B. 103 (1955).
[30]See Isidor Silverman, 21 S.L.R.B. 44 (1958). For a discussion of the N.L.R.B.'s current policy on long-term contracts, see General Cable Corporation, 139 N.L.R.B. No. 111 (1962).

CHAPTER VII

The Board and the Courts

JUDICIAL review of State Board decisions occurs either at the request of the party or parties aggrieved by the Board's final order, or at the request of the Board for the purpose of enforcing its final order. Whether the review be initiated by parties aggrieved by a Board order or by the Board on an enforcement proceeding, the questions before the court are: (1) Are the Board's findings supported by substantial evidence? (2) Was the Board's order proper as a matter of law? This is the approach followed by the courts in determining their scope of judicial review.[1]

The courts, in general, have applied the doctrine of requiring exhaustion of administrative remedies in connection with attempts to invoke relief against Board action. Further, both the delegation of fact-finding authority by the legislature to the Board and the practice of limited judicial review of Board decisions have been upheld in the face of constitutional challenge.[2]

According to the New York State Labor Relations Act, the findings of the Board, if supported by evidence, shall be conclusive.[3] Also, the act provides that only a person aggrieved by a *final order* of the Board may file a petition requesting that the order of the Board be modified or set aside. This is deemed to afford sufficient protection of the interests of aggrieved parties, while at the same time avoiding the delay that might result if the numerous intermediary steps in each controversy were subject to judicial review.

[1]S.L.R.B. v. America Marble Co., 13 Misc. 2d 877, 178 N.Y.S. 2d 109 (Sup.Ct. 1958), *aff'd,* 7 App. Div. 2d 907, 183 N.Y.S. 2d 541 (1st Dept. 1959).
[2]Busch Jewelry Co. v. United Retail Employees' Union, 170 Misc. 482, 10 N.Y.S. 2d 519 (Sup. Ct., N.Y. Co., 1939).
[3]§707.

Consequently, certain actions brought to secure judicial review will not lie, because a final determination of the Board was not involved and hence no order.[4] A certification order or one directing an election is considered to be an interlocutory determination, and thus not reviewable in the first instance. It may only be reviewed if a subsequent unfair labor practice case ensues.[5]

Court Review by Parties

Section 707(4) of the act sets up a method for obtaining judicial review. This section states in part that:

Any person aggrieved by a final order of the Board granting or denying in whole or in part the relief sought may obtain a review of such order in the supreme court of the county where the unfair labor practice in question was alleged to have been engaged in or wherein such person resides or transacts business. . . .

The relationship between the Board and the courts is illustrated in the case of *Stork Restaurant, Inc.* v. *New York State Labor Relations Board.*[6] In this case the Court of Appeals dealt with the problem of the scope of judicial review of Board decisions. In sustaining the Board's order the Court of Appeals applied the "substantial evidence" rule. The court's decision stated in part that:

Judicial review of determinations of an administrative board is often limited, as it has been limited in the New York State Labor Relations Act, by a statutory provision to the effect that "the findings of the board as to the facts, if supported by evidence, shall be conclusive" [§707sd2]. A finding is supported by the evidence only when the evidence is so substantial that from it an inference of the existence of the fact found may be drawn reasonably. . . . The Board must consider and sift all the evidence—accepting the true and rejecting the false—and must base inferences on what it has accepted as true. Choice lies with

---

[4]Wallach's, Inc. v. Boland, 166 Misc. 420, 2 N.Y.S. 2d 541 (Sup. Ct. 1938), *aff'd*, 253 App. Div. 371, 2 N.Y.S. 2d 179 (1st Dept.), *aff'd* 277 N.Y. 345, 14 N.E. 2d 381 (1938); Allen v. Kelley, 191 Misc. 762, 77 N.Y.S. 2d 879 (Sup. Ct. 1948); *aff'd*, 273 App. Div. 963, 79 N.Y.S. 2d 312 (1st Dept. 1948); Domanick v. Triboro Coach Corp., 173 Misc. 911, 18 N.Y.S. 2d 960 (Sup. Ct. 1940), *rev'd*, 259 App. Div. 657, 20 N.Y.S. 2d 306 (1st Dept. 1940).

[5]Hanley v. Boland, 177 Misc. 973, 33 N.Y.S. 2d 673 (Sup. Ct., Albany Co., 1939); Lowell Cab Corp., 170 Misc. 866, 11 N.Y.S. 2d 497 (Sup. Ct., Bronx Co., 1939); Johnson v. Bee Line, Inc., 28 N.Y.S. 2d 18 (Sup. Ct. 1941).

[6]Stork Restaurant, Inc. v. Boland, 282 N.Y. 256, 26 N.E. 2d 247 (1940).

the Board and its finding is supported by the evidence and is conclusive where others might reasonably make the same choice.[7]

Ordinarily, in review proceedings, the parties are limited in their presentation before the courts to the facts and issues contained in the hearings and the Board's final determination. Section 707(2) states explicitly that objections and additional evidence, not urged or adduced before the Board or its agents in the course of the Board's investigations, may not be urged or adduced before the courts *unless* it can be demonstrated that the objections or/and evidence are material *and* that there were reasonable grounds or extraordinary circumstances why these matters were not brought up in the course of the hearings before the Board.

Thus, in the case of *S.L.R.B.* v. *Marlene Transportation Company, Inc., et al.*,[8] the employees attempted to raise a question of Board jurisdiction in the review proceedings before the court. The position of the Board was that the question of jurisdiction had not been raised previously and, therefore, could not be raised before the court. The court upheld the Board's contention, stating in part that:

It must be held that the respondent's failure to raise the issue of jurisdiction before the State board precluded them from asserting it after the termination of the hearings and the issuance of the State board's order. No adequate reason is advanced for respondents' neglect to introduce evidence of its interstate operations at the hearings and no proof proffered to establish that the taxi-cab operations have any relationship to interstate commerce—respondents' assertion that the State board lacks jurisdiction comes too late and cannot justify a review of the order in the absence of timely objection to jurisdiction at the hearing.[9]

If, however, the court finds that there were extraordinary circumstances why evidence was not adduced before the Board, it may remand the case to the Board for the taking of the additional

[7]*Id.* at 273.
[8]S.L.R.B. v. Marlene Transp. Co., 207 Misc. 677, 139 N.Y.S. 2d 621 (Sup. Ct. 1955), *aff'd*, 1 App. Div. 2d 1002, 153 N.Y.S. 2d 532 (1st Dept. 1956). See also Holland v. Edwards, 307 N.Y. 38, 119 N.E. 2d 581 (1954). But see Saratoga Harness Racing Association, Inc. v. S.L.R.B. 6 App. Div. 2d 329, 177 N.Y.S. 2d 401 (3rd Dept.), *aff'd*, N.Y. 2d 960, 161 N.E. 2d 388 (1959).
[9]207 Misc. at 680.

evidence.[10] This procedure again highlights the limitations placed on the courts by Section 707. Part II of Section 707 states that after the Board has taken the additional evidence:

The board may modify its findings as to the facts, or make new findings, by reason of additional evidence so taken and filed, and it shall file *such modified or new findings,* which, *if supported by evidence, shall be conclusive,*[11] and shall file its recommendations, if any, for the modification or setting aside of its original order.

Enforcement Proceedings by Board

The New York State Labor Relations Board has no inherent power to enforce its own orders. When the Board issues its final decision and order, that order carries with it no penalty for non-compliance. Section 707(1) of the act sets up the method by which the Board can obtain enforcement of its orders. This section states in part that:

The Board shall have power to petition the supreme court of the state within the county wherein the unfair labor practice in question occurred or wherein any person charged with the unfair labor practice resides or transacts business...for the enforcement of such order and for appropriate temporary relief or restraining order, and shall certify and file in the court a transcript of the entire record in the proceeding, including the pleadings and testimony upon which such order was made and the findings and order of the board.

The filing of the record with the clerk of the court vests the court with jurisdiction. As in the case of review initiated by parties aggrieved by the Board's order, the court has authority to grant temporary relief while considering the Board's petition for enforce-

---

[10]See Saratoga Harness Racing Ass'n., 18 S.L.R.B. 310 (1955), *remanded,* 6 App. Div. 2d 329, 177 N.Y.S. 2d 401 (3rd Dept. 1958) *aff'd,* 6 N.Y. 2d 960, 161 N.E. 2d 388, 191 N.Y.S. 2d 161 (1959). In this case, the employer raised the question of Board jurisdiction for the first time before the Appellate Division on appeal to set aside the Board's order. The employer's appeal was predicated on the United States Supreme Court decision in the case of Guss v. Utah Labor Relations Board, 353 U.S. 1 (1957), which created the serious federal-state no-man's land jurisdictional problem. Since the Supreme Court's decision was issued subsequent to the decision by Special Term but prior to its enforcement order, the Appellate Division remanded the case to the Board for a consideration of the jurisdictional question. The reason for the action by the Appellate Division was that the decision in the Guss case constituted "extraordinary circumstances."

[11]Italics added.

ment of its order. In making its final determination of the petition, the court may issue a decision enforcing, modifying, or setting aside in whole or in part the Board's order. Here again, however, the court is limited in its scope of judicial review by Section 707 of the act. As previously indicated, the findings of the Board, if supported by (substantial) evidence, are conclusive.

An interesting problem in connection with judicial review occurs in cases where the circumstances have changed between the time of the Board's filing of the petition and the decision by the court. For example, if an employer has complied in whole or in part with the Board's order after the Board has filed its petition, should the reviewing court dismiss the Board's petition in whole or in part? The position of the courts on this point is illustrated in the case of *S.L.R.B.* v. *Harmony Tea Shoppe, Inc.*[12] In this case, the Board applied to the Supreme Court for enforcement of its order. Special Term granted enforcement only insofar as the employer had not already complied with the Board's order. The Board contested this decision, contending that compliance or other events occurring subsequent to the Board's order are not relevant in enforcement proceedings. This contention was upheld by the Appellate Division. The decision of the Appellate Division stated in part that:

There is no need to determine the extent of compliance with the board's orders. An application to enforce such an order properly made should be granted in entirety.... Changes in circumstances or events occurring subsequent thereto are immaterial in an application to the court for an order to enforce the board's order.[13]

The reasoning supporting this result is quite logical and necessary. In fact, to proceed otherwise might make a sham of the Board's orders. Consider the situation which could arise if the court refused to enforce that part of the Board's order which the employer had complied with subsequent to the Board's petition. It is conceivable that an employer could simply wait until the Board's petition had been disposed of by the court and could then

---

[12]Harmony Tea Shoppe, 15 S.L.R.B. 91 (1952), *modified,* 285 App. Div. 1162, 140 N.Y.S. 2d 409 (2nd Dept. 1955), *aff'd,* 2 N.Y. 2d 980, 143 N.E. 2d 337, 163 N.Y.S. 2d 596 (1957).

[13]See also S.L.R.B. v. Timen, 289 N.Y. 644, 44 N.E. 2d 618 (1942).

once again refuse to comply. Since the Board does not have the authority to enforce its own orders, the Board would find itself in the position of again having to petition the courts for enforcement. It is quite obvious that if this approach were followed, the Board's orders could be rendered virtually useless by non-complying employers.

The position of the Board and the courts prevents this type of situation from occurring. By enforcing the Board's petition in its entirety, regardless of events occurring subsequent to the petition, the courts are able to prevent recalcitrant employers from violating the provision of the law. An employer who refuses to comply with a court order enforcing a Board petition may be held in contempt of court. Quite obviously, then, the value of having the court uphold the Board's petition in its entirety rests in the simple circumstance that powers of enforcement rest with the court rather than with the Board.

Judicial Review of Representation Proceedings

Judicial review of representation proceedings is quite limited, if not, for all practical purposes, almost nonexistent. It is a well-established rule that a Board certification or direction of election is an interlocutory determination, not reviewable except in connection with a final order.[14] In essence this means that the only course open to an employer who objects to a Board determination in a representation case is to refuse to bargain with the certified bargaining agent. If the Board issues a cease and desist order in connection with an ensuing unfair labor practice case, the employer then has recourse to judicial review under Section 707(4) of the act. Judicial review of the unfair labor practice would include a review of the Board certification or unit determination, since the unfair labor practice was precipitated by the original Board determination. As a general rule, then, only by the above roundabout procedure can an employer obtain judicial review of a Board determination in a representation proceeding. The theory underlying this is that determinations in representation cases are of a

---

[14]See Wallach's, Inc. v. Boland, 277 N.Y. 345, 14 N.E. 2d 381 (1938).

120

fact-finding nature only and do not result in legal directives to any party.

There may be an exception to the limited scope of judicial review in representation proceedings indicated above. If it can be demonstrated that a Board determination in a representation proceeding is clearly contrary to law, the Board's determination may be immediately reviewable.[15]

Judicial Control of Board Jurisdiction by Actions for Declaratory Judgment

Parties to Board proceedings have on occasion invoked the assistance of the courts through actions for declaratory judgment[16] falling outside the special review procedure established in the statute. The courts recognized early that they were not to prevent the Board from exercising its power in matters over which it had jurisdiction.[17]

It is possible, however, for a party in a proceeding brought by the Board to secure judicial relief on the basis that the Board is exceeding or is outside of its jurisdiction in a particular case. Where a controversy relates to the *power* of the Board to act *at all,* an action for a declaratory judgment may lie. In such cases, it is reasoned, a determination in favor of the plaintiff would render any further proceedings by the Board wholly superfluous.[18]

Thus, the application by an employer for a declaratory judgment on the power of the Board to investigate a situation where two labor organizations, affiliated with the same parent labor organization, claimed the right to represent the plaintiff's employees in collective bargaining was granted. The court ruled that the Board at that time (1941) was without power to investigate the

[15]Bain v. Kelley, 73 N.Y.S. 2d 93 (Sup. Ct. 1947), *aff'd,* 273 App. Div. 883, 77 N.Y.S. 2d 289 (1st Dept.), and 298 N.Y. 592, 81 N.E. 2d 326 (1948).

[16]An action for declaratory judgment is one brought to test out a purely legal issue, such as a question of jurisdiction or statutory interpretation. In the case of an administrative agency its use is likely to be attempted before the administrative proceedings have drawn to a close and before the regular judicial review procedure becomes available.

[17]Domanick v. Triboro Coach Corp., 173 Misc. 911, 18 N.Y.S. 2d 960 (Sup. Ct. 1940), *rev'd,* 259 App. Div. 657, 20 N.Y.S. 2d 306 (1st Dept. 1940).

[18]Bank of Yorktown v. Boland, 280 N.Y. 673 (1939); White v. Boland, 254 App. Div. 356 (1st Dept., 1938).

question as to who represented the employees and was equally without power to direct an election for the purpose of determining the question of representation of the plaintiff's employees. In such a situation, an action for a declaratory judgment for the purpose of determining the power of the Board to act at all could be maintained.[19]

In another action for a declaratory judgment, where a union sought invalidation of a representation election conducted by the Board and claimed that the Board, in declaring void "write-in" ballots naming the plaintiff as the employees' choice and in refusing to allow the plaintiff to intervene and participate in the election, had exceeded its authority, the court held that the Board had acted within its jurisdiction and that, consequently, its actions were not reviewable.[20]

A related problem in the area of Board jurisdiction is that involved in the determination of the propriety of State, as opposed to National Labor Relations Board jurisdiction. This problem will be taken up in the next chapter.

Scope of Judicial Review

The courts, on review, have assumed the responsibility of ascertaining whether the evidence on which a Board order rests is substantial. Is the evidence of consequence? Does it furnish a basis of fact from which the conclusions drawn can reasonably be inferred?

As noted earlier, a determination concerning the substantiality of evidence is deemed a question of law within the domain of the courts. Although this formulation leaves room for considerable flexibility, and may permit a court on occasion to reweigh the evidence on the basis of reviewing the entire record, it is for the Board and not the court to draw inferences from the evidence. The courts recognize that their power of review does not admit a

[19]Rubel Corp. v. Boland, 177 Misc. 638, 31 N.Y.S. 2d 572 (Sup. Ct., N.Y. Co., 1941). See also Great Atlantic and Pacific Tea Co. v. Boland, 176 Misc. 258, 25 N.Y.S. 2d 517 (Sup. Ct. 1941), 261 App. Div. 900 26 N.Y.S. 2d 492 (1st Dept. 1941).
[20]Cody v. Kelley, et al., 184 Misc. 150, 53 N.Y.S. 2d 224 (Sup. Ct., N.Y. Co., 1945).

substitution of their judgment on questions of fact for that of the Board.[21]

There have, of course, been some cases in which the courts have refused to enforce Board orders on the ground that there was insufficient evidence on which to base an order or that there was no statutory authorization for the Board's actions. Under the first circumstance, the courts have construed the term "substantial evidence" to mean evidence which "establishes facts and from which reasonable inferences may be drawn. It does not connote suspicion, imaginative suggestions, surmises or conjectures."[22] It is apparent that in these instances the court has some leeway to so interpret the facts as to make them seem unsubstantial.

The second situation—an absence of legal justification for action —may be a result of one of two factors: there may, in fact, be no statutory authority for Board actions or the court may differ with the Board as to the construction of the act. More often than not, these factors are interdependent. Indeed, absence of power on the part of the Board to act, or lack of jurisdiction, has been the most common type of application of this principle.[23] Most of the in-

[21]S.L.R.B. v. Interborough News Co., 170 Misc. 347, 10 N.Y.S. 2d 396 (Sup. Ct., N.Y. Co., 1939); Collier Serv. Corp v. Boland, 167 Misc. 709, 4 N.Y.S. 2d 480 (Sup. Ct., N.Y. Co., 1938); S.L.R.B. v. Astoria Casket Co., 17 N.Y.S. 2d 13 (Sup. Ct., Queens Co., 1939); S.L.R.B. v. Peerless Wood Products Inc., 170 Misc. 594, 9 N.Y.S. 2d 855 (Sup. Ct., Kings Co., 1939); Stork Restaurant v. Boland, 282 N.Y. 256, 26 N.E. 2d 247 (1940); S.L.R.B. v. Roosevelt Chevrolet Co., 177 Misc. 468, 30 N.Y.S. 2d 381 (Sup.Ct., Queens Co., 1941); S.L.R.B. v. Montgomery Ward & Co., 179 Misc. 298, 38 N.Y.S. 2d 858 (Sup. Ct. 1942), aff'd 266 App. Div. 878, 42 N.Y.S. 2d 840 (2nd Dept.. 1943); S.L.R.B. v. Mill Road Live Poultry Mkt., Inc., 182 Misc. 556, 50 N.Y.S. 2d 631 (Sup. Ct., N.Y. Co., 1943); S.L.R.B. v. Metropolitan Life Ins. Co., 295 N.Y. 839, 66 N.E. 2d 853 (1946); S.L.R.B. v. Union Club of City of New York, 268 App. Div. 516, 52 N.Y.S. 2d 74 (1st Dept. 1944), rev'd, 295 N.Y. 917, 68 N.E. 2d 29 (1946); Freehold Management Corp. v. Kelley, 79 N.Y.S. 2d 447 (Sup. Ct., Westchester Co., 1948); In re DiCarlo 114 N.Y.S. 2d 173 (Sup. Ct., Kings Co., 1949); S.L.R.B. v. Charman Serv. Corp., 201 Misc. 291, 107 N.Y.S. 2d 41 (Sup. Ct. 1951), aff'd, 281 App. Div. 860, 119 N.Y.S. 2d 916 (1st Dept. 1953); Saratoga Harness Racing Ass'n. v. S.L.R.B., 2 Misc. 2d 440, 153 N.Y.S. 2d 488 (Sup. Ct. 1955), modified, 6 A.D. 2d 329, 177 N.Y.S. 2d 401 (3rd Dept. 1958), aff'd, 6 N.Y. 2d 960, 161 N.E. 2d 388 (1959).

[22]Int'l Ry. Co. v. Boland, S.L.R.B. v. Int'l Ry. Co., Frontier Bus & Street Car Employees' Union v. S.L.R.B., 169 Misc. 926, 8 N.Y.S. 2d 643 (Sup. Ct. Erie Co., 1939); S.L.R.B. v. Fordham Electric Co., 266 App. Div. 563, 42 N.Y.S. 2d 875 (1st Dept. 1943); In re Rochester-Penfield Bus. Co., 187 Misc. 239, 63 N.Y.S. 2d 305 (Sup. Ct. 1946), rev'd, 271 App. Div. 1049, 69 N.Y.S. 2d 356 (4th Dept. 1947).

[23]Compare the Erie County Water Authority, 208 Misc. 292, 143 N.Y.S. 2d 379 (Sup. Ct. 1955), rev'd 4 App. Div. 2d 545, 167 N.Y.S. 2d 557 (4th Dept., 1957), aff'd 5 N.Y. 2d 954, 184 N.Y.S. 2d 833 (1959). See ns. 18 and 19 supra.

123

stances of judicial review center on the issue of the substantiality of the evidence supporting the Board's findings. And in most of those the Board has been sustained.

An example of judicial hostility toward the Board and its actions is in *S.L.R.B.* v. *Grief Realty Corp.*[24] The petitioning Board had instituted a proceeding to compel the defendant-owner of an apartment house to bargain collectively with a union and to reinstate an employee with back pay. The Board moved for an order enforcing its order. The Board members had not, however, read the original transcript; only the Trial Examiner's summary report and recommendations were read by the Board members. Consequently, the court refused to enforce the order:

[No] sound view of Section 707 gave the Board the right to make the decision and findings herein without even looking at the testimony and exhibits; this Court should not be expected to enforce the alleged "decision" which is in reality a performed affirmance of a subordinate, [*sic*] it is not too late to insist that this court is not a "rubber stamp" for any "pretended decision" by a quasi-judicial board of laymen.

The court emphasized the law's provision that the Board shall have the power to "petition" the Supreme Court for enforcement of its order, and not that it is the duty of the court to acquiesce.

Although this decision was subsequently reversed,[25] it illustrates some judicial attitudes toward one of the problems of the administrative process.

Tangential Relations between Board and Courts

A rather persistent problem has arisen in connection with cases dealing with the status of building superintendents. It is quite common for building superintendents to receive, as part of their compensation, a rent-free apartment. Upon discriminatory release from employment, should these employee-tenants be entitled to occupancy of these apartments (secured by temporary restraint of employers' efforts to evict), pending Board consideration of the formers' protest? May these employees press a suit in equity when

[24]S.L.R.B. v. Grief Realty Corp., 188 Misc. 549, 70 N.Y.S. 2d 288 (Sup. Ct. 1947), *rev'd*, 272 App. Div. 928, 71 N.Y.S. 2d 91 (2nd Dept. 1947).
[25]*Ibid.*

the power of the State Labor Relations Board has been invoked on the plaintiff's behalf?

The initial judicial reactions to plaintiff appeals for a temporary relief restraining eviction were negative. To allow both administrative and judicial treatment of the problems would result in frustration and perhaps a conflict of decisions. The court conceived the issue as allowing for either judicial or administrative treatment, but not both. If the issue were to be determined by the court, this might deprive the Board of the very function which the act specifically conferred upon it. Judicial opinion considered the eviction to be only a possible unfair labor practice, without taking cognizance of the fact that, as a result of this unfair labor practice, the individuals were left homeless or liable to legal strictures if they discounted the eviction notices. Since equity was not to interfere to maintain an employee in his position, it likewise should not interfere to maintain him in his apartment—which is a part of his salary. The threat of irreparable harm to be done was not seen as clearly by the courts as it was by the plaintiffs.[26]

As early as 1948, Justice Rabin had recognized the circumstances as being inequitable, but he believed that the court was precluded by the Labor Relations Act from intervening in matters of this sort.[27] More recently, however, there have been decisions recognizing the inequity of these circumstances and granting injunctive relief in tenant-employee, landlord cases on the basis of the irreparable harm which might be caused the plaintiff if his plea were to be denied.[28]

Moreover, it has been held that a building superintendent may not be removed from the premises pending the determination of a charge of discriminatory discharge for the reason that the applicable provision of the Civil Practice Act (Section 1410) permitted eviction only where the superintendent's employment had been

[26]Beazer v. Bluttal, 186 Misc. 234, 60 N.Y.S. 2d 668 (Sup. Ct., N.Y. Co., 1946); Gomeringer v. Natrel Realty Corp., 64 N.Y.S. 2d 361 (Sup. Ct., Bronx Co., 1946); Cammarata v. Bargus Realty Co., 191 Misc. 467, 77 N.Y.S. 507 (Sup. Ct., Bronx Co., 1948); Parrish v. Anndebor Realty Corp., 84 N.Y.S. 2d 183 (Sup. Ct., Bronx Co., 1948).

[27]Weir v. Mosale Realty, Inc., 83 N.Y.S. 2d 529 (Sup. Ct., Bronx Co., 1948).

[28]Maguire v. Ardea Realty Corp., 111 N.Y.S. 2d 756 (App. Div., 1st Dept., 1952), memorandum); Romanisky v. Siglon Realty Corp., 122 N.Y.S. 2d 171 (Sup. Ct., Bronx Co., 1953).

"lawfully terminated." The issue of lawful termination in such a case was a matter for the determination of the State Board, and pending such determination a temporary injunction was to be issued in order to prevent inequity and hardship which would have resulted in the event of immediate eviction.[29]

On the other hand, courts have asserted jurisdiction over actions to enjoin breach of contract and to restrain the commission of violent and unlawful acts, despite earlier Board treatment of the same conduct. To deny this function, it was reasoned, would be to make the courts subservient to the Board.[30]

Where a court, in a proceeding under the Arbitration Act (Sections 1458 and 1459 of the Civil Practice Act), was seeking to determine the question of whether or not there was a proper submission to arbitrate, and the determination of this question turned on whether or not the defendant unions represented a majority of the employees, the court asserted power to resolve all questions necessary to that determination. The defendant unions claimed unsuccessfully that the court was without jurisdiction to determine whether they did in fact represent a majority of the plaintiff's employees and that such a question must be referred to the State Labor Relations Board.[31]

Finally, in a case involving an attempt on the part of the Board to intervene in a contract action to which it was not a party, the question before the court was whether or not the Board was so entitled. The Board claimed that its right to intervene arose under Section 706, subdivision 1 of the act. The court, however, stated that:

...the legislature [in passing labor legislation] did not make the Supreme Court of the State subservient to the N.Y.S.L.R.B. The Board was not given any power...to interpret, enforce, or abrogate any contract made by any two parties, particularly where it is not a party to the contract.[32]

[29]Spezio v. Sutphin-Flushing Realty Corp., 17 Misc. 2d 960, 181 N.Y.S. 2d 933 (Sup. Ct., Queens Co., 1958). But see Comacho v. Burgos, 14 Misc. 2d 602, 183 N.Y.S. 2d 445 (Sup. Ct., N.Y. Co., 1958); Clark v. Murphy, 15 Misc. 2d 851, 183 N.Y.S. 2d 457 (Sup. Ct., N.Y. Co., 1958).
[30]S.L.R.B. v. Holland Laundry, 294 N.Y. 480, 63 N.E. 2d 68 (1945).
[31]Busch Jewelry Co., Inc. v. United Retail Employees' Union, Local 830, 170 Misc. 482, 10 N.Y.S. 2d 519 (Sup. Ct., N.Y. Co., 1939).
[32]United Baking Co., Inc. v. Bakery & Confectionery Workers' Union, 257 App. Div. 501, 505, 14 N.Y.S. 2d 74, 80 (3rd Dept., 1939).

To hold that exclusive jurisdiction was given to the New York State Labor Relations Board by the act would nullify the powers of the Supreme Court and go against public policy. The court, presumably, distinguished between a private action to enforce a contract and the Board's power to decide that a contract was not a bar to an election. Situations are, of course, conceivable where a conflict might arise where one union is suing to enforce an agreement whereas, that agreement not being deemed a bar, another union has won a representation election.

Observations

As is true of many administrative agencies, judicial review does not play a large role, in quantitative terms, insofar as the work of the New York State Labor Relations Board is concerned. Of a total of 12,769 unfair labor practice cases closed up to the end of 1962, only 815 required formal cease and desist orders. An even smaller number necessitated judicial intervention to secure compliance, and in only nine instances was enforcement refused by the courts. The importance of judicial review need not, because of these facts, be minimized, of course, because it undoubtedly plays its restraining role by its availability. It is noteworthy, however, that the Board does its work largely without the active intervention of the courts.

CHAPTER VIII

The Jurisdiction of the State Board and Its Relationship to the N.L.R.B.

THE principal jurisdictional limitation upon the New York State Labor Relations Board is to be found in Section 715 of the act which provides that:

The provisions of this article shall not apply to: (1) employees of any employer who concedes to and agrees with the board that such employees are subject to and protected by the provisions of the national labor relations act or the federal railway labor act; or (2) employees of the state or of any political or civil subdivision or other agency thereof; or (3) employees of any charitable, educational or religious association or corporation, no part of the net earnings of which inures to the benefit of any private shareholder or individual, except that the provisions of this article shall apply to...employees of a nonprofit making hospital or residential care center.[1]

A further limitation is to be found in the definition of "employees" contained in Section 701 which excludes

any individual employed by his parent or spouse or in the domestic service of any person in his home, or any individuals employed only

---

[1]The final clause in this section was added in 1963. N.Y. Lab. Law § 715 (Supp. 1963). "Non-profit hospital or residential care center" are, however, defined in a manner as to include only those located in New York City. The propriety of collective bargaining by hospital employees poses issues of labor relations policy beyond the scope of this study. For discussion, see Hepton, *Battle for the Hospitals* (1963).

for the duration of a labor dispute, or any individuals employed as farm laborers.

Unquestionably, however, the most significant limitation upon the Board's power flows from the circumstance that the National Labor Relations Act and the Federal Railway Labor Act regulate a substantial proportion of labor relations within New York State. Although this circumstance, as we shall see, deprives the State Board of jurisdiction over the labor relations of employers whose business affects interstate commerce sufficiently to be subject to federal control, the jurisdiction of the State Board is nevertheless not without significance insofar as large numbers of small firms employing relatively few employees are concerned. Based on the circumstance that 94 percent of business establishments in New York State employ twenty or fewer employees, 85 percent employ fewer than eight employees, and 74 percent employ three or fewer, Chairman Kramer of the New York State Labor Relations Board has estimated that approximately 90 percent of the business establishments in New York State are subject to the jurisdiction of the State Board.[2] The history of the process of delineating this jurisdictional line between State and National Boards is the principal subject of this chapter.

Early Developments

The National Labor Relations Board has, since its inception in 1935, been empowered to adjust unfair labor practices and questions concerning representation when they affect interstate commerce. In recognition of the exclusive character of this congressional grant of power under the Supremacy and Commerce Clauses of the Constitution, and in order to avoid unnecessary jurisdictional conflict, the New York State Labor Relations Act provides, as we have noted, that it

shall not apply to the employees of any employer who concedes to and agrees with the board that such employees are subject to and protected by the provisions of the national labor relations act or the federal railway labor act.

[2] Report of the Joint Legislative Committee on Industrial and Labor Conditions, 117 (1960).

Because this recognition of federal supremacy is somewhat ambiguous, and because the National Board has never fully exercised its jurisdiction, problems have arisen at the borderline as to which agency, state or federal, is empowered to regulate the labor relations of particular employers and groups of employees.

Most frequently this has occurred when an employer claims that his workers are "subject to and protected by" the N.L.R.A., and therefore under the jurisdiction of the N.L.R.B. One of the most difficult problems in this regard has been the situation where the National Board refuses jurisdiction over a particular employer whose business *does* affect interstate commerce. Are the employees still "protected by" federal legislation, or does the state act apply?

As early as 1937, the National and New York Boards realized the possibility of a jurisdictional conflict between them. Consequently, they developed informal clearance and referral procedures. Furthermore, in an effort to single out industries they considered purely local,[3] and therefore under the coverage of state legislation, they concluded the following agreement:

[3]With respect to proof of interstate as opposed to intrastate activities, the burden of proof always falls on the Respondent. The most frequently cited case on this point is Roxy Cleaners and Dyers, 11 S.L.R.B. 209 (1948), where it was stated at 210: "Where...jurisdiction rests *prima facie* with this Board, an employer who asserts that the New York Act may not constitutionally be applied to him, has the burden of coming forward with proof that interstate commerce is substantially affected. Particularly is that true here, for the transactions upon which the employer relies are matters peculiarly within his own knowledge. We see nothing in this record to compel a holding that this Board is without jurisdiction."

This was not the first case on this issue, but it is illustrative of the Board's reasoning in those cases involving Respondents which claim interstate involvement and then fail to show it adequately. See, for example, Gristede Bros., Inc., 5 S.L.R.B. 382 (1942); Prudential Ins. Co. of America, 9 S.L.R.B. 636 (1946); Progressive Drug Co., 9 S.L.R.B. 628 (1946); Hippodrome Parking Space, Inc., 11 S.L.R.B. 207 (1948); Daniel the Caterer, 11 S.L.R.B. 297 (1948); J. H. Penny, Inc., 11 S.L.R.B. 329 (1948); Long Island Water Corp., 11 S.L.R.B. 399 (1948); and Lottie's Dogwood Room, 11 S.L.R.B. 632 (1948).

Slightly different were those cases in which the Respondents claimed to be in industries which "indirectly affected" interstate commerce. Citing the Schechter Poultry decision, 295 U. S. 495 (1935), the State Board has held that it was incorrect to assume that anything which affects interstate commerce comes automatically within the reach of the federal commerce power. In the matter of Herbert Bayard Swope, 12 S.L.R.B. 199 (1949), for example, the Board stated that "activities local in their immediacy do not become interstate and national because of distant repercussions." See also New Garden Theatre, 12 S.L.R.B. 244 (1949); Cook Dry Cleaning Co., 12 S.L.R.B. 285 (1949); Ajax Transp. Co., 12 S.L.R.B. 594 (1949); First Mechanized Washers, Inc., 12 S.L.R.B. 536 (1949); and Regal Shoe Co., 12 S.L.R.B. 722 (1949).

130

Unless there are unusual circumstances, the New York State Labor Relations Board will assume jurisdiction over all cases arising in the following trades and industries, without clearing, except as a matter of record, with the National Board's officials:

1. Retail stores,
2. Small industries which receive all or practically all raw materials from within the State of New York, and do not ship any material proportion of their product outside the State,
3. Service trades (such as laundries),
4. Office and residential buildings,
5. Small and clearly local public utilities (this includes local traction companies, as well as gas and electric light corporations),
6. Storage warehouses,
7. Construction operations,
8. Other obviously local businesses.

Two years later, in 1939, the first case involving a question of federal-state jurisdiction arose before the State Board. In *Davega-City Radio, Inc.,*[4] it was conceded that the employer was in fact within the jurisdiction of the N.L.R.B., primarily because almost half his merchandise was shipped to him from out-of-state sources and approximately one-sixth of his sales were made to customers in other states. Since the national agency had not asserted jurisdiction, however, the state agency reasoned that it could proceed to enforce the provisions of the state act against the company.

The employer appealed to the state courts,[5] claiming that by virtue of Article VI of the Federal Constitution (i.e., the "supremacy clause"), the national law had preempted the State Board from taking any action in this field. The case reached the Court of Appeals, which found no merit in the employer's contention. It held:

To permit State enforcement of a State law consistent with a Federal law on the same subject until such time as the appropriate Federal agency asserts its own jurisdiction in no way lessens the supremacy of the National laws as required by Article VI of the Constitution.[6]

The next year, 1940, saw two more cases in which the Board applied the *Davega-City* doctrine to interstate businesses. In *Vim*

[4]1 S.L.R.B. 137 (1937).
[5]Davega-City Radio v. S.L.R.B., 281 N. Y. 13, 22 N.E. 2d 145 (1939).
[6]*Id.* at 281 N.Y. 24–25, 22 N.E. 2d 149 (1939).

Electric Co.,[7] the question was raised of whether employees who resided in New York but worked in stores located in New Jersey could be included within the appropriate New York bargaining unit. And in the *John Hancock Mutual Life Insurance Co.* case,[8] the employer claimed that since it was a foreign corporation, the New York Board did not have jurisdiction. In both cases, the Board found that the N.L.R.B. had not asserted jurisdiction, and therefore asserted its own. In many similar cases up to 1947,[9] the Board followed a similar line of reasoning in assuming control. Its position was that where the federal agency had not *in fact* asserted jurisdiction, the state remained free to act, and this result held true even if the absence of National Board action was attributable to a failure to invoke potential federal jurisdiction.

Jurisdiction over Supervisory Employees

The next important case, *Allegheny Ludlum Steel Corp.*,[10] involved the question of whether the State Board could entertain a representation petition from the company's foremen. The employer argued that he was engaged in interstate commerce, and that the state's action in certifying a foremen's union was against federal policy, since the N.L.R.B. in *Maryland Drydock Co.*[11] had ruled that such persons do not constitute an appropriate bargaining unit. The assertion of state jurisdiction was upheld at all three levels of New York courts,[12] with the Supreme Court declaring that "...only in a case where the intention of Congress to give to the Federal Board *exclusive* control over the entire field is clearly manifested can the power of the State to act be superseded."[13]

The New York Board was also upheld in the state courts in

[7]3 S.L.R.B. 377 (1940).

[8]3 S.L.R.B. 98 (1940).

[9]See, for example, Goldsmith & Perlman, 7 S.L.R.B. 242 (1944); American Emblem Co., 8 S.L.R.B. 1 (1945); S. G. Tilden, Inc., 8 S.L.R.B. 335 (1945); Peters Bros. Rubber Co., 8 S.L.R.B. 385 (1945); Central Paint & Varnish Works, Inc., 9 S.L.R.B. 413 (1946); United Cigar-Whelan Stores Corp., 9 S.L.R.B. 353 (1946); Bank of Manhattan Co., 10 S.L.R.B. 86 (1947).

[10]7 S.L.R.B. 103 (1944).

[11]49 N.L.R.B. 733 (1943).

[12]Allegheny Ludlum Steel Corp. v. Kelly, 184 Misc. 47, 49 N.Y.S. 2d 762 (Sup. Ct. 1944), *aff'd*, 269 App. Div. 805, 56 N.Y.S. 2d 196 (4th Dept., 1945), *aff'd*, 295 N.Y. 607, 64 N.E. 2d 352 (1945).

[13]184 Misc. 51, 49 N.Y.S. 2d 766, italics added.

another case[14] dealing with supervisory employees in the same year, 1945. Here, the company refused to obey the subpoenas of the Board, claiming (1) that the N.L.R.B. alone had jurisdiction over businesses in interstate commerce, and (2) that foremen as supervisory employees were "employers" rather than employees within the meaning of the act and could not constitute an appropriate bargaining unit. Both arguments were rejected by the Board and state courts.

The Meaning of "Protected by"

The State Board's 1946 decision in *Harris, Upham & Co.*[15] presents two interesting problems in the field of federal as opposed to state regulation. In this case, the union sought to file a representation petition with the N.L.R.B., but the federal agency referred it to the New York Board. Challenging the state's jurisdiction nevertheless, the employers pointed out that there had been prior action by the National Board when, in 1944, it conducted a representation election among their stock telephone-booth clerks. Therefore, argued the employers, state law could not now be applied.

The State Board rejected this contention. It stressed the fact that in the instant case the telephone-booth operators were only one group involved in the proceeding before it. "The controversy concerning representation here presented is a current controversy affecting a unit which includes not merely the employees involved in the 1944 proceeding before the National Board, but other employees of the Company as well," it said. "The processing of that prior case by the National Board does not preclude this Board from acting in the instant controversy."[16]

The second issue was over interpretation of the provision of the act that employees who are "subject to and protected by" the provisions of the N.L.R.A. shall be exempt from its coverage. The employers argued that there was no separate meaning of the words "subject to" and "protected by," and that even though the

---

[14]S.L.R.B. v. Bethlehem Steel Co., 295 N.Y. 601, 64 N.E. 2d 350 (1945).

[15]9 S.L.R.B. 570 (1946). For other cases where the State Board assumed control after the N.L.R.B. refused to consider the petition, see The Maintenance Co., 9 S.L.R.B. 113 (1946); S. G. Tilden, Inc., 9 S.L.R.B. 144 (1946); W. H. H. Chamberlain, Inc., 9 S.L.R.B. 487 (1946); Manufacturers Trust Co., 10 S.L.R.B. 476 (1947).

[16]9 S.L.R.B. 573.

National Board would not entertain a petition of their employees, these workers were, nonetheless, "protected by" the national act. The New York Board's reply was:

It hardly seems that the [federal]Legislature could have intended the words "protected by" to have no meaning of their own. It is more reasonable to suppose that the Legislature intended the words "protected by" to have their usual significance and to relate to the actual application of the respective statutes.... Protection connotes actual availability of safeguards or remedies. The sense of this is clear, for if the words "protected by" mean only "subject to," then the mere fact that employees are "subject to" the National Act would oust this Board of jurisdiction; and, in that event, if the National Board should decline to entertain a petition, as it has done here, the employees would be without protection under either statute.[17]

Decisions of the Supreme Court of the United States

The New York Board suffered an important reversal in 1947 when the Supreme Court of the United States overturned the decisions of the Board and the New York Court of Appeals in the *Allegheny Ludlum* and *Bethlehem* cases, *supra*.[18] The Supreme Court declared that the N.L.R.B.'s policy concerning foremen was "an exercise of its discretion to determine that such units were not appropriate for bargaining purposes" and, therefore, was not an "administrative concession that the nature of these appellants' business put their employees beyond reach of federal authority."[19] And since the State Board's general attitude toward foremen was essentially different from federal policy, and since the businesses of both employers (steel manufacturing) were clearly under federal jurisdiction and not covered by the federal-state agreement of 1937, the Court concluded that "it is beyond the power of New York State to apply its policy to these appellants as attempted herein."

Thus, by the Supreme Court's decision, there was created a partial "no-man's land" in interstate commerce. That is to say, an area was carved out where the National Board would not, and the

[17]*Id.* at 576–577.
[18]Bethlehem Steel Co. v. S.L.R.B., 330 U.S. 767 (1947).
[19]*Id.* at 775.

State Board could not, regulate. But it should be noted that this was *only* in those areas where the state's policy was essentially different from that of the National Board.

Approximately a month after the *Allegheny Ludlum* and *Bethlehem* ruling, *supra*, the National and State Boards concluded a second agreement[20] which spelled out what effect this decision had on the previous pact which they had made. It read as follows:

Sec. 204.1. Agreement with *New York State Labor Relations Board.*— The National Labor Relations Board has agreed with the New York State Labor Relations Board as follows:

(a) In the opinion of both Boards, there is nothing in the decision of the Supreme Court in the cases of *Bethlehem Steel Co.* v. *New York State Labor Relations Board,* and *Allegheny Ludlum Steel Corp.* v. *William J. Kelley, et al.,* Nos. 55 and 76, October Term, 1946, decided April 7, 1947, forbidding or disapproving such collaborative arrangements as are contained in the existing understanding between the New York State Labor Relations Board and the National Labor Relations Board....

(b) The existing understanding shall be continued in full force and effect in its present form until revoked, modified, or superseded by a new agreement between the Boards.

In summarizing the period from 1937 to 1947, then, it would appear that up to the time of the *Allegheny* and *Bethlehem* cases, *supra,* the State Board followed the rule that where the N.L.R.B. did not actually exercise its jurisdictional powers over employers involved in interstate commerce in particular cases, it felt free to act when called upon. This was somewhat limited by the Supreme Court's ruling, in that the Board was not to have carte blanche in those fields where the N.L.R.B. normally exercised its jurisdiction and where the state approach was opposed to national policy. Naturally, the State Board had also assumed authority in those areas which the federal agency had ceded it by the 1937 agreement.

Effect of Section 10(a) of Taft-Hartley

The next development came with the passage of the Labor-Management Relations Act (Taft-Hartley Act) of 1947. Section 10 (a) of the statute allows the N.L.R.B.:

[20]Federal Register, May 28, 1947.

135

to cede to [a state agency] jurisdiction over any cases in any industry (other than mining, manufacturing, communications, and transportation except where predominantly local in character) even though such cases may involve labor disputes affecting commerce, unless the provision of the State or Territorial statute applicable to the determination of such cases by such agency is inconsistent with the corresponding provision of this Act or has received a construction inconsistent therewith.[21]

The N.L.R.B. has never utilized this power to cede jurisdiction, maintaining that no state or territorial statute met the requirements imposed by the Congress.

The first case in which the State Board dealt with this new section was *Stone's Clothes Shop*.[22] There, the employer owned and operated a retail clothing store in White Plains, New York, as well as three stores in New Jersey and one in Connecticut. The out-of-state purchases of the stores constituted 58 percent of the total purchase. The employer contended (1) that the *Allegheny Ludlum* and *Bethlehem* decisions divested the Board of jurisdiction, and (2) that Section 10(a) of the federal act also rendered the Board powerless to act because it invalidated the previous agreements of the national and state agencies. The New York Board

---

[21]The assumptions apparently underlying this section are (1) that the N.L.R.B. cannot grant states jurisdiction over the mining, manufacturing, communication, and transportation industries, nor can the states assume control over them; and (2) that where the N.L.R.B. has not ceded jurisdiction over a particular industry involved in interstate commerce, the states cannot regulate that industry. Thus, during the three-year period preceding the establishment of the 1950 jurisdictional standards by the National Board, the State Board refused jurisdiction in several cases where there was prior N.L.R.B. treatment in the same or similar cases. See, for example, Red Arrow Bonded Messenger Corp., 11 S.L.R.B. 203 (1948); Buffalo Industrial Bank, 11 S.L.R.B. 205 (1948); Buffalo General Laundries, Inc., 11 S.L.R.B. 275 (1948); Hoffman Packing Co., 12 S.L.R.B. 512 (1949).

There were other cases which would, in any event, have been left with the National Board. Where a local New York State operation was considered to be an integral part of a larger multistate operation, the Board recognized the interstate nature of the Respondent's business. For example, Grandview Dairy Inc., 11 S.L.R.B. 112 (1948); Joan Barrie, 11 S.L.R.B. 471 (1948); Sanitary Automatic Candy Corp., 12 S.L.R.B. 357 (1949). In other instances, the percentage of business done outside the state, involving either the importing of raw materials or the exporting of finished products or parts, was determining. Corevent Corp., 11 S.L.R.B. 462 (1948); Seymour Products, Inc., 12 S.L.R.B. 46 (1949); Optical Service, Inc., 12 S.L.R.B. 529 (1949); Imperial Engraving Co., 12 S.L.R.B. 559 (1949). 357 (1949).

[22]11 S.L.R.B. 413 (1948).

refused to accept either contention, stating that, in the first place, Section 10(a) did not overturn any preexisting pact. "Since Section 10(a) is declaratory of the National Board's power prior to enactment of Section 10(a)," the Board noted, "that section does not affect a prior cession of jurisdiction, made in the exercise of a power which that section affirms.[23] And since the 1937 agreement granted state control over retail stores, the Board assumed jurisdiction of the case—with the important proviso that in its decision there was no conflict between the state and federal statutes.

1950 N.L.R.B. Jurisdictional Standards

In 1950, the N.L.R.B. announced, largely in terms of the dollar volume of the employer's business, the "yardsticks" which had evolved in determining whether it would assume jurisdiction over interstate businesses. Following these standards, the State Board divested itself of control over the following types of cases: (1) businesses whose operations were directly related to interstate industries;[24] and (2) concerns which met the dollar volume standard and the other criteria relating to the nature of the operation and the extent and type of interstate operations.[25]

And, conversely, the State Board found that it had control over the following categories of firms: (1) those whose operations were "small";[26] (2) those which did not meet the requisite dollar volume established by the N.L.R.B.;[27] (3) those which did not indicate

[23]*Id.* at 417.

[24]L. B. Auto Sales, Inc., 13 S.L.R.B. 111 (1950). Jackson Motor Co., 13 S.L.R.B. 143 (1950); Zyle Realty Corp., 13 S.L.R.B. 267 (1950); Anco Enterprises, Inc., 13 S.L.R.B. 320 (1950); Modern Cleaners Co., 13 S.L.R.B. 342 (1950); and Metro Hoist & Body Co., 14 S.L.R.B. 308 (1951).

[25]Central Paper Mill Supply Co., 13 S.L.R.B. 347 (1950); Michaels & Co., 13 S.L.R.B. 414 (1950); Goodwin's Inc., 13 S.L.R.B. 699 (1950); Elite Specialty Metal Co., 15 S.L.R.B. 467 (1952); Gustavo Stanzione, 15 S.L.R.B. 66, 73 (1952); W. C. Williams Corp., 16 S.L.R.B. 23 (1953); Curtis Elevator Co., 16 S.L.R.B. 31 (1953); National Radio Distributors' Corp., 16 S.L.R.B. 329 (1953).

[26]Dasher Foundry & Machine Corp., 13 S.L.R.B. 114 (1950). Herbert Strausser, Inc., 13 S.L.R.B. 532 (1950); Chapin Constr. Co., 15 S.L.R.B. 128 (1952).

[27]Park East Foundation, Inc., 14 S.L.R.B. 54 (1951); Commercial Stationery Co., 14 S.L.R.B. 177 (1951); Park West Foundation, Inc., 14 S.L.R.B. 536 (1951); Department Stores Serv. Co., 14 S.L.R.B. 600 (1951); Royal Concourse Co., 14 S.L.R.B. 618 (1961); Benjamin's Inc., 15 S.L.R.B. 344 (1952); Royal Concourse Co., 15 S.L.R.B. 524 (1952); Sterling Optical Co., 16 S.L.R.B. 800 (1953).

substantial proof of interstate commerce;[28] and (4) those in industries where there was no indication of congressional intent to regulate the industry.[29]

1951 Federal-State Relations

Two important developments on the question of federal-state relations occurred in 1951. Both involved litigation before the courts, and both were concerned with taxicab companies in New York City.

In the first, *S.L.R.B. v. Charman Serv. Corp.,*[30] the issue raised before the Supreme Court of New York County was whether, in determining its jurisdictional power over an employer, the State Board should base its decision on the operations of the entire taxicab industry of the city (in this case, New York City) or on the operations of the individual employer in the case before it. The Board adopted the latter viewpoint, and the Supreme Court agreed, stating that

it does not follow that where some or many of the employers in an industry do affect [interstate] commerce, the National Board thereby acquires jurisdiction over all employers in that industry, even those whose individual acts do not affect commerce.[31]

The second case[32] arose out of the circumstance that employees of the Taxi Transit Co. had filed unfair labor practice charges before both the N.L.R.B. and the New York Board in 1949. The

[28]Dean Furn. Co., 13 S.L.R.B. 536 (1950); United Tel. Answering Serv., Inc., 14 S.L.R.B. 197 (1951); I. Howard Lehman, 14 S.L.R.B. 251 (1951); The Steak Joint, 14 S.L.R.B. 301 (1951); Chalfin Machine Products, Inc., 14 S.L.R.B. 394 (1951); Master Platers Corp., 15 S.L.R.B. 673 (1952).

[29]Jackson & Perkins Co., 14 S.L.R.B. 355 (1951). Here the Respondent was in the nursery stock business and claimed to be engaged in a business which substantially affected interstate commerce. The employees involved in the particular dispute were farm laborers, and therefore not within the coverage of the national act. The State Board thought that although Congress, in the National Board Appropriation Act of 1951, had chosen not to regulate this particular employer-employee relationship, it had placed no restriction on state action. Under the circumstances, the states were free to act, irrespective of whether the employer's business substantially affected interstate commerce. The State Board then dismissed the case itself for the reason that the employees involved were farm laborers excluded from the statute.

[30]201 Misc. 291, 107 N.Y.S. 2d 41 (Sup. Ct. 1951), aff'd, 281 App. Div. 860, 119 N.Y.S. 2d 916 (1st Dept. 1953).

[31]201 Misc. 295–296, 107 N.Y.S. 2d 46.

[32]N.L.R.B. v. S.L.R.B., 126 N.Y.L.J. 72 (S.D.N.Y. 1951).

state agency had notified the N.L.R.B. that charges had been filed with it, and the latter had voiced no objections to the processing of the case on the state level. By 1950, however, the National Board had reversed its previous policy of not asserting jurisdiction over the taxicab industry and had begun to entertain petitions from cab drivers. In the instant case, the N.L.R.B. asked the United States District Court of Southern New York to enjoin any further action by the New York agency which affected the employees of Taxi Transit or those involved in the *Charman* case, *supra* (which case was still pending before the New York County Supreme Court). The District Court dismissed the motion, primarily because (1) there was serious doubt as to the interstate character of the employers' businesses, and (2) "the delay [by the National Board in asserting its jurisdiction] obviously should be taken into consideration in determining whether to grant the extraordinary remedy of a preliminary injunction."[33]

No-Man's Land

The problem of the "no-man's land" arose again in the case of *Wags Transp. Sys.* (1953).[34] Here again, the New York Board recognized that the employer's business did affect interstate commerce, but maintained that this case was different from the *Bethlehem* and *Allegheny Ludlum* cases, *supra,* where the Board was prohibited from acting because of previous federal action in the field which was not in accord with state policy. In the present case, the Board believed that there would be no potential conflict with the N.L.R.B., since the latter had declined to assert jurisdiction over the type of business in which Wags was engaged at the time the charges were brought before the State Board (1948). Consequently,

[33]As of 1952 (Cambridge Taxi Co., 101 N.L.R.B. 1328), the National Board stated that it would assert jurisdiction only where two factors were present: (1) The employer is either the sole taxicab company operating in the area served by its cabs, which services instrumentalities of commerce, or is the holder of a contract license or franchise from some instrumentality or commerce, granting to the employer the privilege or right to serve, either exclusively or concurrently with others, a depot or terminal of such instrumentality; and (2) The employer derives a substantial portion of its total revenue directly from carrying passengers to and from terminals or depots of these instrumentalities of commerce.
[34]16 S.L.R.B. 386.

Where the National Board refuses to assert jurisdiction, labor disputes must be subject to regulation by the States or they will not be regulated at all. Labor disputes may, or may not, substantially affect interstate commerce, but they invariably have an immediate and direct impact upon the local community in which they occur. We do not believe that Congress...ever intended to create a no-man's land in which labor disputes would be entirely unregulated because of federal inaction.[35]

These arguments were not accepted, however, either by the Supreme Court of New York County or by the Appellate Division. The lower court decided that the N.L.R.B. had "exclusive power in all cases touching interstate commerce, *to the total exclusion of state power.*"[36] The Appellate Division tempered somewhat the Supreme Court's decision by declaring: "There being *no clear showing* that the National Board would not have assumed jurisdiction and also in the absence of a cession agreement under Section 10(a) of the Taft-Hartley Act, the appellant could not assert jurisdiction."[37]

This no-man's land became even larger in 1954 when the N.L.R.B. substantially *raised* the floor below which it would not go in handling cases. This reflected the new majority view of the National Board that it should restrict its authority to those "labor disputes [which] would have a pronounced impact upon the flow of interstate commerce."[38]

[35]*Id.* at 389.

[36]S.L.R.B. v. Wags Transp. Sys., 130 N.Y.S. 2d 731, 735 (Sup. Ct. 1954), italics added.

[37]S.L.R.B. v. Wags Transp. Sys., 284 App.Div. 883, 884, 134 N.Y.S. 2d 603, 604 (1st Dept. 1954), italics added.

[38]Breeding Transfer Co., 110 N.L.R.B. 493 (1954). For several years after the establishment of the N.L.R.B.'s 1954 standards, the decisions by the State Board on whether to assume jurisdiction were essentially of the same nature as prior to their release. Where the evidence substantially proved that the employer was engaged in interstate commerce and that its operations exceeded the minimum requirements specified in the N.L.R.B.'s formula, it recognized that it was without jurisdiction. Slater Sys., N.Y., Inc., 17 S.L.R.B. 250 (1954); B/G Foods, Inc., 20 S.L.R.B. 208 (1957); Diamond Auto Glass Corp., 20 S.L.R.B 337 (1957).

The majority of cases prior to 1957 were, however, decided against Respondents who claimed that the National Board had exclusive jurisdiction. The bases for these decisions, once again, were related to the dollar volume requirements and to lack of substantial proof. Dollar volume: Philbern Thermometer Co., 17 S.L.R.B. 434 (1954); Washington Mirror Works, Inc., 17 S.L.R.B. 646 (1954); Hosler Cadillac Co., 18 S.L.R.B. 113 (1955); Whitbread's Sons Lumber Co., 19 S.L.R.B. 328 (1956): Le Boff's, Inc., 20 S.L.R.B. 27 (1957). Lack of proof: C. I. Beverage Distrib., Inc.,

In the case of *Raisch Motors* (1955),[39] the N.L.R.B. had made a definite statement that it would not assert its jurisdiction over the employer, principally because the volume of direct and indirect inflow of goods and out-of-state sales was far less than required by the 1954 standards. For the New York Board, this satisfied the Appellate Division's requirement in the *Wags Transp.* case, *supra,* that there be a "clear showing" that the National Board would not assume control. Consequently, there could be no conflict between the two agencies, and the Board ruled that it could regulate the present dispute.

It was the United States Supreme Court's decision in *Guss v. Utah Labor Relations Board*[40] in 1957 which met directly the issue of whether a state board could assume jurisdiction over an employer in interstate commerce where the N.L.R.B. had refused to assert its own control. The Court's decision was that the states had *no authority* to act with respect to a labor dispute "affecting interstate commerce" in the area "pre-empted" by the N.L.R.B., regardless of that Board's decision not to exercise its control over such disputes. This meant that a decision such as the New York Board's in the *Raisch Motors* case, *supra,* was no longer controlling.

Influenced by this decision and by an additional congressional allotment for the fiscal year 1958–1960, the N.L.R.B. in 1958 announced its third set of jurisdictional standards which broadened the area in which it would act.[41]

The position which the State Board took in cases like *Wags Transp.* and *Raisch Motors, supra,* was finally vindicated in 1959 when Congress passed the Labor-Management Reporting and Disclosure (Landrum-Griffin) Act. Section 14 of the National Labor Relations Act was amended as follows:

Nothing in this Act shall be deemed to prevent or bar any agency or the courts of any State...from assuming and asserting jurisdiction

---

18 S.L.R.B. 120 (1955). Vel Cab Corp., 20 S.L.R.B. 161 (1957); Consol. Beer & Soda Distrib., 20 S.L.R.B. 359, 417 (1957).

[39] 18 S.L.R.B. 94 (1955).

[40] 353 U.S. 1 (1957).

[41] See National Labor Relations Board, Twenty-Third Annual Report (for the fiscal year ended 1958), p. 8.

over labor disputes over which the Board declines...to assert jurisdiction.

Consequently, in two representation proceedings over which the National Board refused to exercise its authority,[42] the state took jurisdiction, even though the petitions were filed before the 1959 act, on the basis that they were "prospective in operation, not retrospective." In unfair labor practices,[43] however, the Board took a different stand—14(c)(2) is not retroactive to such cases— "despite the manifest inequities involved." In all interstate cases arising after the passage of the legislation, however, the New York Board can assume control and apply its own statute where there is no actual assertion of authority on the part of the N.L.R.B.

The jurisdictional accommodation between state and federal boards has been further facilitated by an advisory opinion procedure adopted by the N.L.R.B. and designed to elicit that Board's view on jurisdictional questions.[44] The operation of that procedure is illustrated by several cases involving racetrack stable employees of horse owners.[45] The employers challenged State Board jurisdiction on the grounds that they were engaged in interstate commerce and therefore subject to exclusive federal regulation. The National Board, however, issued advisory opinions, declining jurisdiction over such employers,[46] thus leaving the state agency free to proceed.

As a practical matter, however, the present practice appears to be to urge the moving party before the State Board to take its case to the N.L.R.B. whenever the activities of the employer appear to satisfy N.L.R.B. jurisdictional standards. This is done in the informal stage of administrative investigation. If the federal agency, acting through one of its field representatives, declines to assert

[42]Augi's Taxi, 23 S.L.R.B. 467 (1960); Sullivan County Harness Racing Ass'n., 21 S.L.R.B. 379 (1958).

[43]Saratoga Harness Racing Ass'n., 23 S.L.R.B. 63 (1960); Troy Spring Works, Inc., 23 S.L.R.B. 199 (1960).

[44]National Labor Relations Board, Rules and Regulations, Subpart H, Secs. 102.98–102.110.

[45]Howard Jacobson, 24 S.L.R.B. No. 46 (1961); Norman Robert McLeod, 24 S.L.R.B. No. 45 (1961); Robert Nelson Blackburn, 24 S.L.R.B. No. 44 (1961); John W. Galbreath & James P. Conway, 24 S.L.R.B. 177 (1961).

[46]William H. Dixon, 130 N.L.R.B. 1204 (1961); Meadow Stud, Inc., 130 N.L.R.B. 1202 (1961). But see Hirsch v. McCulloch, 303 Fed 2d 208, 49 L.R.R.M. 2828 (C.A.D.C. 1962).

jurisdiction, the matter may then be renewed before the State Board which will deem itself to be free to proceed. This informal procedure has the advantage of consuming a matter of a few weeks instead of requiring the several months it takes to secure a formal advisory opinion from the full N.L.R.B. in Washington. Thus it appears that a reasonably effective accommodation of the adjacent jurisdiction of the two labor relations agencies has now been established.

CHAPTER IX

Concluding Observations

IN THIS concluding chapter some of the proposals which have been advanced for modification of the New York State Labor Relations Act and its administration are discussed. These fall into two general categories. The first involves proposed changes in the administrative organization of the New York State Labor Relations Board. The second mainly involves changes in the substantive provisions of the statute.

Administrative Reorganization

The single most drastic proposal for administrative reorganization of the New York State Labor Relations Board was advanced in Commissioner Benjamin's 1942 report, *Administrative Adjudication in the State of New York*. The proposal was as follows:

My recommendation is that there be established two boards, independent of each other, each consisting of three members appointed by the Governor, by and with the advice and consent of the Senate, and removable by the Governor for cause. The terms of office of the members of each board would be staggered (as are the terms of the present Board) to expire at two-year intervals. It is an essential part of my proposal that there should be corresponding terms of office for members of the two boards, so that (except for temporary variations that might be caused by death, resignation or removal) both boards should be made up, in the same proportions, of appointees of the same appointing power. . . .

Generally, I recommend that one of the new boards (which I suggest calling the State Labor Relations Board) should have the function of adjudication in unfair labor practice cases, and in representation cases should have the functions of adjudication (including the adjudication of objections to the conduct of elections) and formal certification of bargaining representatives; and that the other board (which I suggest calling the State Labor Relations Authority) should exercise all other functions, including the investigation of charges with respect to unfair labor practices and of controversies concerning the representation of employees, the negotiation of voluntary adjustments of alleged violations of the Act, the determination whether or not to issue complaints with respect to alleged unfair labor practices and the issuance of such complaints, the litigation of unfair labor practice cases before the Board, the supervision of voluntary agreements relating to the selection of bargaining representatives, the presentation of evidence or argument at hearings before the Board in representation cases where that is necessary to supplement the presentation by the other parties, the conduct of elections (whether held on consent or by direction of the Board), and the litigation of all enforcement and other proceedings in court. The allocation of staff would follow corresponding lines, the Board's staff to include trial examiners and other personnel necessary to assist it in adjudication, the Authority's staff to include trial attorneys and other personnel necessary to assist it in its varied functions. The personnel of the regional offices in Albany and Buffalo would, in this allocation, fall under the jurisdiction of the Authority. Each board would have the power to make rules and regulations within the sphere of its authority.[1]

The purpose of the foregoing suggestions was, plainly, to accomplish, through *external* separation, a complete division between the functions of prosecuting and of adjudication both of which were then, and continue now to be, blended in a single agency. Commissioner Benjamin's recommendation has, to this date, not been adopted. The main reasons for the recommendation were that no *internal* separation of functions can ever be quite complete, that the possibility of undesirable commingling of functions therefore always exists, and that consequently there persists the likelihood of at least an *appearance* of unfair prejudging, if not of actual unfairness.

It is of interest to observe that, on a somewhat more modest scale, this proposal of Commissioner Benjamin was echoed at the federal level in the Taft-Hartley amendment separating the office

[1]Benjamin, *Administrative Adjudication in the State of New York* 48–49 (1942).

of General Counsel from the National Labor Relations Board in 1947. Similar proposals have subsequently been advanced in connection with the State Board. Indeed, a more complete separation of executive and prosecuting responsibilities from the judicial function of the N.L.R.B. was suggested in 1960 by an advisory panel to the United States Senate Committee of Labor and Public Welfare.[2]

The persistent reappearance of suggestions along these lines, focusing particularly upon labor relations agencies, implies that this field of regulation continues to be more volatile and controversial than many other areas of administrative activity, for most administrative agencies function on the basis of a unitary command structure. My own conclusions are somewhat tentative. I am, as I have indicated on other occasions, persuaded that we need to rethink in broad terms the questions of the role of administrative agencies and of their efficacy as instruments of government.[3] On the other hand, my investigations of the New York State Labor Relations Board lead me to the conclusion that the drastic surgery proposed by Commissioner Benjamin in connection with this particular agency is probably not necessary. Thus, I am persuaded from my scrutiny of the Board's procedures described in earlier chapters that the internal separation of functions presently practiced works well to avoid unfairness in the particular case. The insulation of the Trial Examiner is illustrative. At the same time, the agency is left free to implement a vigorous *general* policy, as it is doing, for instance, in the field of "paper locals."

Proposed Substantive Amendments

It is not surprising that most proposals in this area are along lines which would bring the State Labor Relations Act (which retains most of its original Wagner Act character) more into conformity with the National Labor Relations Act, as amended both in 1947 and 1959 by the Taft-Hartley and Landrum-Griffin

[2]Advisory Panel on Labor-Management Relations Law to the Senate Committee on Labor and Public Welfare, Report on Organization and Procedure of the National Labor Relations Board, S. Doc. No. 81, 86th Cong., 2d Sess. (1960).

[3]Hanslowe, Neo-Liberalism: An Analysis and Proposed Application, 9 J. Pub. L. 96 (1960); The Malaise of the Administrative Process, 1963 Duke L. J. 477.

amendments, respectively. A sample of these proposals will convey their general aim.

An elaborate statutory proposal was made by the New York Chamber of Commerce in 1958, which is summarized in the Report of the New York State Joint Legislative Committee on Industrial and Labor Conditions, 1958 (pp. 115–116) as follows:

As a guide to the deliberations of this Committee, we outline below the amendments which we recommend for adoption:

1. "Findings and Policy" should be modernized.

2. Eliminate supervisors from coverage of Act so as to avoid the conflict arising from dual loyalties to an employer and to a Union.

3. Set up separate and independent General Counsel, and provide statutory separation between the investigatory and prosecuting functions of the Board, on the one hand, and its judicial functions, on the other.

4. Enunciate the right of employees to refrain from collective activities as well as to engage in them.

5. Eliminate closed shop and hiring hall, and limit obligation under union security clause to paying dues and uniform initiation fee.

6. Declare as Union unfair labor practices:

a. Restraint or coercion of employees in their rights under the Act.

b. Enforcement of illegal Union security measures.

c. Refusal to bargain.

d. To require excessive initiation fees.

e. Featherbedding demands.

7. Guarantee right of free speech.

8. Define duty to bargain in good faith and provide for reasonable notice to other party and Mediation Board before terminating contract or striking.

9. Amend rules governing proper bargaining units to exclude guards and professional employees from units which include production employees.

10. Provide for decertification proceedings by employees and proceedings to de-authorize a union security arrangement.

11. Place employer petitions for election on the same footing as union petitions for election.

12. Prohibit more than one election in a year. Also correct New York's present highly unfair rule which prohibits even permanent replacements of economic strikers from voting, and provide rules governing eligibility or non-eligibility of replaced economic strikers.

13. Provide for non-Communist affidavits for union officials.

14. Provide for filing of financial statements by unions.

15. Provide statute of limitations for unfair labor practices.

16. Empower Board to arbitrate jurisdictional disputes and empower parties to obtain injunctions against strikes or picketing occurring in such disputes.

17. Empower Board to apply for temporary injunction against either an employer or a union after complaint of unfair labor practice is issued.

That proposal, if it had been enacted, would have brought the New York State Labor Relations Act into substantial conformity with the National Labor Relations Act (as it stood prior to its 1959 amendments). The close similarity between this proposal and the Taft-Hartley amendments to the National Labor Relations Act was very likely motivated, in part at least, by the "no-man's land" problem created by the United States Supreme Court's decision in the *Guss* case, which was discussed in the previous chapter. The theory apparently was that, by bringing the state statute into conformity with the federal law, the National Labor Relations Board might have been persuaded to cede jurisdiction to the State Board, thereby enabling the latter to fill the "no-man's land." That particular reason for conforming the state act to the federal statute has, of course, now been removed by the federal legislation in 1959 which empowers the states to assume jurisdiction in any situation where the National Labor Relations Board declines to do so. Thus, whatever other reasons there might be for amending the state act, it is no longer necessary precisely to duplicate the federal statute for reasons of the "no-man's land" problem.

The position of the New York Chamber of Commerce in 1960 was reflected by the following legislative program:

1. Guarantee employees against restraint and coercion by unions as well as by employers.

2. Empower our courts to halt blackmail and coercive picketing.

3. Guarantee workers the right to a secret ballot election where a question of representation arises.

4. Protect the results of Labor Board elections for one year.

4a. Permit decertification proceedings after one year, as permitted by Federal law.

5. Guarantee rights of free speech to all.

6. Forbid persons who are, or who have been members of the Communist Party, or who have been convicted of certain specified crimes, from serving as officers of a union or as labor relations consultants, or as officers of an employer association dealing with a labor organization, for a period of time after termination of Communist Party membership, or after conviction or end of imprisonment.

7. Prohibit demands for make-work rules and thereby eliminate their triple consequences of (a) saddling of the public with arbitrary and unnecessarily high prices, (b) loss of business to New York State employers due to the competitive handicaps such make-work rules impose, and (c) inflationary results.

8. Abolish the closed shop—permit union security provisions of the nature permitted by Federal law.

8a. In providing security for unions, the need to protect workers against excessive or discriminatory dues and initiation fees should be met.

9. Require unions, as well as companies, to bargain in good faith.

10. Revise present rule which denies permanent employees hired as replacements for economic strikers the right to vote in the selection of their own collective bargaining agent.

11. Eliminate evasion of responsibility and flouting of authority by requiring unions to designate the Secretary of State to accept service of process on their behalf.

Likewise in 1960, a majority of the Committee on Labor Law of the New York State Bar Association advanced the following position.

Among the subjects on which the committee feels legislative consideration is needed are:

1. Statutory grant of free speech to employers.

2. Statutory regulation of the respective rights of replaced economic strikers and of their replacements to vote in labor board elections. Although it is not entirely clear from board decisions, there is considerable ground for believing that under the Board's rules replacements of economic strikers may not vote even though they are permanent employees.

3. Drawing of a statutory line of demarcation between rank-and-file employees and their supervisors which would prevent combining

supervisors and those whom they supervise in a single bargaining unit.

4. Examination into the justification for continuing the closed shop in the State of New York. Under the present law, employees may be required by contract to be members of a union before they can seek employment.

5. Statutory definition and regulation of unfair labor practices by unions, such as (a) refusal by a union to bargain in good faith, and (b) practicing of coercion and restraint on employees in the exercise of their right to choose or refrain from choosing a bargaining representative.[4]

Note should also be taken of a somewhat more limited legislative proposal, introduced by Assemblyman John L. Ostrander in 1960, intended to deal with the problem of organizational picketing by minority unions. The proposal would have added the following language to Section 705(3) of the act:

Where a labor organization is picketing an employer to become the representative of his employees and does not represent or claim to represent a majority of his employees, and where there is no other exclusive bargaining representative representing or claiming to represent the employees, the employer or his representative may file a petition with the board after the seventh day from the commencement of such picketing, alleging that there is a question or controversy concerning the representation of his employees. When such a petition has been filed, the board shall forthwith direct an election in such unit as the board finds to be appropriate with the name of such labor organization listed on the ballot as a nominee for exclusive bargaining representative of the employees. If such labor organization fails to receive a majority of the votes cast in the election, it shall be an unlawful labor practice on the part of such labor organization to continue such picketing and may be prevented from so doing by the board as provided in section seven hundred six, of this article, until after one year from the date of such election.[5]

An assessment of these proposals requires them to be placed in a somewhat broader context. Of particular significance in this regard is the difference in treatment which the State Anti-Injunction statute has received at the hands of the New York courts, as contrasted with that of the Norris-LaGuardia Act. Unlike the strict

[4]New York State Bar Association, Report of Committee on Labor Law 2–3 (1960).
[5]Assembly; No. 4521; Int. 4297; Print 4521 (1960).

and literal reading which the federal courts accorded the latter statute, the New York courts have pursued a path of rather flexible interpretation of the concept "labor dispute."[6]

While the New York cases, to be sure, are not always free from doubt, the following are the more important types of situations in which the state courts have lifted the restrictions of the Anti-Injunction statute and have issued injunctions restraining union activity: (1) mass picketing and picketing involving violence or threats of violence;[7] (2) picketing directed at self-employed employers;[8] (3) make-work pressure, at least in some situations;[9] (4) some forms of secondary boycott picketing;[10] (5) picketing by a union which has lost a representation election;[11] (6) jurisdictional disputes picketing, at least in some cases;[12] (7) picketing intended to induce breach of contract;[13] (8) recognition picketing by a minority union.[14] Thus, several of the union activities which would be proscribed as unfair labor practices by the above proposals are already enjoinable by the courts in New York State.

Against this list must be balanced the New York courts' generally sympathetic attitude toward peaceful picketing, especially when it is directed toward customers at the primary employers' site or is for organizational purposes. It must also be conceded that the line which the New York courts attempt to maintain between organizational and recognitional picketing is difficult to perceive in theory and equally difficult to draw in practice.[15]

It is also worth noting that some of the proposals being advanced,

[6]See Seidenberg, The Labor Injunction in New York City, 40–95 (1953).
[7]Busch Jewelry Co. v. United Retail Employees' Union Local 830, 281 N.Y. 150, 22 N.E. 2nd 320 (1939).
[8]Zweibon v. Goldberg, 20 N.Y.S. 2d 272 (Sup. Ct., Kings Co., 1940); Gips v. Osman, 258 App. Div. 789, 16 N.Y.S. 2d 101 (1st. Dept. 1939).
[9]Opera on Tour Inc. v. Weber, 285 N.Y. 348, 34 N.E. 2d 349 (1941).
[10]Elizabeth Arden Sales Corp. v. Hawley, 176 Misc. 821, 28 N.Y.S. 2d 936, aff'd 261 App. Div. 953, 27 N.Y.S. 2d 423 (1st. Dept., 1941).
[11]LaManna v. O'Grady, 278 App. Div. 77, 103 N.Y.S. 2d 476 (1st. Dept., 1951).
[12]Florsheim Shoe Store Co. v. Retail Shoe Salesmen's Union, 288 N.Y. 188, 42 N.E. 2d 480 (1942).
[13]Assoc. Flour Haulers & Warehousemen, Inc. v. Sullivan, 168 Misc. 315, 5 N.Y.S. 2d 982 (Sup. Ct., King's Co., 1938); Stern-Fair Corp. v. Moving Picture Operators Union, Local 306, 139 N.Y.S. 2d 145 (Sup. Ct., Queen's Co., 1954); Greater City Master Plumbers Association, Inc., v. Kahme, 6 N.Y.S. 2d 589 (Sup. Ct., N.Y. Co., 1937).
[14]Goodwin v. Hagedorn, 303 N.Y. 300, 101 N.E. 2d 967 (1951).
[15]Wood v. O'Grady, 307 N.Y. 532, 122 N.E. 2d 386 (1954).

while entailing restrictions upon the State Board's statutory authority, would involve little, if any, change in the Board's present practice. This would be true, for instance, of proposals requiring the holding of secret ballot elections, protecting the results of elections for one year, and guaranteeing rights of free speech to all.

Still other proposals are of minor significance. This would seem to be true of the proposed imposition, upon unions, of a duty to bargain in good faith. The corresponding Taft-Hartley unfair labor practice has not played a significant role. In addition, the New York Board has held that an employer's duty to bargain is suspended in the face of the union's taking an adamant and unyielding position in negotiations.[16]

A word should be said about proposals to prohibit the closed shop, an important facet of which is the question of the right of access to union membership. Here again, the issue in New York is somewhat less sharp than might appear on the surface because, while the New York courts seem to have refused to recognize a right to join a union,[17] they have, by protecting the employment rights of those unreasonably excluded, significantly limited the incentive to restrict admission. Specifically, the courts have developed the rule that a union cannot at the same time have a closed shop and be a closed union.[18] The dimensions of this problem have been further curtailed by the State Antidiscrimination Act.[19] If legislation is, nevertheless, deemed desirable in this area, it might be suggested that the state, instead of mimicking the somewhat rigid and cumbersome federal provisions on the union shop, might wish to consider adopting the approach of the Massachusetts Labor Relations Act.[20] This is one of tolerating the closed shop, but of prohibiting discrimination in employment against employees whose union membership has been unfairly denied or terminated.

The fundamental issue posed by most of the proposals set forth above is, of course, whether or not a program of substantial amendment of the New York State Labor Relations Act, similar to the Taft-Hartley and Landrum-Griffin amendments of the National

[16]Matter of Malgarinos, 16 S.L.R.B. 211 (1953).
[17]Miller v. Ruehl, 166 Misc. 479, 2 N.Y.S. 2d 394 (Sup. Ct., Erie Co., 1938).
[18]Clark v. Curtis, 297 N.Y. 1014, 80 N.E. 2d 536 (1948).
[19]N.Y. Civil Rights Law, N.Y. Session Laws 1940, Ch. 9, §43, par. 1.
[20]Massachusetts Labor Relations Act, §§4, 6A, Annotated Laws of Massachusetts, Ch. 150 A, §§4 and 6A, as amended by Laws 1947, c. 657.

Labor Relations Act, should be undertaken. This issue is so super-charged with political volatility that the author is, frankly, reluctant to strike the spark that might set off the explosion! Indeed, the issue is so large as to appear beyond the competence of the isolated and somewhat insulated solitary academician. Timorousness, therefore, suggests the wiser course of outlining some considerations to be taken into account by those urging or opposing so fundamental a revision.

Basic among these considerations are some of the facets of New York law to which I have previously alluded, and in the context of which the proposals for amendment, I have suggested, must be considered. These, as I have intimated, signify to me that a good many of these proposals are not as farreaching as they might appear. The proposals, instead, to some not quite precisely defined extent, would represent codifications, refinements, or modest modifications of existing law. This has significance both for the proponents and the opponents of amendment. The proponents would not gain as much as might appear to them on the surface. Nor would the opponents of amendment lose as much. The question to be posed to both contending groups, then, is whether their respective, opposing, massive, all-out positions are worth the effort necessary to achieve or to maintain them. This leads to the related question of whether this sort of "all-or-nothing" dialogue is a very fruitful or effective way of conducting the debate. Furthermore, the question might be raised of whether, in considering amendments to the New York State Labor Relations Act, the aping of what has been done at the federal level poses the most imaginative and creative line of approach possible.

Perhaps the state and the affected private groups should give serious thought to reviewing a statute now over a quarter of a century old. If so, I think it should be done by the method of comprehensive tripartite study and in as dispassionate an atmosphere as is possible under the circumstances. Furthermore, such a study should be undertaken with imagination, with a willingness to consider novel approaches, leaving shibboleths and entrenched positions behind. I am persuaded that only such an approach would entail the reasonable likelihood of producing a balanced and well-drawn new statute having a broad sense of acceptability.

Statistical Tables Describing Activities of the New York State Labor Relations Board

Table 1. Analysis of Cases Filed, July 1, 1937–December 31, 1962.

	1962		Total 1937–1962	
	Cases	Percent of Total Filed	Cases	Percent of Total Filed
Total cases filed (all types)................	1,267	100%	39,047	100%
Charges of unfair labor practices............	418	33%	12,885	33%
Representation petitions by employees........	799	63%	24,113	62%
Representation petitions by employers........	50	4%	2,049	5%
Total cases closed (all types)*..............	1,217		38,815	
Number of employees involved..............	6,140		988,628	
In unfair labor practice charges...........	1,816		223,838	
In representation petitions...............	4,324		764,790	
Cases filed by:				
A.F. of L. unions**.....................			15,901	
C.I.O. unions**........................			6,330	
A.F. of L.–C.I.O. unions**..............	711		6,095	
Independent unions.....................	432		5,969	
Individual employees...................	74		2,703	
Employers (representation petitions).......	50		2,049	

Source: Twenty-sixth Analysis of Decisions, New York State Labor Relations Board: For the Year Ended December 31, 1962.
    *Pending Cases, December 31, 1962: 232.
    **Separate figures for A.F. of L. and C.I.O. prior to the merger of these two labor organizations in December 1955. Thereafter listed under A.F. of L.-C.I.O. unions.
    For the disposition of closed cases, see Table 4.

Table 2. Labor Relations Inquiries Processed.

	1962	Total 1959–1962
Total inquiries processed	3,734	15,112
Disposition:		
Representation petitions filed	133	445
Unfair labor charges filed	99	375
Information furnished re. Act and/or Board procedure	656	2,825
Referred to other governmental agency	2,036	8,776
Miscellaneous	810	2,691

Note: The above include personal interviews, written and telephonic inquiries. Statistics of inquiries processed prior to 1959 not included.

Table 3. Board Action in Relation to Strike Cases, July 1, 1937–December 31, 1962.

	1962	Total 1937–1962
Cases filed involving strikes	102	3,431
Number of employees affected	768	81,797
Cases in which Board was instrumental in settling strikes	37	2,894
Number of employees affected	370	60,692
Cases in which contemplated strike action was withheld pending Board action*	45	1,510
Number of employees affected	829	87,709

*Approximate figures.

Table 4. Disposition of Closed Cases, July 1, 1937–December 31, 1962.

	Unfair Labor Practice Cases		Representation Cases Filed by Employees		Representation Cases Filed by Employer		Total Cases All Types		
	1962	Total 1937–1962	1962	Total 1937–1962	1962	Total 1937–1962	1962	Total 1937–1962	
Cases closed before hearing authorized:									
By adjustment	188	5,369	268	6,524	13	620	469	12,513	32.3%
By reference to Mediation Board	...	14	...	5	...	4	...	23	...
By withdrawal	53	3,250	181	5,578	8	465	242	9,293	23.9%
By consent stipulation:									
Certification following consent comparison	...	...	...	342	...	2	...	344	.9%
Certification following consent election	...	...	116	4,876	1	112	117	4,988	12.9%
Dismissal following consent election	...	...	65	1,802	4	71	69	1,873	4.8%
By dismissal:									
On the merits	18	1,043	8	256	3	174	29	1,473	3.8%
Lack of prosecution by party filing	8	454	5	485	1	43	14	982	2.5%
No jurisdiction:									
Religious or charitable organization	...	8	...	26	...	...	...	34 }	
Educational institution	...	6	...	8	...	...	...	14 }	
Farm labor	...	2	...	2	...	...	...	4 }	.3%
Employee of city or state	...	4	...	1	...	...	...	5 }	
Acts prior to July 1, 1937	...	9	...	...	...	...	...	9 }	
Jurisdictional conflict	...	6	...	61	...	2	...	69 }	
Declined jurisdiction because of commerce	...	359	3	403	2	22	5	784	2.0%

Charge of refusal to bargain or petition involving only one employee (before 1942)	...	7	...	52	...	...	...	59 } .3%
Union no longer in existence	...	3	...	8	...	...	...	11 }
Union superseded by new organization	...	...	...	29	...	...	...	29 }
Consolidated with, or superseded by, another charge or petition	...	75	1	109	...	...	1	184	.5%
Total cases closed before hearing authorized	267	10,609	647	20,567	32	1,515	946	32,691	84.2%
Cases closed after hearing authorized:									
By adjustment during or following hearing (petitions)	...	...	46	561	4	135	50	696	1.8%
By adjustment before final decision by Board (unfair labor charges):									
Adjusted after issuance of complaint but before hearing began	25	257	...	...	...	...	25	257	
Adjusted while hearing in progress	13	398	...	...	...	...	13	398	
Adjusted after close of hearing and before issuance of any Intermediate Report of Trial Examiner	10	225	...	...	...	...	10	225	} 2.4%
Adjusted after close of hearing and issuance of Trial Examiner's Intermediate Report	1	64	...	...	...	...	1	64	
By withdrawal during or following hearing; no adjustment	6	84	23	490	1	59	30	633	1.7%
By dismissal on the merits by Board decision*	13	278	5	401	7	166	25	845	2.2%
Cease and desist orders: (total 815 or 2.1%)									
Compliance secured	19	686	...	...	...	...	19	686	1.8%
Enforcement refused by courts	...	9	...	...	...	...	...	9	...
Closed, miscellaneous	7	111	...	...	...	...	7	111	.3%

157

Table 4. (continued)

	Unfair Labor Practice Cases		Representation Cases Filed by Employees		Representation Cases Filed by Employer		Total Cases All Types		
	1962	Total 1937–1962	1962	Total 1937–1962	1962	Total 1937–1962	1962	Total 1937–1962	
By certification during or following hearing	...	...	46	789	...	6	46	795	2.1%
By certification following ordered election	...	...	23	704	1	35	24	739	1.9%
By dismissal after ordered election	...	...	17	401	3	72	20	473	1.2%
Terminated by decision	...	...	...	5	1	53	1	58	.1%
By dismissal, declined jurisdiction because of commerce	...	48	...	85	...	2	...	135	.3%
Total cases closed after hearing authorized	94	2,160	160	3,436	17	528	271	6,124	15.8%
Total cases closed	361	12,769	807	24,003	49	2,043	1,217	38,815	100.0%

*Since the Board was established, in 1937, it has found violations of the Act and issued cease and desist orders in 815 cases. In addition to the 806 cases already closed as noted, there are at present seven cases in which Board cease and desist orders have issued and which are open awaiting compliance before enforcement proceedings are instituted in the courts; and two cases awaiting compliance after court enforcement of the Board's decision.

The figure of 815 cease and desist orders contrasts with 278 unfair labor practice cases dismissed on the merits by Board decision after hearing. It should be compared to the total of 12,769 unfair labor practice cases closed in the twenty-five and one-half year period. 1,043 of these cases were dismissed on the merits before hearing. Cease and desist orders were required in only 6.3% of all unfair labor practice cases closed.

Table 5. Summary of Elections, July 1, 1937–December 31, 1962.

	Total 1962	Total 1937–1962
Elections held	236	7,748
Consent	194	6,326
Ordered	42	1,422
Eligible voters	1,658	326,269
Votes cast	1,442	288,506
Percent of eligibles voting	87%	88.4
Blank ballots	0	560
Void ballots	14	2,690
Challenged ballots	110	6,991
Elections Participated in:		
A.F.L.*		3,966
C.I.O.*		1,593
A.F.L.–C.I.O.*	131	1,099
Independent union**	121	1,683
Single employer union †	1	151
No union ‡	204	6,847
Neither union §	31	714
Elections won by:		
A.F.L.*		2,509
C.I.O.*		928
A.F.L.–C.I.O.*	69	619
Independent union	68	861
Single employer union	0	100
No union	83	2,351
Neither union	6	96
Total votes cast:#		
A.F.L.*		151,462
C.I.O.*		124,543
A.F.L.–C.I.O.*	878	37,391
Independent union	674	64,524
Single employer union	59	24,055
No union	1,208	170,975
Neither union	241	84,258
Number of votes cast for:		
A.F.L.*		68,364
C.I.O.*		58,813
A.F.L.–C.I.O.*	452	31,039
Independent union	340	27,367
Single employer union	13	13,255
No union	482	71,256
Neither union	39	9,172

Footnotes on p. 160.

Footnotes to Table 5

*Separate figures AFL and CIO shown up to December 1955 when these two labor organizations merged. Thereafter listed under AFL-CIO.

**"Independent union" refers to a labor organization unaffiliated with either the AFL or the CIO, and whose membership includes the employees of more than one employer.

†"Single employer union" refers to an independent organization whose membership is limited to the employees of a single company. Under Section 705 of the Act, company dominated unions cannot be placed on any ballot.

‡"No union" refers to place on ballot for vote against the union in elections involving a single union.

§"Neither union" refers to place on ballot for vote against either union in elections involving two unions.

#Figures refer only to elections in which indicated union appeared on ballot.

Time Consumed in Disposition of Cases*

Representation Cases. For all representation cases closed during 1961, in both the informal or preliminary stage and the formal or hearing stage, the average time from filing of petition to closing was thirty-three days and the median time was twenty-eight days. In the informal stage, (excluding consent election agreement cases), the average time was twenty days and the median was sixteen days. In those cases in which consent election agreements were obtained during the informal stage, the average time from the date of filing of the petition to the date of closing, (by certification or dismissal after the election), was thirty-three days and the median was thirty-two days.

For representation cases closed in the formal stage, following hearings and Board decisions, the average time from the filing to the certification or dismissal, (after the election), was seventy-six days and the median was seventy-one days.

Unfair Labor Practices Cases. For all unfair labor practice cases closed during 1961, in both the informal and formal stages, the average time from filing to closing was sixty-seven days and the median was forty-one days. In the informal stage, the average time from filing to closing was thirty-four days and the median was twenty-eight days.

For those unfair labor practice cases which were processed through the formal stage, the average time from the date of the filing of the charge to Board decision was 204 days, with a median of 200 days. This includes the time for processing through the informal stage as well as the authorization for issuance of complaint and notice of hearing, the formal hearing, the issuance by the trial examiner of his intermediate report, the time for filing of exceptions and briefs, oral argument, and to Board decision.

---

*Letter from A. M. Goldberg, executive secretary, N.Y.S.L.R.B. (February 1, 1963).

Sample Decisions

Exhibit 1. Intermediate Report in an Unfair Labor Practice Case

NEW YORK STATE LABOR RELATIONS BOARD

In the Matter of THE SULLIVAN COUNTY HARNESS RACING ASSOCIATION, INC. -and- HOWARD SHELDON AND GILBERT ROSELMAN	} CASE NO. SU-34754

APPEARANCES:

Richard J. Horrigan, Esq.,
for the Board

Henry G. Friedlander, Esq., and
Leon Greenberg, Esq.,
for the Respondent

INTERMEDIATE REPORT
of the
TRIAL EXAMINER

Statement

Upon the basis of a charge filed July 26, 1961, by Howard Sheldon and Gilbert Roselman, the New York State Labor Relations Board, herein called the Board, on October 20, 1961, issued its complaint alleging that The Sullivan County Harness Racing Association, Inc., herein called the Respondent, had engaged in, and is engaging in, certain unfair labor practices in violation of Section 704, subdivisions 4 and 5, of the New York State Labor Relations Act, herein called the Act.

The complaint, charge and notice of hearing were duly served upon Respondent, and upon Howard Sheldon.

On or about October 30, 1961, Respondent filed an answer, denying, in substance, the material allegations of the complaint.

A hearing was duly held on November 20 and 21, 1961 and January 23 and March 13, 1962, before the undersigned Trial Examiner, duly designated by the Board.

At the hearing, on the motion of the Board's litigation attorney, the allegations of the complaint referring to Gilbert Roselman, who did not appear at the hearing to testify, were withdrawn.

During the hearing, and at the close of the entire case, Respondent moved to dismiss the complaint, alleging failure of proof. Decision thereon was reserved. For the reasons appearing hereinafter, the undersigned will recommend that the said motions be granted.

Upon consideration of the entire record, and from his observation of the witnesses, the undersigned recommends that the Board make the following:

FINDINGS OF FACT

I. The Respondent

The complaint alleges, the answer admits, and the undersigned finds, that Respondent, The Sullivan County Harness Racing Association, Inc, a domestic corporation, operates a race track at Monticello, Sullivan County, State of New York.

II. The Union

Building Service Employees International Union, Local 32E, AFL-CIO, herein called Local 32E, is a labor organization which exists and is constituted for the purpose, in whole or in part, of collective bargaining or of dealing with employers concerning grievances, terms or conditions of employment, or of other mutual aid or protection.

III. The Alleged Unfair Labor Practices

The complaint alleges, in substance, that on or about July 22, 1961 and July 25, 1961, Respondent discharged Howard Sheldon, its employee, and failed and refused to reinstate him for the reason that he joined or assisted the Union and had engaged in concerted activities for the purposes of collective bargaining and other mutual aid and protection and that Respondent thereby engaged in unfair labor practices in violation of Section 704, subdivisions 4 and 5, of the Act.

Sheldon was first employed by Respondent as a pari-mutuel cashier at Respondent's race track during the 1960 season. He was rehired for the same position for the 1961 season which commenced in mid-June, 1961.[1]

On July 14th, Sheldon was suspended by Respondent. He was reinstated on July 21st and discharged on July 22nd.

The evidence concerning Sheldon's suspension, his reinstatement and his subsequent discharge, will be discussed below.

Sheldon's Union Activities

Sheldon testified that on July 3rd he met with William Merkel, an official of Local 32E, and agreed to organize Respondent's pari-mutuel employees on behalf of Local 32E. According to Sheldon, he that night commenced compiling, with the assistance of Roselman and another employee, a mailing list of the pari-mutuel employees from information he procured from them

---

[1] All dates mentioned herein are in 1961, unless otherwise indicated.

at the track. Sheldon testified that he informed the employees with whom he spoke that a new union was organizing the pari-mutuel employees.

On July 12th, at the Lenape Hotel, in Liberty, New York, Sheldon met with Henry Chartier, president of Local 32E, and other officials of Local 32E. Sheldon testified that he conferred with them for about one hour in the hotel lobby and that during this conversation there came into the lobby the son-in-law (later identified as Albert Van Dyke) of Frank Cipriani, president of Independent Harness Mutuel Employees of New York State, the union with which Respondent has a collective bargaining agreement covering Respondent's pari-mutuel employees. Sheldon also testified that a Mr. Wolger, described by Sheldon as head of the money room at the Respondent's track, also came into the hotel lobby during the conference with the officials of Local 32E.

Sheldon testified that he signed a Local 32E designation card on or about July 8th or July 11th.[2]

According to Sheldon, on the same day that he first signed the designation card for Local 32E, he received a batch of designation cards which he proceeded, with the assistance of Roselman, to get signed by various of Respondent's pari-mutuel employees. Sheldon first testified that he and Roselman solicited signatures at the track, mostly in the lavatory, or at the employees' homes, and that he and Roselman had succeeded in getting 75 to 80 such cards signed by Respondent's employees. Later in his testimony, he said that over 100 designation cards had been signed by employees and that he had personally procured 99 percent of them. Sheldon also testified that he devoted about three-and-a-half to four weeks getting these cards signed and that he turned them over to Merkel on August 4th.

During the course of Sheldon's cross-examination by Respondent's counsel, the Board's litigation attorney produced, at the request of Respondent's counsel, the Local 32E designation cards filed with the Board in connection with a representation petition, Case No. SE-34769, filed on August 7th. When the cards were exhibited to Sheldon, he identified them by stating that "most of them" were the cards that he had delivered to Merkel on August 4th.

The cards produced and identified by Sheldon were 47 in number, 27 of which were dated after July 22nd, the date of Sheldon's discharge, 15 were undated, one dated July 1st, and included the 2 cards signed by Sheldon and 2 cards signed by Roselman, one of which was undated.

After the Local 32E cards were produced at the hearing, as noted above, Sheldon gave several different versions of how many cards had been signed prior to his discharge. After testifying that only 5 or 6 cards had been signed prior to July 22nd, he finally admitted, when pressed by Respondent's counsel, that only 4 cards had been signed before his discharge and that these included the 2 undated cards signed by himself and Roselman.

---

[2]The designation card which was offered in evidence by the Board's litigation attorney was undated. During his cross-examination, Sheldon identified another Local 32E designation card signed by him and dated July 26th. Sheldon explained that he signed the latter card because the first card had been "misplaced."

On re-direct examination, Sheldon testified as follows:

"Q. Now, as you know, the cards that we found in the case of the petition filed by 32E, amounted to 47 cards. Were there any other cards over and above this 47 that you and Roselman turned over to 32E?

A. I thought there were 70 or 75 cards. A lot came in the mail, too. I don't see any of the mailed cards here.

Q. So you believed that you turned over the difference between the 47 and the 75?

A. I thought there were more, yes.

Q. And do you know when you turned over those additional cards above the 47 to 32E, was it before or after your discharge?

A. Well, it was before my discharge.

Q. Approximately how long before?

A. Some were handed in before and some were after.

Q. I believe you told Mr. Friedlander that you had about four signed of these 47 before your discharge. Now, how many of the others?

A. Well, the great majority of the cards were signed after my discharge.

Q. Well, the difference between this 47 and the 75 or so that you claim, would be 25 or 30 cards over and above the 47?

A. Yes.

Q. Will you tell us, please, your best recollection as to how many of these 25 or 30 were turned over before July 22nd and how many were turned over after July 22nd?

A. I would say the majority were.

Q. And leaving approximately how many of the 25 or 30 that were turned over before?

A. Five or six."

On further cross-examination, Sheldon could identify by name, only one employee who allegedly had signed a card that would be among the "missing" 25 to 30 cards.

Respondent's Knowledge of
Sheldon's Union Activities

Sheldon testified that on July 21st (nine days after the Lenape Hotel meeting), Cipriani asked him what he had been doing at the Lenape Hotel with officials of Local 32E. Sheldon also testified that on July 22nd, Al Pitts, assistant mutuel manager of Respondent's track, said to him as he handed him a copy of Respondent's letter discharging him, "That's what you get for being a wise-guy with unions." On July 24th, two days after Sheldon's discharge, Sheldon, accompanied by Cipriani, met with Leon Greenberg, Respondent's personnel director and house counsel, and asked for reinstatement. According to Sheldon, Greenberg told him, "I was responsible for getting you the job here. I thought you were a young aggressive fellow and now you try to hurt me with these unions."

Cipriani denied that his son-in-law or anyone else had informed him that Sheldon had been seen in the Lenape Hotel with officials of Local 32E or that he had observed Sheldon soliciting signatures for Local 32E at the track. He testified that it was not until after Sheldon's discharge that he heard that Sheldon had been seeking signatures for Local 32E.

164

Greenberg denied that he had told Sheldon at any time that he had been discharged for union activities or that he knew, until after Sheldon's discharge, that Sheldon had engaged in any union activities. Cipriani, who was present at the conference between Greenberg and Sheldon, corroborated Greenberg's denial that Greenberg had made the statement attributed to him by Sheldon.

Pitts, too, denied the anti-union remark attributed to him by Sheldon and allegedly made at the time Pitts handed him a copy of the letter of discharge on July 22nd.

Sheldon's Suspension, Reinstatement and Discharge

Although Sheldon's suspension on July 14th is not alleged in the complaint to be a violation of the Act, it will be discussed here as it provides a background of prior offenses similar to that for which Respondent contends that Sheldon was discharged.

Sheldon did not work on July 14th and 15th. On July 14th John H. Crawford, Respondent's pari-mutuel manager, notified Greenberg by letter, a copy of which was sent to Cipriani as president of Independent Harness Mutuel Employees of New York State, that Sheldon was being suspended indefinitely for "continuous violation of the rules and regulations of the Pari-Mutuel Department."

The Respondent offered in evidence a memorandum dated July 14th from Franklin E. Devlin, president and general manager of the Respondent, addressed to Crawford, asking him to investigate a complaint that had been made by a patron of the track to the effect that Sheldon had been abusive to a lady guest when she attempted to cash a ticket at Sheldon's window.

Crawford's testimony in this connection, contained a number of serious discrepancies and self-contradictions, such as, stating at one point that Sheldon had been suspended because he had not reported for work on July 14th and that Devlin's complaint had had no bearing on his decision to suspend Sheldon, and testifying later that both reasons figured in the decision to suspend Sheldon. He so testified despite the fact that he had also stated that Devlin's letter may not have been brought to his attention until after July 14th and that he did not know of Devlin's memorandum at the time he suspended Sheldon. Significantly, in a letter to Cipriani, dated July 16th, in reply to a request by Cipriani for information concerning the specific charges against Sheldon, Crawford made no mention of the absence of Sheldon on July 14th, as the reason for the suspension but referred only to Devlin's complaint about Sheldon's conduct toward a woman patron.

It should also be noted that Crawford, in this same letter, stated that Sheldon was suspended after a hearing in his office during which he presented him with Devlin's memorandum. Crawford first testified that he called Sheldon into his office on July 14th and confronted him with Devlin's complaint. When Crawford's attention was called to the fact that he had testified that Sheldon was suspended for failure to report for work on July 14th, and therefore was absent that day, he changed his testimony to state that Sheldon first learned about his suspension on July 17th.

While from the foregoing recital of the conflicts in Crawford's testimony, it clearly appears that he was not a very reliable witness, the fact that a complaint had been made that Sheldon had been abusive to a patron of the track seems fairly clear, and is corroborated, in a large part, by Sheldon's own testimony that he had been suspended after having been informed by Crawford that he had "yelled" at a customer.

Sheldon was reinstated to his job on July 21st and he worked that night. The next day, Saturday, July 22nd, there was a "doubleheader" (racing programs both in the afternoon and evening) at the track. After the final race of the afternoon session, Sheldon was handed a sealed envelope by Al Pitts, the assistant mutuel manager. The envelope contained a copy of a letter from Crawford to Greenberg, dated July 22nd, notifying Greenberg that Sheldon had been discharged for "constant violation of the rules and regulations of the Pari-Mutuel Department." Sheldon was not permitted to work during the evening races.

Concerning the reason for Sheldon's discharge, Greenberg testified that during the afternoon races, Joseph Dunnigan of Baltimore, Maryland, a friend of his and his guest at the track that day, told him that he had been insulted and abused by a cashier when he sought to cash a winning ticket. Greenberg, accompanied by Dunnigan, went to Sheldon's booth, where Dunnigan pointed out Sheldon as the cashier who had insulted him.

According to Greenberg, he immediately instructed Crawford to discharge Sheldon at once. Greenberg testified that Sheldon was discharged for insulting Mr. Dunnigan and for the earlier incident involving the woman customer. Crawford prepared the discharge letter and had Pitts deliver a copy thereof to Sheldon at the track, as noted above.

Sheldon testified that the following Monday, July 24th, he spoke to Greenberg in Greenberg's office. Sheldon was accompanied by Cipriani. According to Sheldon, Greenberg stated that Sheldon was through at the track because he had yelled at a member of the Board of Directors. When Sheldon asked to be confronted with the person who had made the complaint, Greenberg agreed to arrange for such a meeting. On August 12th Sheldon met with Greenberg and Dunnigan in Greenberg's office.

Sheldon testified that during this meeting Dunnigan accused him of speaking "acidly" (as Sheldon put it) to him, during the incident at Sheldon's window on July 22nd, but he was not permitted to question Dunnigan.

Greenberg testified that at the meeting, Dunnigan repeated to Sheldon what he had told Greenberg on July 22nd. According to Greenberg, Dunnigan told Sheldon that he [Sheldon] had said to him "What the hell are you coming in late for?—I have a good notion not to cash that [the ticket] out for you."

Conclusions

When Sheldon's testimony is reduced to its final essence, it appears that the sum of his activities on behalf of Local 32E prior to his discharge, was in getting four (including himself and Roselman) out of 130 employees in the pari-mutuel department to sign cards for Local 32E; in preparing a mailing list; and in being allegedly seen conferring with officials of Local 32E.

Sheldon was the sole witness called by the Board. The only evidence offered by the Board that Respondent may have had knowledge of these activities of Sheldon's in behalf of Local 32E, was Sheldon's testimony concerning alleged anti-union remarks made to him by Greenberg and Pitts, and Cipriani's alleged inquiry nine days after the event, as to what he was doing at the Lenape Hotel with officials of Local 32E.

Sheldon's testimony, as demonstrated above, was highly unreliable and was lacking in basic truthfulness in many respects. Under the circumstances, the factual conflicts between the testimony of Sheldon and that of Respondent's witnesses as to Respondent's knowledge of Sheldon's union activities must be resolved in Respondent's favor, largely because of Sheldon's lack of credibility. The undersigned finds that the more persuasive testimony of Greenberg, Pitts and Cipriani, denying the statements attributed to them by Sheldon should be credited. Accordingly, the undersigned finds that the Board has failed to prove that Respondent, before Sheldon's discharge, had any knowledge of Sheldon's activities on behalf of Local 32E, such as they were, and thus that any anti-union consideration could have motivated Sheldon's discharge.

There was considerable testimony in the record as to Cipriani's supervisory status or lack thereof, a determination of which question would be crucial to a finding as to whether Cipriani's alleged knowledge of Sheldon's activities was chargeable to Respondent. However, since Sheldon's testimony in this respect was proven unreliable, and Cipriani's denial has been credited it is unnecessary to decide whether Cipriani was a supervisor.

One additional comment is appropriate at this point. The record is clear, despite the general unsatisfactory testimony of Crawford given in connection with the reason for suspending Sheldon on July 14th, that two serious complaints against Sheldon had, in fact, been made. Apart from Sheldon's testimony that he could not remember either incident involved in the complaints, the record is devoid of any credible evidence that the complaints did not arise as testified to by Respondent's witnesses.

In view of the lack of substantial union activities on the part of Sheldon, prior to his discharge, or knowledge thereof by Respondent, and indispensable element in establishing an illegal discharge, the undersigned must find that the Board has failed to meet the burden of proving that Respondent had discriminated against Sheldon, in violation of Section 704, subdivisions 4 and 5, of the Act, as alleged in the complaint.

It will be recommended that the complaint herein be dismissed.

CONCLUSIONS OF LAW

Upon the basis of the foregoing recommended Findings of Fact and upon the entire record in this proceeding, the undersigned recommends that the Board find and conclude as a matter of law:

1. The Sullivan County Harness Racing Association, Inc. is an employer within the meaning of Section 701, subdivision 2, of the Act.

2. Building Service Employees International Union, Local 32E, AFL-CIO, is a labor organization within the meaning of Section 701, subdivision 5, of the Act.

3. By discharging Howard Sheldon, Respondent did not require its employees as a condition of employment to refrain from joining, forming or assisting a labor organization of their own choosing and did not thereby engage in unfair practices within the meaning of Section 704, subdivision 4, of the Act.

4. By discharging Howard Sheldon, Respondent did not discourage membership in a labor organization of its employees' own choosing, by discriminating in regard to hire and tenure and other terms and conditions of employment and has not thereby engaged in unfair labor practices within the meaning of Section 704, subdivision 5, of the Act.

RECOMMENDATION

Upon the basis of the foregoing recommended Findings of Fact and Conclusions of Law and upon the entire record in this proceeding, the undersigned recommends that the complaint herein be dismissed.

Dated: New York, N. Y.
    August 23, 1962

OSCAR FORSTER
TRIAL EXAMINER

Exhibit 2. Board Decision in an Unfair Labor Practice Case

NEW YORK STATE LABOR RELATIONS BOARD

In the Matter of THE SULLIVAN COUNTY HARNESS RACING ASSOCIATION, INC. -and- HOWARD SHELDON[1]	25 SLRB NO. 110 CASE NO. SU-34754 Oct. 19, 1962

APPEARANCES:

Richard J. Horrigan, Esq.,
for the Board

Leon Greenberg, Esq.,
by Henry G. Friedlander, Esq.,
for the Respondent

DECISION
and
ORDER

On August 23, 1962, Oscar Forster, Esquire, Trial Examiner, issued his Intermediate Report herein, a copy of which is annexed hereto and made a part hereof. He found that Respondent had not engaged in the unfair labor practices alleged in the complaint.

Copies of the Intermediate Report were duly served on all parties. The Board's litigation attorney filed exceptions thereto on September 4, 1962.

The Board, having considered the entire record in the proceeding, the Intermediate Report and the exceptions thereto, accepts the recommendations of the Trial Examiner and adopts his discussion of the evidence in the Intermediate Report as the opinion of the Board herein.

Upon its consideration of the entire record, the Board makes the following:

FINDINGS OF FACT

1. Respondent, The Sullivan County Harness Racing Association, Inc., is engaged in the operation of a race track at Monticello, Sullivan County, State of New York.

2. Building Service Employees International Union, Local 32E, AFL-CIO, herein called the Union, is a labor organization which exists and is constituted for the purpose, in whole or in part, of collective bargaining or of dealing with employers concerning grievances, terms or conditions of employment or of other mutual aid or protection.

3. On or about July 22, 1962, Respondent discharged Howard Sheldon, theretofore employed by it as a pari-mutuel clerk.

---

[1]The allegations of the complaint alleging the unlawful discharge of Gilbert Roselman having been withdrawn, the title is amended accordingly.

4. Respondent did not discharge Howard Sheldon because of his membership in, or activities on behalf of, the Union.

CONCLUSIONS OF LAW

Upon the basis of the foregoing Findings of Fact and upon the entire record in this proceeding, the Board finds and concludes as a matter of law:

1. Respondent, The Sullivan County Harness Racing Association, Inc., is an employer within the meaning of Section 701, subdivision 2, of the Act.

2. Building Service Employees International Union, Local 32E, AFL-CIO, is a labor organization within the meaning of Section 701, subdivision 5, of the Act.

3. By discharging Howard Sheldon, Respondent has not engaged in unfair labor practices within the meaning of Section 704, subdivisions 4 and 5, of the Act.

ORDER

Upon the basis of the foregoing Findings of Fact and Conclusions of Law and pursuant to Section 706, subdivision 3, of the New York State Labor Relations Act, it is hereby

ORDERED, that the complaint herein be, and the same hereby is, dismissed.

Dated: New York, N. Y.
October 19, 1962

JAY KRAMER, Chairman

JAMES AMADEI, Member

MARTIN GREENE, Member

Exhibit 3. Board Decision in a Representation Case

NEW YORK STATE LABOR RELATIONS BOARD

In the Matter of THE SQUARE SANITARIUM, INC., owner and operator of WESTCHESTER SQUARE HOSPITAL -and- THE NEW YORK STATE NURSES ASSOCIATION, Petitioner -and- LOCAL 144, HOTEL & ALLIED SERVICE EMPLOYEES' UNION, Intervenor	25 SLRB NO. 117 CASE NO. SE-35178 Nov. 8, 1962

APPEARANCES:

Sugarman, Kuttner & Fuss, Esqs.,
by Howard L. Kuttner, Esq., and
E. L. Sugarman, Esq., and
Sanford H. Markham, Esq.,
for the Employer

Robert H. Jones, III Esq.,
for the Petitioner

Vladeck and Elias, Esqs.,
by Judith Vladeck, Esq., and
Carl Rachlin, Esq.,
for the Intervenor

DECISION
and
DIRECTION OF ELECTION

The New York State Nurses Association, herein called the Petitioner, filed its petition herein, pursuant to Section 705 of the New York State Labor Relations Act, on December 21, 1961.

A hearing was duly held before Robert J. Lawler, Esquire, Trial Examiner, on March 5, 6 and 19, and May 3 and 4, 1962. At the hearing, the Trial Examiner granted the motion of Local 144, Hotel & Allied Service Employees' Union, herein called the Intervenor, for leave to intervene. His ruling is hereby affirmed.

Upon its consideration of the entire record, the Board renders the following decision:

I. The Employer

The Square Sanitarium, Inc., a domestic corporation, owns, operates, manages and controls the Westchester Square Hospital, a proprietary hospital located at 2475 St. Raymond Avenue, Borough of The Bronx, City and State of New York.

II. The Jurisdiction of the Board

The Employer contends that the Board does not have jurisdiction of its labor relations because of the interstate nature of its operations.

The National Labor Relations Board has declined to assert jurisdiction over proprietary hospitals.[1] In *Leedom* v. *Fitch Sanitarium, Inc.*, 294 F 2d 251, 253, the United States Circuit Court of Appeals, District of Columbia Circuit, upheld the National Board's declination, stating: "that although the activities of proprietary hospitals are 'not wholly unrelated to commerce,' their operations 'are essentially local in nature and therefore the effect on commerce of labor disputes involving such hospitals is not substantial enough to warrant the exercise of the Board's jurisdiction.'"

Since the National Board has declined to assert jurisdiction over proprietary hospitals, this Board is expressly authorized to assert such jurisdiction by Section 14(c) of the National Labor Relations Act, as amended.[2]

Accordingly, we find that we have jurisdiction of the instant proceeding.

III. Undisputed Matters

It is undisputed, and we find and conclude, that, in fact and within the meaning of the Act: a question or controversy concerning representation exists.

IV. The Petitioner

The Employer contends that the Petitioner is not a labor organization within the meaning of the Act because, the Employer argues, the Petitioner's certificate of incorporation and by-laws do not give it the authority to engage in collective bargaining or to enter into collective bargaining agreements.

Section 701(5), of the Act defines a "labor organization," as follows:

"The term 'labor organization' means any organization which exists and is constituted for the purpose, in whole or in part, of collective bargaining, or of dealing with employers concerning grievances, terms or conditions of employment, or of other mutual aid or protection. . ."

In *Metropolitan Life Insurance Company*, 10 SLRB 638, 684, the Board observed:

"The Act requires no particular form of organization. The principal inquiry, rather, is whether the purported labor organization exists and is constituted for the purpose, in whole or in part, of collective bargaining."[3]

The Petitioner is a corporation organized under the Membership Corporation Law of the State of New York. It was formed in 1902, and its certificate

---

[1]*Flatbush General Hospital*, 126 N.L.R.B. 144.

[2]*Blackburn*, 24 S.L.R.B. 190, 191–5; *Walsh*, 24 S.L.R.B. 434, 435; *Dunetz, et al.*, 25 S.L.R.B. 177; *Klar (Program Publishing Co.)*, 25 S.L.R.B. No. 76.

[3]See also *The Brunswick Home, Inc.*, 18 S.L.R.B. 458, 463–465; *Radio City Music Hall Corporation*, 20 S.L.R.B. 20, 22–23.

of incorporation, as amended in 1949, states that among its purposes are "to promote and protect the health and welfare of nurses;...and to do all things necessary, proper, incidental, suitable, useful and conducive to the complete accomplishment of the foregoing purposes in their broadest sense." The Petitioner's by-laws includes among its objectives "to promote and protect the economic and general welfare of nurses" and "to represent nurses and serve as their state spokesmen with allied, professional and governmental groups and with the public."

We find that the Petitioner's purposes, although set forth in general terms, are broad enough to encompass those which would include the normal subjects of collective bargaining, even though the latter phrase, as such, is not used. Substance, not legalistic formalities, is the primary consideration. That the Petitioner may also have other purposes does not, of itself, preclude a finding that it is a "labor organization" within the meaning of Section 701(5), of the Act,[4] so long as those other purposes are not inconsistent with or antithetical to those set forth in the Act.[5]

The Petitioner, in practice, has functioned as a labor organization by negotiating with various voluntary hospitals and agreeing to changes in working conditions, although these agreements have not been reduced to executed written bilateral agreements.[6] It has over 3,000 designation cards signed by registered nurses authorizing it to be "my exclusive representative for the purposes of bargaining collectively with my employer about my wages, hours, employment conditions and every other matter involving or affecting my employment." The Petitioner's House of Delegates unanimously adopted an "Economic Security Program" which states, as an objective, the improvement of the economic security of registered nurses by organization and education, declares that employers are obligated to deal justly with registered nurses through their authorized representatives, and disavows the right to strike. Contrary to the Employer's assertion, this disavowal of the right to strike does not affect the Petitioner's status as a labor organization.[7] Although Section 713 of the Act protects the right of employees to strike, the definition of "labor organization" in Section 701(5) does not require such an organization to exercise this right.[8] In view of the type of work here involved, such a disavowal is entirely understandable. Indeed, Section 700 makes it clear that one of the very purposes of the Act is to remove the causes of industrial strife by providing resort to the Board as an available alternative. If we were to deny Petitioner access to the machinery of the Board, we would remove this peaceful alternative.

---

[4]*Railway Mail Association* v. *Corsi*, 293 N.Y. 315, 320–321.

[5]Contrast *Metropolitan Jockey Club*, 6 S.L.R.B. 366, 381; *Phillips (Fanshaw Bar and Restaurant)*, 10 S.L.R.B. 790, 794; *Schaller (Lucullus Cake Shop)*, 14 S.L.R.B. 361, 363–365; *Charlie Banks Wines & Liquors, Inc.*, 19 S.L.R.B. 352, 357–358; *LeBoff's, Inc.*, 20 S.L.R.B. 262, 265–266; *Helsid Realty Corp., et al.*, 22 S.L.R.B. 326, 333.

[6]See *Humble Oil and Refining Co.*, 1962 CCH, N.L.R.B., parag. 11, 180 (Case No. 22-RC-1444, February 13, 1962).

[7]Most collective agreements contain a voluntary no-strike clause, and it has been held that an agreement not to strike is implicit in a contractual arbitration clause. (*I.B.T.* v. *Lucas Flour Co.*, 369 U.S. 95).

[8]*Humble Oil and Refining Co.*, *supra*.

The Petitioner's amended certificate of incorporation was approved by the New York State Board of Standards and Appeals pursuant to Section 9-a of the New York General Corporation Law and Section 11-1a of the New York Membership Corporation Law which require approval by that Board of any certificate of incorporation which "specifies among the purposes, the organization of working men and women and wage earners for their mutual betterment, protection and advancement or for the regulation of hours of labor, working conditions and wages..." In a contested matter, the New York City Department of Labor also found that the Petitioner is a "labor organization" and certified it as exclusive bargaining representative.[9] It is also denominated a "labor organization" in the New York State Department of Labor's "Directory of Labor Organizations in New York State."[10]

The Petitioner has complied with the requirements imposed upon labor organizations by the Labor and Management Improper Practices Act, (New York State Labor Law, Article 20-A) and the federal "Labor-Management Reporting and Disclosure Act of 1959."

On the evidence, we find and conclude that The New York State Nurses Association exists and is constituted for the purpose, in whole or in part, of collective bargaining, or of dealing with employers concerning grievances, terms or conditions of employment, or of other mutual aid or protection, and is a labor organization in fact and within the meaning of Section 701(5) of the Act.

V. The Appropriate Unit

The Petitioner contends that the appropriate unit consists of all the registered professional nurses. The Employer contends that the appropriate unit consists of all the registered professional nurses, the licensed practical nurses and the nurses' aides. Both would exclude supervisors. The Intervenor contends that the nurses' aides are covered by a contract between it and the Employer, and should not be included in a unit with either of the other groups.

As we have often pointed out:

"The Board's primary consideration in determining the bargaining unit is to group employees who have a mutual interest in wages, hours, working conditions, and other subjects of collective bargaining. Although the Board decides each case on its own facts, it has found that the following are criteria of mutual interest: similarity of duties or functions, of wages or method of computing compensation, of working conditions, of qualifications or skills; interdependence or interchangeability of function; interchange or transfer of employees from one category of employment to another; the desires of the employees; the form of self-organization; and the collective bargaining experience in the establishment, and in the industry. The Board also considers the organization of the employer's business, and its own prior decisions affecting the same establishment or the same industry."[11]

---

[9]*New York State Nurses Association*, 2 N.Y.C.D.L. Nos. 24 and 25.

[10]See *Railway Mail Association* v. *Corsi*, 293 N.Y. 315, 320.

[11]Board's Twenty-Fourth *Annual Analysis of Decisions* (1960), p. 13.

At the time of the hearing herein, the Employer's registered professional nursing staff consisted of 18 full-time head nurses, 18 part-time head nurses, 7 full-time assistant head nurses, 5 full-time staff nurses and 18 part-time staff nurses.[12] The licensed practical nursing staff consisted of 9 full-time head nurses and 5 part-time head nurses, 30 full-time staff nurses and 15 part-time staff nurses. In addition the Employer employed 50 nurses' aides.

The salary brackets of the three groups are different. The full-time registered professional nurses receive $355 to $370 per month and the part-time registered professional nurses receive $18 a day, except for one who receives $15 per day. The full-time licensed practical nurses receive $200 to $290 per month and the part-time licensed practical nurses receive $14 to $16 per day, except for one who receives $13 per day and another who receives $18 per day. The nurses' aides receive $173 to $210 per month.

The qualifications, education, training, and licenses of the three groups also differ. Section 6901 (2)(a) of the Education Law, provides:

"A person practices nursing as a registered professional nurse within the meaning of this article who for compensation or personal profit performs any professional service requiring the application of principles of nursing based on biological, physical and social sciences, such as responsible supervision of a patient requiring skill in observation of symptoms and reactions and the accurate recording of the facts, and carrying out of treatments and medications as prescribed by a licensed physician or by a licensed dentist and the application of such nursing procedures as involves understanding of cause and effect in order to safeguard life and health of a patient and others."

Section 7901 (2)(b) of the Education Law provides:

"A person practices nursing as a licensed practical nurse within the meaning of this article who for compensation or personal profit performs such duties as are required in the physical care of a patient and in carrying out of medical orders as prescribed by a licensed physician or by a licensed dentist requiring an understanding of nursing but not requiring the professional service as outlined in paragraph a."

The Education Law and the Commissioner of Education have different requirements for a license as a registered professional nurse and as a licensed practical nurse. The registered professional nurse must be a high school graduate, have obtained a diploma from a registered school of nursing having a minimum course of two years or completed a one, two or three year course in a registered collegiate institution, and pass a two day written examination in medical, surgical, obstetric, pediatric and psychiatric nursing.[13] The licensed practical nurse is only required to have completed the eighth grade, completed a nine month course of study, and successfully pass a one day written examination in subjects determined by the Board of Examiners of Nurses.[14] The State has established no standards or minimum requirements for nurses' aides.

[12]Supervision is by the director of nursing services and four assistant directors, all of whom are required to be registered professional nurses.

[13]Education Law, Section 6905; Regulations, Commissioner of Education, Sections 5, 14, 61.

[14]Education Law, Section 6906; Regulations, Commissioner of Education, Section 61.

The Employer contends that the work of the registered professional nurses and of the licensed practical nurses in the Westchester Square Hospital is interchangeable. The record shows that in some respects they do perform the same duties.[15] However, the Employer's director of nursing testified: that the licensed practical nurses are subject to closer supervision than the registered professional nurses; that licensed practical nurses acting as head nurses always have registered professional nurses to consult; and the more serious the patient's condition the more important it is to have a registered professional nurse rather than a licensed practical nurse assigned to the patient. Moreover, there are certain duties which only a registered professional nurse may perform. The nurses' aides do general bedside care (such as feeding, bathing, giving enemas, taking temperature and pulse), assist the head or staff nurse, act as a messenger, assist patients in and out of bed, and take patients to x-ray and operating rooms. They do not give medication or treatment.

Organizational activity among the three groups is different.[16] Only registered professional nurses may become members of Petitioner. Licensed practical nurses have an organization of their own, Licensed Practical Nurses of New York, Inc., which does not admit registered professional nurses to membership. Nurses aides are represented by the Intervenor which has a contract with the Employer covering them.[17]

In view of the differences in education, training, qualifications, licenses, skills, duties, and wages, and the separate organization of the three groups, we find that the registered professional nurses do not have sufficient common interests with the licensed practical nurses and the nurses' aides to warrant placing them all in the same unit. As separately licensed[18] professional[19] employees, the registered professional nurses properly constitute a separate bargaining unit.

Upon consideration of the entire record, we find and conclude that, in order to insure to the employees concerned the full benefit of their right to self-organization, to collective bargaining and otherwise to effectuate the policies of the Act, all head registered professional nurses, assistant head registered professional nurses, and staff registered professional nurses (excluding supervisory employees) employed by The Square Sanitarium, Inc., at Westchester Square Hospital, 2475 St. Raymond Avenue, Borough of The Bronx, City and State of New York, constitute a unit appropriate for the purposes of collective bargaining, in fact and within the meaning of Section 705(2), of the Act.

---

[15] Although material, duties are not the sole factor in determining the appropriate unit. (*Erie County Water Authority*, 23 S.L.R.B. 151, 159).

[16] See Board's Report (1937–1939), pp. 142–144; Fourth *Annual Report* (1940), pp. 105–106; Sixth *Annual Report* (1942), p. 56; *Akap Inc. (Aly's Hat Box)*, 24 S.L.R.B. 3, 10.

[17] This contract covers porter, maids, kitchen and cafeteria workers, orderlies, elevator operators, and others, as well as nurses' aides.

[18] *Galbreath, et al.*, 24 S.L.R.B. 470, 472, and cases there cited.

[19] *Mason (Royal Hospital)*, 2 S.L.R.B. 273, 274–275; *Revere Copper and Brass, Incorporated, etc.*, 8 S.L.R.B. 351, 354–5; *Park West Foundation, Inc.*, 14 S.L.R.B. 536, 539; *L. H. Martin Value Center, Inc.*, 25 S.L.R.B. No. 86.

VI. The Election

We shall conduct an election by secret ballot among the employees in the appropriate unit to determine their desires concerning representation for the purposes of collective bargaining.

It was stipulated that the employees eligible to vote in any election shall include regular part-time employees, in addition to full-time employees. We accept this stipulation in substance, and shall direct that part-time employees who were employed at least one day a week in each of any 10 of the 13 calendar weeks immediately preceding the date of the Direction of Election shall be eligible to vote.[20]

Since the Intervenor does not claim, and has not established, any interest among the employees in the appropriate unit, we shall not place its name on the ballot.

DIRECTION OF ELECTION

By virtue of and pursuant to the power vested in the New York State Labor Relations Board by the New York State Labor Relations Act, it is hereby

DIRECTED, that, as part of the investigation authorized by the Board, an election by secret ballot shall be conducted within twenty (20) days from the date hereof, under the supervision of the Board or its agents, at a time, place, and during hours to be fixed by the Board, among all full-time employees in the unit found appropriate in "Section V", above, employed during the payroll period immediately preceding the date of this Direction of Election and all part-time employees in the unit found appropriate in "Section V", above, employed at least one day a week in each of any 10 of the 13 calendar weeks immediately preceding the date of this Direction of Election (other than those who have voluntarily quit or who had been discharged for cause before the date of the election), to determine whether or not they desire to be represented for the purposes of collective bargaining in respect to rates of pay, wages, hours of employment and other conditions of employment by The New York State Nurses Association.

Dated: New York, N. Y.
    November 8, 1962

JAY KRAMER, Chairman

JAMES AMADEI, Member

MARTIN GREENE, Member

---

[20]See *Hillson Limousine Service, Inc.,* 24 S.L.R.B. 458, 464.

Text of Article 20—
New York State Labor Relations Act

SECTION 700—Findings and Policy

The economic necessity for employees to possess full freedom of association, actual liberty of contract and bargaining power equal to that of their employers, who are frequently organized in corporate or other forms of association, has long been sanctioned by public opinion, and recognized and affirmed by legislatures and the highest courts. As the modern industrial system has progressed, there has developed between and among employees and employers an ever greater economic interdependence and community of interest which have become matters of vital public concern. Employers and employees have recognized that the peaceable practice and wholesome development of that relationship and interest are materially aided by the general adoption and advancement of the procedure and practice of bargaining collectively as between equals. It is in the public interest that equality of bargaining power be established and maintained. It is likewise recognized that the denial by some employers of the right of employees freely to organize and the resultant refusal to accept the procedure of collective bargaining, substantially and adversely affect the interest of employees, other employers, and the public in general. Such denial creates variations and instability in competitive wage rates and working conditions within and between industries and between employees and employers engaged in such industries, and by depressing the purchasing power of wage earners and the profits of business, and tends (a) to produce and aggravate recurrent business depressions, (b) to increase the disparity between production and consumption, (c) to create unemployment with its attendant dangers to the health, peace and morals of the people, and (d) to increase public and private expenditures for relief of the needy and the unemployed.

When some employers deny the right of employees to full freedom of association and organization, and refuse to recognize the practice and procedure of collective bargaining, their actions lead to strikes, lockouts and other forms of industrial strife and unrest which are inimical to the public safety and welfare, and frequently endanger the public health.

Experience has proved that protection by law of the right of employees to organize and bargaining collectively, remove certain recognized sources of industrial strife and unrest, encourages practices fundamental to the friendly adjustment of industrial disputes arising out of differences as to wages, hours or other working conditions, and tends to restore equality of bargaining power between and among employers and employees, thereby advancing the interests of employers as well as employees.

In the interpretation and application of this article, and otherwise, it is hereby declared to be the public policy of the state to encourage the practice and procedure of collective bargaining, and to protect employees in the exercise of full freedom of association, self-organization and designation of representatives of their own choosing for the purposes of collective bargaining, or other mutual aid and protection, free from the interference, restraint or coercion of their employers.

All the provisions of this article shall be liberally construed for the accomplishment of this purpose.

This article shall be deemed an exercise of the police power of the state for the protection of the public welfare, prosperity, health and peace of the people of the state.[1]

SECTION 701—Definitions. When used in this article:

1. The term "person" includes one or more individuals, partnerships, associations, corporations, legal representatives, trustees, trustees in bankruptcy, or receivers.

2. The term "employer" includes any person acting on behalf of or in the interest of an employer, directly or indirectly, with or without his knowledge, but a labor organization or any officer or agent thereof shall only be considered an employer with respect to individuals employed by such organization.

3. The term "employees" includes but is not restricted to any individual employed by a labor organization; any individual whose employment has ceased as a consequence of, or in connection with, any current labor dispute or because of any unfair labor practice, and who has not obtained any other regular and substantially equivalent employment; and shall not be limited to the employees of a particular employer, unless the article explicitly states otherwise, but shall not include any individual employed by his parent or spouse or in the domestic service of any person in his home, or any

---

[1]As amended by Chapter 689 of the Laws of 1940. Section 700 was amended so as to emphasize the community of interest rather than the area of conflict between employers and employees.

individuals employed only for the duration of the labor dispute, or any individuals employed as farm laborers.

4. The term "representatives" includes a labor organization or an individual whether or not employed by the employer of those whom he represents.

5. The term "labor organization" means any organization which exists and is constituted for the purpose, in whole or in part, of collective bargaining, or of dealing with employers concerning grievances, terms or conditions of employment, or of other mutual aid or protection and which is not a company union as defined herein.

6. The term "company union" means any committee, employee representation plan or association of employees which exists for the purpose, in whole or in part, of dealing with employers concerning grievances or terms and conditions of employment, which the employer has initiated or created or whose initiation or creation he has suggested, participated in or in the formulation of whose governing rules or policies or the conducting of whose management, operations or elections the employer participates in or supervises or which the employer maintains, finances, controls, dominates, or assists in maintaining or financing, whether by compensating anyone for service performed in its behalf or by donating free services, equipment, materials, office or meeting space or anything else of value, or by any other means.

7. The term "unfair labor practice" means only those unfair labor practices listed in section seven hundred four.

8. The term "labor dispute" includes, but is not restricted to, any controversy between employers and employees or their representatives as defined in this section concerning terms, tenure or conditions of employment or concerning the association or representation of persons in negotiating, fixing, maintaining, changing, or seeking to negotiate, fix, maintain or change terms or conditions of employment, or concerning the violation of any of the rights granted or affirmed by this article, regardless of whether the disputants stand in the proximate relation of employer and employee.

9. The term "board" means the labor relations board created by section seven hundred two.

10. The term "policies of this article" means the policies set forth in section seven hundred.

11. The term "non-profitmaking hospital or residential care center" means an organized residential facility for the medical diagnosis, treatment and care of illness, disease, injury, infirmity or deformity which is located in a city having a population of one million or more and which is maintained and operated by an association or corporation, no part of the net earnings of which inures to the benefit of any private shareholder or individual.

12. The term "employee of a non-profitmaking hospital or residential care center" means any person employed or permitted to work by or at a non-profitmaking hospital or residential care center but shall not include any person employed or permitted to work: (a) as a member of a religious order; (b) in or for such a non-profitmaking hospital or residential care center,

which work is incidental to or in return for charitable aid conferred upon such individual and not under any express contract of hire; or (c) as a volunteer.[2]

SECTION 702—Labor Relations Board. 1. There is hereby created in the department of labor a board to be known as the New York State labor relations board which shall be composed of three members who shall be appointed by the governor, by and with the advice and consent of the senate. Each member of the board at the time of his appointment shall be a citizen of the United States and a resident of the State of New York, and shall have been a qualified elector in the state for a period of at least one year next preceding his appointment. No member of the board during his period of service as such shall hold any other public office. One of the original members shall be appointed for a term of two years, one for a term of four years and one for a term of six years, but their successors shall be appointed for terms of six years each, except that any individual chosen to fill a vacancy shall be appointed for the unexpired term of the member whom he is to succeed. The governor shall designate one member to serve as chairman of the board. Any member of the board may be removed by the governor for inefficiency, neglect of duty, misconduct or malfeasance in office, and for no other cause, after being given a copy of the charges and an opportunity to be publicly heard in person or by counsel.

2. A vacancy in the board shall not impair the right of the remaining members to exercise all the powers of the board, and two members of the board shall, at all times, constitute a quorum. The board may adopt an official seal and prescribe the purposes for which it shall be used.

3. The board shall at the end of every year make a report in writing to the governor, stating in detail the work it has done in hearing and deciding cases and otherwise, and it shall sign and report in full an opinion in every case decided by it.

4. Each member of the board shall devote his entire time to the duties of his office and shall not engage in any other business, vocation or employment. The board shall appoint an executive secretary and such attorneys, trial examiners and directors for local areas and such other employees, and fix such salaries or other compensation therefor, as it may from time to time find necessary for the proper performance of its duties. The reasonable and necessary traveling and other expenses of the members of the board and other officers and employees of the board, while actually engaged in the performance of their duties shall be paid from the state treasury upon the audit and warrant of the comptroller, upon vouchers approved by the chairman. Attorneys appointed under this section may, at the direction of the board, appear for and represent the board in any case at court. The board may establish or utilize such regional, local, or other agencies and utilize such voluntary and uncompensated services as may from time to time be needed.[3]

[2]Subsections 11 and 12 were added in 1963.

[3]This section was last amended by Chapter 311 of the Laws of 1954. All amendments to this section since 1937 have been for the purpose of changing the salaries of the Board members, and to provide for traveling expenses.

5. All employees of the board shall be appointed by the board in accordance with the provisions of the civil service law and rules.[4]

6. The principal office of the board shall be in the city of Albany, but it may meet and exercise any or all of its powers at any other place within the state. The board may, by one or more of its members or by such agents or agencies as it may designate, conduct in any part of this state any proceeding, hearing, investigation, inquiry, or election necessary to the performance of its functions. A member who participates in any such proceeding shall not be disqualified from subsequently participating in a decision of the board in the same case.

7. The board shall have authority from time to time to make, amend and rescind such rules and regulations as may be necessary to carry out the provisions of this article including the determination of the life of the selected representatives. Such rules and regulations shall be effective upon publication in the manner which the board shall prescribe.

8. Neither the board nor any of its agents or employees shall engage in any effort to mediate, conciliate or arbitrate any labor dispute, but nothing contained in this subdivision shall be construed to prevent the board, its agents or employees, from engaging in any effort to obtain voluntary adjustments and compliance with the terms and provisions of this article and in accordance with its purposes and policy.[5]

9. Notwithstanding the provisions of any other law, neither the industrial commissioner nor any board or other agency of the department of labor shall in any way direct, review, modify or reverse any decision or finding of the board nor shall the industrial commissioner or any board or other agency of the department of labor supervise or control the board in the exercise of any powers or in the performance of any duties under this article.

SECTION 703—Rights of Employees. Employees shall have the right of self-organization, to form, join, or assist labor organizations, to bargain collectively through representatives of their own choosing, and to engage in concerted activities, for the purpose of collective bargaining or other mutual aid or protection, free from interference, restraint, or coercion of employers, but nothing contained in this article shall be interpreted to prohibit employees from exercising the right to confer with their employer at any time, provided that during such conference there is no attempt by the employer,

---

[4]As amended by Chapter 4 of the Laws of 1940. Prior to 1940 the Board did not have a specific group of trial examiners. If the board members could not handle a case, the case was assigned to outside attorneys or to members of the Board's staff of attorneys. This practice was challenged under Section 702(5) of the Labor Law on the grounds that these attorneys had to be appointed from the eligible lists of the Civil Service Commission. This contention was upheld by the Court of Appeals in the case of *Metropolitan Life Insurance Company v. Boland*, 281 N.Y. (1939). As a result of this decision Section 702(5) was amended to the above.

[5]As amended by Chapter 126 of the Laws of 1940. The purpose of this amendment was to obtain legislative approval of the Board's policy of attempting to consummate voluntary adjustments and compliance without formal hearings.

directly or indirectly, to interfere with, restrain or coerce employees in the exercise of the rights guaranteed by this section.[6]

SECTION 704—Unfair Labor Practices. It shall be an unfair labor practice for an employer:

1. To spy upon or keep under surveillance, whether directly or through agents or any other person, any activities of employees or their representatives in the exercise of the rights guaranteed by section seven hundred three.

2. To prepare, maintain, distribute or circulate any blacklist of individuals for the purpose of preventing any of such individuals from obtaining or retaining employment because of the exercise by such individuals of any of the rights guaranteed by section seven hundred three.

3. To dominate or interfere with the formation, existence, or administration of any employee organization or association, agency or plan which exists in whole or in part for the purpose of dealing with employers concerning terms or conditions of employment, labor disputes or grievances, or to contribute financial or other support to any such organization, by any means, including but not limited to the following: (a) by participating or assisting in, supervising controlling or dominating (1) the initiation or creation of any such employee organization or association, agency, or plan, or (2) the meetings, management, operation, elections, formulation or amendment of constitution, rules or policies, of any such employee organization or association, agency or plan; (b) by urging the employees to join any such employee organization or association, agency or plan for the purpose of encouraging membership in the same; (c) by compensating any employee or individual for services performed in behalf of any such employee organization or association, agency or plan, or by donating free services, equipment, materials, office or meeting space or anything else of value for the use of any such employee organization or association, agency or plan; provided, that an employer shall not be prohibited from permitting employees to confer with him during working hours without loss of time or pay.

4. To require an employee or one seeking employment, as a condition of employment, to join any company union or to refrain from forming, or joining or assisting a labor organization of his own choosing.

5. To encourage membership in any company union or discourage membership in any labor organization, by discrimination in regard to hire or tenure or in any term or condition of employment: Provided that nothing in this article shall preclude an employer from making an agreement with a labor organization requiring as a condition of employment membership therein, if such labor organization is the representative of employees as provided in section seven hundred five.

6. To refuse to bargain collectively with the representatives of employees, subject to the provisions of section seven hundred five.

7. To refuse to discuss grievances with representatives of employees, subject to the provisions of section seven hundred five.

---

[6]As amended in Chapter 773 of the Laws of 1940. This section was amended so as to remove any doubt concerning the right of employees to confer with their employer at any time, provided that no attempt be made by the employer to interfere with the rights of the employees as guaranteed under the act.

8. To discharge or otherwise discriminate against an employee because he has signed or filed any affidavit, petition or complaint or given any information or testimony under this article.

9. To distribute or circulate any blacklist of individuals exercising any right created or confirmed by this article or of members of a labor organization, or to inform any person of the exercise by any individual of such right, or of the membership of any individual in a labor organization for the purpose of preventing individuals so blacklisted or so named from obtaining or retaining employment.

10. To do any acts, other than those already enumerated in this section, which interfere with, restrain or coerce employees in the exercise of the rights guaranteed by section seven hundred three.

SECTION 705—Representatives and Elections. 1. Representatives designated or selected for the purposes of collective bargaining by the majority of the employees in a unit appropriate for such purposes or by the majority of the employees voting in an election conducted pursuant to this section shall be the exclusive representatives of all the employees in the appropriate unit for the purposes of collective bargaining in respect to rates of pay, wages, hours of employment, or other conditions of employment: Provided, that employees, directly or through representatives, shall have the right at any time to present grievances to their employer.

2. The board shall decide in each case whether, in order to insure to employees the full benefit of their right to self-organization, to collective bargaining and otherwise to effectuate the policies of this article, the unit appropriate for the purposes of collective bargaining shall be the employer unit, multiple employer unit, craft unit, plant unit, or any other unit; provided, however, that in any case where the majority of employees of a particular craft, or in the case of a non-profitmaking hospital or residential care center where the majority of employees of a particular profession or craft, shall so decide the board shall designate such profession or craft as a unit appropriate for the purpose of collective bargaining.[7]

3. Whenever it is alleged by an employee or his representative, or by an employer or his representative, that there is a question or controversy concerning the representation of employees, the board shall investigate such question or controversy and certify in writing to all persons concerned the name or names of the representatives who have been designated or selected. In any such investigation the board shall provide for an appropriate hearing upon due notice, either in conjunction with a proceeding under section seven hundred six or otherwise, and may conduct an election by secret ballot of employees, or use any other suitable method to ascertain such representatives (either before or after the aforesaid hearing), provided, however, that the board shall not have authority to investigate or determine any question or controversy between individuals or groups within the same

[7]As amended by Chapter 518 of the Laws of 1942. The amendment simply added "multiple employer unit" to the types of units which the board would consider appropriate for the purposes of collective bargaining. Further amended in 1963 to deal with non-profit hospitals.

labor organization nor between labor organizations affiliated with the same parent labor organization concerning the internal affairs of any labor organization but nothing contained in this proviso shall be deemed to preclude the board from investigating and determining which, if any, of affiliated groups or labor organizations have been designated or selected by employees as their representatives for the purposes of collective bargaining within the meaning of this article.[8]

4. The board shall have power to determine who may participate in the election and to establish the rules governing any such election: Provided, that no election need be directed by the board solely because of the request of an employer or of employees prompted thereto by their employer, nor shall any individuals employed only for the duration of a strike or lockout be eligible to vote in such election; and provided further, that no such election shall be conducted under the employer's supervision, or, except as may be required by the board, on the employer's property, during working hours, or with his participation or assistance.[9]

5. If at an election conducted pursuant to this section three or more nominees for exclusive collective bargaining representatives appear on the ballot and no one of them receives a majority of the votes cast at the election, the two nominees who received the highest number of votes shall appear on the ballot of a second election to be conducted hereunder, and the one receiving a majority of the votes cast at the second election shall be the exclusive representative of all the employees in such unit for the purpose of collective bargaining in respect to rates of pay, wages, hours of employment, or other conditions of employment.

6. A labor organization nominated as the representative of employees shall be listed by name on the ballots authorized by sub-division three of this section. In any investigation conducted by the board pursuant to this section the board may make a finding as to whether any committee, employee representation plan, or association of employees involved is a company union, and if any such committee, employee representation plan, or association of employees be found to be a company union, it shall not be listed on the ballots, certified or otherwise recognized as eligible to be the representative of employees under this article.

---

[8]As amended by Chapter 750 of the Laws of 1940 and Chapter 1034 of the Laws of 1957. The 1940 amendment made it mandatory upon the Board to conduct investigations in representation cases initiated by petitions filed by employers. This amendment simply put a legislative stamp upon a policy which the board had generally followed anyway. The 1957 amendment removed the prior limitation on the Board's authority to conduct elections among labor unions affiliated with the same parent labor organization. The 1957 amendment further provides that the board shall *not* have the authority to investigate the internal affairs of any labor union.

[9]As amended by Chapter 634 of the Laws of 1940 and Chapter 518 of the Laws of 1942. The 1940 amendment permitted the Board, if it deemed it to be necessary, to hold elections on the employer's property during working hours, or with the employer's assistance. The 1942 amendment simply changed the wording from "no election shall be directed" to "no election need be directed".

SECTION 706—Prevention of Unfair Labor Practices. 1. The board is empowered and directed, as hereinafter provided, to prevent any employer from engaging in any unfair labor practice. This power shall not be affected or impaired by any means of adjustment, mediation or conciliation in labor disputes that have been or may hereafter be established by law.

2. Whenever a charge has been made that any employer has engaged in or is engaging in any unfair labor practice, the board shall have power to issue and cause to be served upon such employer a complaint stating the charges in that respect and containing a notice of hearing before the board at a place therein fixed to be held not less than seven days after the serving of said complaint. Any such complaint may be amended by the board or its agent conducting the hearing at any time prior to the issuance of an order based thereon. The person so complained of shall have the right to file an answer to the original or amended complaint not less than five days after the service of such original or amended complaint and to appear in person or otherwise to give testimony at the place and time set in the complaint. In the discretion of a member or agent conducting the hearing, or of the board, any other person may be allowed to intervene in the said proceeding and to present testimony. In any such proceeding the board or its agent shall not be bound by technical rules of evidence prevailing in the courts of law or equity.

3. The testimony taken at the hearing shall be reduced to writing and filed with the board. Thereafter, in its discretion, the board upon notice may take further testimony or hear argument. If upon all the testimony taken the board shall determine that the respondent has engaged in or is engaging in any unfair labor practice, the board shall state its findings of fact and shall issue and cause to be served on such respondent an order requiring such respondent to cease and desist from such unfair labor practice, and to take such further affirmative or other action as will effectuate the policies of this article, including, but not limited to (a) withdrawal of recognition from and refraining from bargaining collectively with any employee organization or association, agency or plan defined in this article as a company union or established, maintained or assisted by any action defined in this article as an unfair labor practice; (b) awarding of back pay; (c) reinstatement with or without back pay of any employee discriminated against in violation of section seven hundred four, or maintenance of a preferential list from which such employee shall be returned to work; (d) reinstatement with or without back pay of all employees whose work has ceased or whose return to work has been delayed or prevented as the result of the aforementioned or any other unfair labor practice in respect to any employee or employees or maintenance of a preferential list from which such employees shall be returned to work. Such order may further require such person to make reports from time to time showing the extent to which the order has been complied with. If upon all the testimony the board shall be of the opinion that the person or persons named in the complaint have not engaged in or are not engaging in any such unfair labor practice, then the board shall make its findings of fact and shall issue an order dismissing the complaint.

4. Until a transcript of the record in a case shall have been filed in a

court, as hereinafter provided, the board may at anytime, upon reasonable notice and in such manner as it shall deem proper, modify or set aside, in whole or in part, any finding or order made or issued by it.

5. The board shall not require as a condition of taking action or issuing any order under this article, that employees on strike or engaged in any other lawful, concerted activity shall discontinue such strike or such activity.

6. The board shall consider all complaints or petitions filed with it and conduct all proceedings under this article with all possible expedition.

SECTION 707—Judicial Review. 1. The board shall have power to petition the supreme court of the state within the county wherein the unfair labor practice in question occurred or wherein any person charged with the unfair labor practice resides or transacts business, or if such court be on vacation or in recess, then to the supreme court of any county adjoining the county wherein the unfair labor practice in question occurred or wherein any person charged with the unfair labor practice resides or transacts business, for the enforcement of such order and for appropriate temporary relief or restraining order, and shall certify and file in the court a transcript of the entire record in the proceeding, including the pleadings and testimony upon which such order was made and the findings and order of the board. Upon such filing, the court shall cause notice thereof to be served upon such person, and thereupon shall have jurisdiction of the proceeding and of the question determined therein, and shall have power to grant such temporary relief or restraining order as it deems just and proper, and to make and enter upon the pleadings, testimony, and proceedings set forth in such transcript a decree enforcing, modifying, and enforcing as so modified, or setting aside in whole or in part the order of the board.

2. No objection that has not been urged before the board, its member, agent or agency, shall be considered by the court, unless the failure or neglect to urge such objection shall be excused because of extraordinary circumstances. The findings of the board as to the facts, if supported by evidence, shall be conclusive. If either party shall apply to the court for leave to adduce additional evidence and shall show to the satisfaction of the court that such additional evidence is material and that there were reasonable grounds for the failure to adduce such evidence in the hearing before the board, its member, agent, or agency, the court may order such additional evidence to be taken before the board, its member, agent, or agency, and to be made a part of the transcript. The board may modify its findings as to the facts, or make new findings, by reason of additional evidence so taken and filed, and it shall file such modified or new findings, which, if supported by evidence, shall be conclusive, and shall file its recommendations, if any, for the modification or setting aside of its original order.

3. The jurisdiction of the supreme court shall be exclusive and its judgment and decree shall be final, except that appeals shall lie to the appellate division of said court and to the court of appeals, in the manner and subject to the limitations provided in the civil practice act irrespective of the nature of the decree or judgment or the amount involved.[10]

---

[10]As amended by Chapter 210 of the Laws of 1942. The appeal procedure was slightly changed to provide for review of Board decisions up to and including the court of appeals, subject to the limitations of the civil practice act.

4. Any person aggrieved by a final order of the board granting or denying in whole or in part the relief sought may obtain a review of such order in the supreme court of the county where the unfair labor practice in question was alleged to have been engaged in or wherein such person resides or transacts business by filing in such court a written petition praying that the order of the board be modified or set aside, or if such court be on vacation or in recess, then to the supreme court of any county adjoining the county wherein the unfair labor practice in question occurred or wherein any such person resides or transacts business. A copy of such petition shall be forthwith served upon the board, and thereupon the aggrieved party shall file in the court a transcript of the entire record in the proceeding, certified by the board, including the pleading and testimony and order of the board. Upon such filing, the court shall proceed in the same manner as in the case of an application by the board under subdivision one of this section, and shall have the same exclusive jurisdiction to grant to the board such temporary relief or restraining order as it deems just and proper, and in like manner to make and enter a decree enforcing, modifying and enforcing as so modified, or setting aside in whole or in part the order of the board; and the findings of the board as to the facts shall in like manner be conclusive.

5. The commencement of proceedings under subdivisions one and four of this section shall not, unless specifically ordered by the court, operate as a stay of the board's order.

6. When granting appropriate temporary relief or a restraining order, or making and entering a decree enforcing, modifying and enforcing as so modified or setting aside in whole or in part an order of the board, as provided in this section, the jurisdiction of courts sitting in equity shall not be limited by acts pertaining to equity jurisdiction of courts.

7. Petitions filed under this article shall be heard expeditiously and shall be considered and determined upon the transcript filed, without requirement of printing. Upon the filing of a record in the supreme court, the case shall be heard with greatest possible expedition, and shall take precedence over all other matters except matters of the same character.

SECTION 708—Investigatory Powers. For the purpose of all hearings and investigations, which, in the opinion of the board, are necessary and proper for the exercise of the powers vested in it by sections seven hundred five and seven hundred six.

1. The board, or its duly authorized agents or agencies, shall at all reasonable times have access to, for the purpose of examination, and the right to examine, copy or photograph any evidence, including payrolls or list of employees, of any person being investigated or proceeded against that relates to any matter under investigation or in question. Any member of the board shall have power to issue subpoenas requiring the attendance and testimony of witnesses and the production of any evidence that relates to any matter under investigation or in question before the board, its member, agent, or agency, conducting the hearing or investigation. Any member of the board, or any agent or agency designated by the board for such purposes, may administer oaths and affirmations, examine witnesses, and receive evidence.

2. If any witness resides outside of the state, or through illness or other

cause is unable to testify before the board or its member, agent, or agency conducting the hearing or investigation, his or her testimony or deposition may be taken within or without this state, in such manner and in such form as the board or its member, agent or agency conducting the hearing may by special order or general rule, prescribe.

3. In case of contumacy or refusal to obey a subpoena issued to any person the supreme court of any county within the jurisdiction of which the inquiry is carried on or within the jurisdiction of which said person guilty of contumacy or refusal to obey is found or resides or transacts business, upon application by the board shall have jurisdiction to issue to such person an order requiring such person to appear before the board, its member, agent, or agency, there to produce evidence if so ordered, or there to give testimony touching the matter under investigation or in question; and any failure to obey such order of the court may be punished by said court as a contempt thereof.

4. Upon any such investigation or hearing, the board, a member thereof, or an officer duly designated by the board to conduct such investigation or hearing, may confer immunity in accordance with the provisions of section two thousand four hundred forty-seven of the penal law.[11]

5. Complaints, orders, and other process and papers of the board, its member, agent, or agency, may be served either personally or by certified or registered mail or by telegraph or by leaving a copy thereof at the principal office or place of business of the person required to be served. The verified return by the individual so serving the same setting forth the manner of such service shall be proof of the same, and the return post-office receipt or telegraph receipt therefor when registered and mailed or telegraphed as aforesaid shall be proof of service of the same. Witnesses summoned before the board, its member, agent, or agency shall be paid the same fees and mileage that are paid witnesses in the courts of this state, and witnesses whose depositions are taken and the person taking the same shall severally be entitled to the same fees as are paid for like services in the courts of this state.[12]

6. All process of any court to which application may be made under this article may be served in the county wherein the person or persons required to be served reside or may be found.

7. The several departments, commissions, divisions, authorities, boards, bureaus, agencies and officers of the state or any political subdivision or agency thereof, shall furnish the board, upon its request, all records, papers, and information in their possession relating to any matter before the board.

SECTION 709—Punitive Provision. Any person who shall wilfully resist, prevent, impede, or interfere with any member of the board or any of its agents or agencies in the performance of duties pursuant to this article, or who shall in any manner interfere with the free exercise by employees of

[11]As amended by Chapter 891 of the Laws of 1953. The amendment allows the board to grant immunity from punishment acording to Section 2447 of the penal law to witnesses appearing before board investigations.

[12]As amended by Chapter 65 of the Laws of 1956. This amendment simply authorizes the mailing of process by certified mail.

their right to select representatives in an election directed by the board pursuant to section seven hundred and five, shall be punished by a fine of not more than five thousand dollars or by imprisonment for not more than one year, or both.

SECTION 710—Public Records and Proceedings. Subject to rules and regulations to be made by the board, the complaints, orders and testimony relating to a proceeding instituted by the board under section seven hundred six may be made public records and be made available for inspection or copying. All proceedings pursuant to section seven hundred and six shall be open to the public.

SECTION 711—Estimate of Annual Administrative Expenses; How Paid. Prior to the fifteenth day of November of each year, the industrial commissioner shall submit to the director of the budget for his approval an estimated budget of the administrative expenses of the New York state labor relations board for the ensuing fiscal year. All moneys appropriated to the department or the board, for the use of the board, shall be expended and audited in the manner provided for all other expenditures under the supervision of the industrial commissioner.

SECTION 712—Repeal of Inconsistent Provisions. Insofar as the provisions of this article are inconsistent with the provisions of any other general, special or local law, the provisions of this article shall be controlling.

SECTION 713—Limitations. Nothing in this article shall be construed so as to interfere with, impede or diminish in any way the right of employees to strike or engage in other lawful, concerted activities, except that it shall continue to be unlawful for the employees of a non-profitmaking hospital or residential care center, or their representatives, or any other persons to engage in or to induce or encourage, or to attempt to engage in or to induce or encourage any strike, work stoppage, slowdown or withholding of goods or services by such employees or other persons at such hospital or residential care center, provided, however, that nothing herein shall be construed to prohibit publicity, other than picketing, for the purpose of truthfully advising the public that a grievance or dispute, as defined in section seven hundred sixteen of this article, exists at such hospital or residential care center, as long as such publicity does not have the effect of inducing any persons to withhold goods or services at such hospital or residential care center.

It shall be unlawful for a non-profitmaking hospital or residential care center to institute, declare or cause, or to attempt to institute, declare or cause any lockout of the employees of such hospital or residential care center.[13]

SECTION 714—Separability. If any clause, sentence, paragraph, or part of this article or the application thereof to any person or circumstances, shall, for any reason, be adjudged by a court of competent jurisdiction to be in-

---

[13]As amended in 1963 to deal with strikes and lock-outs in certain non-profit hospitals.

valid, such judgment shall not affect, impair, or invalidate the remainder of this article, and the application thereof to other person or circumstances, but shall be confined in its operation to the clause, sentence, paragraph, or part thereof directly involved in the controversy in which such judgment shall have been rendered and to the person or circumstances involved. It is hereby declared to be the legislative intent that this article would have been adopted had such invalid provisions not been included.

SECTION 715—Application of Article. The provisions of this article shall not apply to: (1) employees of any employer who concedes to and agrees with the board that such employees are subject to and protected by the provisions of the national labor relations act or the federal railway labor act; or (2) employees of the state or of any political or civil subdivision or other agency thereof; or (3) employees of any charitable, educational or religious association or corporation, no part of the net earnings of which inures to the benefit of any private shareholder or individual, except that the provisions of this article shall apply to (a) employees of any such charitable, educational or religious association or corporation whose services are performed in connection with the operation of a building owned or operated by such an association or corporation and used or occupied as a commercial or industrial enterprise operated for the production of profit, irrespective of the purposes to which such profit may be applied, and which employees are not engaged in the charitable, educational or religious activities of such association or corporation and (b) employees of a non-profitmaking hospital or residential care center.[14]

SECTION 716—Grievances and Disputes in Non-profitmaking Hospitals and Residential Care Centers. 1. As used in this section "grievance" means any controversy or claim arising out of or relating to the interpretation, application or breach of the provisions of an existing collective bargaining contract. As used in this section "dispute" means all other controversies, claims or disputes between the employees of a non-profitmaking hospital or residential care center, or their representatives, and such hospital or residential care center concerning wages, hours, union security, seniority or other economic matters, including, but not limited to, controversies, claims or disputes arising in the course of negotiating, fixing, maintaining, changing or arranging such terms or conditions.

2. Every collective bargaining contract between the employees of a non-profitmaking hospital or residential care center, or their representatives, and such hospital or residential care center which does not contain provisions for the final and binding determination of grievances shall be deemed to include provision for the submission of such grievances, upon the request

---

[14]As amended by Chapter 463 of the Laws of 1946 and Chapter 764 of the Laws of 1955. The 1946 amendment added the provision starting "except that the provisions of this article shall apply etc." The 1955 amendment limited the exemptions of employees of charitable, educational and religious associations and corporations to apply only to employees of those associations or corporations where no part of the net earnings inured to the benefit of private shareholders or individuals. Further amended to apply to the employees of certain non-profit hospitals.

of either or both parties, to arbitration pursuant to such rules as may be established from time to time by the New York state board of mediation.

3. Every collective bargaining contract between the employees of a non-profitmaking hospital or residential care center, or their representatives, and such hospital or residential care center which does not contain provisions for the final and binding determination of disputes shall be deemed to include provisions for:

(a) the appointment of a fact-finding commission by the New York state board of mediation upon the request of both parties to the dispute, or by the industrial commissioner upon his own motion and upon certification by such board that in its opinion efforts to effect a voluntary settlement of the dispute have been unsuccessful. Such fact-finding commission shall have all the powers and duties, including the power to make recommendations for the settlement of the dispute, as are vested in a board of inquiry by article twenty-two of this chapter; and

(b) the submission of the dispute to arbitration, pursuant to such rules as may be established from time to time by the New York state board of mediation, by such board of mediation upon the request of both parties to the dispute, or by the industrial commissioner upon his own motion and upon certification by such board of mediation that in its opinion efforts to effect a voluntary settlement of the dispute have been unsuccessful.

4. In the absence of a collective bargaining contract between the employees of a non-profitmaking hospital or residential care center, or their representatives, and such hospital or residential care center, the New York state board of mediation and the industrial commissioner may, in the manner and upon the conditions provided in subdivision three of this section, exercise all of the powers vested in them by the provisions of such subdivision of such section.

5. Nothing in this section shall be deemed to affect, impair or alter any collective bargaining contract between the employees of a non-profitmaking hospital or residential care center, or their representatives, and such hospital or residential care center which was executed prior to July first, nineteen hundred sixty-three, during the term of such contract.

6. The supreme court shall have jurisdiction, to confirm, modify, correct or vacate any arbitration award made pursuant to the procedure established by this section, in the manner provided by article eighty-four of the civil practice act. The supreme court shall have jurisdiction, upon such notice as it deems appropriate, to restrain or enjoin any violation of the provisions of this section or section seven hundred thirteen and to grant such other and further equitable relief as may be appropriate. The provisions of section eight hundred seventy-six-a of the civil practice act shall not apply to an action or proceeding instituted pursuant to this section or section seven hundred thirteen.

SECTION 717—Short Title. This article shall be known and may be cited and referred to as the "New York state labor relations act."

Text of General Rules and Regulations of the New York State Labor Relations Board

Effective May 1, 1951*

Article I—Definitions

Section 1. The terms "person," "employer," "employees," "representatives," "labor organization," "company union," "unfair labor practice" and "labor dispute," as used herein, shall have the meanings set forth in Section 701 of the New York State Labor Relations Act.

Section 2. Act; Board: The term "Act," as used herein, shall mean the New York State Labor Relations Act, and the term "Board" shall mean the New York State Labor Relations Board.

Section 3. Regional Attorney: The term "Regional Attorney," as used herein, shall mean the agent designated by the Board as Regional Attorney for a particular local area.

Section 4. Board's Attorney: The term "Board's Attorney," as used herein, shall mean the agent designated by the Board to act as its attorney in any proceeding or hearing before the Board or its Trial Examiner.[1]

Section 5. Trial Examiner: The term "Trial Examiner," as used herein, shall mean the Board, its Member, agent or agency conducting a hearing.

Section 6. Labor Relations Examiner: The term "Labor Relations Examiner," as used herein, shall mean the agent designated by the Board to conduct conferences and to investigate charges of unfair labor practice and petitions for investigation and certification of representatives filed with the Board.[2]

Section 7. Parties: The term "party" or "parties" as used herein in connection with proceedings under Section 706 of the Act, shall mean the respondent-employer, or employers, the person or organization making the charge, and any other persons or labor organizations whose intervention in the proceeding has been permitted by the Board or Trial Examiner, except as limited by the Board or Trial Examiner in granting such permission. As used herein in connection with proceedings under Section 705 of the Act, "party" or "parties" shall mean the employer, or employers, the person or labor organization filing the petition, any other person or organization designated in the notice of hearing and served therewith, and any other

---

*These 1951 General Rules and Regulations represent the most recent amendments to the Board's Rules. The original 1937 preliminary Rules and Regulations were amended in 1940, 1941, 1943, and 1951. The major historical changes in the Board's Rules are indicated in the footnotes.

[1]This section was added by the 1940 General Rules and Regulations.

[2]This section was added by the 1943 amendments to the General Rules and Regulations.

persons or labor organizations whose intervention has been permitted by the Board or Trial Examiner, except as limited by the Board or Trial Examiner in granting such permission.[3]

Article II—Procedure under Section 705 of the Act for the Investigation and Certification of Representatives

Petition

Section 8. Petition; Filing: A petition for investigation pursuant to Section 705 of the Act may be filed with the Board by employees, employers or their representatives. The petition shall be in writing. The original shall be signed and verified before any person authorized to administer an oath. The original and three copies of the petition shall be filed with the Board. Petition forms will be supplied by the Board upon request.[4]

Section 9. Petition of Employee or Representative; Contents: A petition, when filed by an employee or his representative shall contain:

    (a) The name and address of the petitioner;

    (b) The name and address of the employer or employers concerned and the general nature of the business and the approximate number of employees;

    (c) The approximate percentage and volume of sales to and purchases from, points outside New York State, and any other facts concerning interstate commerce, if any. If such information is unknown to the petitioner, the petition shall so state;[5]

    (d) The classification of employees in the bargaining unit or units claimed to be appropriate, the number of employees therein, the names and addresses of any other individuals or labor organizations who claim to be the representatives of any of the employees in the alleged bargaining unit or units;

    (e) An allegation that a question or controversy exists concerning representation and a concise statement setting forth the nature thereof;

    (f) A request that the Board certify the petitioner as the collective bargaining representative of the employees within the bargaining unit or units claimed to be appropriate.[6]

Section 10. Petition of Employer or Representative; Contents: Such petition, when filed by an employer shall contain:

---

[3]This section was added by the 1940 General Rules and Regulations. The wording was slightly changed in 1943, but had no effect upon Board procedure.

[4]The wording of this section was changed in 1940, 1943, and 1951. Again, the change in wording was only slight and had no effect upon Board procedure.

[5]This section was amended in 1951 to provide for more detailed information concerning the interstate character of the employer's business. Prior to 1951 the section asked for "The approximate percentage of sales made to points outside New York State, or the approximate amount of business transacted outside New York State, and any other facts concerning interstate commerce, if any;" The 1951 change in this section illustrates the federal-state jurisdictional problem created by Section 10(a) of Taft-Hartley.

[6]This part of Section 9 was added in 1943.

(a) The name and address of the petitioning employer;

(b) The general nature of the business and the approximate number of employees;

(c) The approximate percentage and volume of sales to and purchases from, points outside New York State and any other facts concerning interstate commerce, if any;[7]

(d) The classification of employees in the bargaining unit or units claimed to be appropriate, and the number of employees employed in such bargaining unit or units;

(e) The names and addresses of any individuals or labor organizations who claim to represent any of the employees in the alleged bargaining unit or units;

(f) An allegation that a question or controversy exists concerning representation and a concise statement setting forth the nature thereof.

Section 11. Sufficiency of Petition: No petition in a proceeding under Section 705 of the Act shall be dismissed for failure of the petitioner to set forth in the petition all the information required.[8]

Section 12. Notice of Pending Petitions: Upon the filing of a petition under Section 705 of the Act, notice thereof, including the date when such petition was filed, the name and address of the employer affected and the nature of his business, the unit claimed to be appropriate and the name of the person or organization filing the same, shall be posted on the public docket maintained by the Board.[9]

Section 13. Petition; Withdrawal or Amendment: At any time before the issuance of a notice of hearing on a petition for investigation and certification, the Board may permit the amendment of the petition or its withdrawal in whole or in part. At any time after the issuance of such notice of hearing, the Board, upon motion, may permit withdrawal of the petition in whole or in part, and the Board or the Trial Examiner may permit amendment thereof.[10]

Investigation and Elections

Section 14. Investigation; Ascertainment of Desires of Employees; Notice: In the course of its investigation of a question or controversy concerning representation, the Board may direct an election or elections, or use other suitable methods to ascertain the wishes of employees, either in conjunction with a proceeding instituted under Section 706 of the Act or otherwise. When a hearing has been directed, the Board or its agent shall prepare and cause to be served upon the parties a notice of hearing before a Trial

---

[7]See n. 5 *supra.*

[8]This section was added in 1940. Although it was not contained in the 1937 Preliminary Rules and Regulations it was, nevertheless, a Board policy from the very beginning not to dismiss petitions solely on the basis of deficiencies in content.

[9]This section was added in 1943. The practice of posting these petitions on the Board's public docket was actually started in 1940. The Board found that this procedure was more efficient and effective than sending out individual notices to interested parties. The Board presently uses both of these methods to inform parties.

[10]This section was added in 1940, and the wording was slightly changed in 1943.

ᴀ a time and place fixed therein. A copy of the petition shall be with the notice of hearing.

Section 15. Elections; Terms and Conditions: If the Board determines, as a part of its investigation of a question or controversy concerning representation, that an election or elections by secret ballot shall be held, it shall provide that such election or elections be conducted by an agent of the Board at such time and place and upon such terms or conditions as he or the Board may specify.

Section 16. Determination of Representatives on Consent: Subject to the approval of the Board, the parties to a representation proceeding may waive a hearing and agree on the method by which the Board shall determine the question of representation.[11]

Section 17. Procedure Following Elections; Objections: Upon the conclusion of any election or elections, the Board, its Labor Elections Supervisor or other agent shall prepare a report as to the result of the election or elections. The Board shall cause this report to be served upon the parties. Within five (5) days thereafter, any party may serve upon all other parties, and file with the Board (with proof of service) an original and three (3) copies of objections to the election or elections or to the report thereon. The objections shall contain a concise statement of the facts constituting the grounds of objection. The Board may direct oral argument to be heard before it, or direct that hearings be held before a Trial Examiner, or otherwise investigate or make its determination with respect to the objections or to any challenged ballots.[12]

Certifications

Section 18. Certification of Representatives: The Board, upon the completion of its investigation, shall certify to the parties the name or names of the representatives selected, if any, or make other disposition of the matter.

Section 19. Certification; Life of; Exceptions: When a representative has been certified by the Board, such certification shall remain in effect for one year from the date thereof, and thereafter until such time as it shall be made to appear to the Board that the certified representative does not represent a majority of the employees within an appropriate unit. In any case where unusual or extraordinary circumstances require such action, or where probable cause is shown that such action may be necessary to prevent the occurrence or continuation of an unfair labor practice, the Board, in its discretion, may shorten or extend the life of the original certification. When the Board shall find that during the life of a certification the employer has refused to bargain collectively with the certified representative, the time of the con-

---

[11]This section was added in 1940. The wording was changed in 1943 with no change in Board procedure.

[12]The wording of this section has been slightly changed since 1937. In 1943 the sentence beginning "The objections shall contain a concise..." was added.

196

tinuance of such refusal to bargain shall not be a part of the time limited in computing the life of the certification.[13]

Article III—Procedure under Section 706 of the Act for the Prevention of Unfair Labor Practices

Charge

Section 20. Charge: A charge that any employer has engaged in or is engaging in any unfair labor practice may be made by any person or labor organization.

Section 21. Charge; Form; Filing: A charge shall be in writing. The original shall be signed and verified before any person authorized to administer an oath. The original and three (3) copies of the charge shall be filed with the Board. Charge forms will be supplied by the Board upon request.

Section 22. Contents of Charge: A charge shall contain:
  (a) The full name and address of the person or labor organization making the charge;
  (b) The full name and address of the employer or employers against whom the charge is made;
  (c) Upon information and belief, the general nature of the employer's business, the approximate number of its employees, the approximate percentage and volume of sales to and purchases from, points outside New York State, and any other facts concerning interstate commerce, if any;[14]
  (d) An enumeration of the subdivision or subdivisions of Section 704

---

[13]This section contains two significant changes from the wording of the 1937 Preliminary Rules and Regulations:
(a) The 1937 Rules provided for a certification for one year "provided however, that in any case where unusual or extraordinary circumstances require such action, or where such action may be necessary to prevent the occurrence or continuation of an unfair labor practice, the Board, in its discretion, may fix the life of such representative for a lesser period, or may, prior to the expiration of such year... certify the same or another person or organization as the representative designated or selected, or may extend the period of the original certification, or make other disposition of the matter." This wording was amended in 1940 to read as the present Section 19. The amendment made the certification good for a period of one year "and thereafter until such time as it shall be made to appear to the Board that the certified representative does not represent a majority of the employees in the appropriate unit." This change in wording shifts the burden of proof with regard to the life of the certification from the party seeking to extend the certification beyond one year to the party seeking to limit the certification to one year.
(b) Another portion of this section added in 1940 was the sentence beginning "When the Board shall find that during the life of a certification..." The purpose of this addition was to prevent employers from taking the position that they had no duty to bargain with a certified representative after the one year period, even though the one year might have been partially or completely consumed in court action.
[14]See n. 5 *supra.*

of the Act which are alleged to have been violated by the employer or employers, and, in the event it is alleged that any employee has been discharged, refused employment, or suffered discrimination in violation of the Act, the name of such employee.

Section 23. Charge; Withdrawal: A charge, or any part thereof, may be withdrawn only with the consent of the Board and upon such conditions as the Board may deem proper.

Section 24. Charge; Amendment: A charge or any part thereof may be amended in the discretion of the Board or the Trial Examiner, at any time before the issuance of the final decision and order by the Board.[15]

Section 25. Charge; Not Part of Complaint; Other Disposition:

(a) A charge shall not be part of the complaint.

(b) If the Board in its discretion shall determine that no complaint shall issue on a charge filed with it, the Board may make such other disposition of the charge or any part thereof as it may deem proper.[16]

Complaint

Section 26. Complaint; Notice of Hearing: After a charge has been filed, if it appears to the Board that formal proceedings should be instituted, the Board may issue and cause to be served upon the parties a complaint in the name of the Board, containing a concise statement as to the alleged violations of the Act and a notice of hearing before a Trial Examiner at a place fixed therein, and at a time not less than seven (7) days after the service of the complaint.[17]

Section 27. Complaint; Supplemental Complaint; Amendment: In the discretion of the Board or the Trial Examiner, a supplemental complaint may be issued or a complaint may be amended upon motion of the Board's Attorney or upon the Board's own motion, upon due notice to all parties, at any time before the issuance of the final decision and order.[18]

Section 28. Complaint; Withdrawal: A complaint or supplemental complaint or amended complaint, or any part thereof, may be withdrawn by the Board on its own motion, or on motion of Board's Attorney, at any time before the issuance of a final decision and order, upon notice to all parties.

Answer

Section 29. Answer; Filing; Service: The party or parties against whom the complaint is issued shall have the right to file an answer within five (5)

---

[15]This section was added in 1940, and the wording has subsequently been changed with no effect upon Board procedure.

[16]This section was added in 1940.

[17]The 1937 Preliminary Rules and Regulations stated that the hearing would be before a Trial Examiner or a member of the Board. As of 1942 Board members were appearing less and less frequently as Trial Examiners.

[18]Provisions for the amendment of the complaint were found in the 1937 Rules. The 1951 amendments added the provision for a supplemental complaint to this section. This additional wording simply verified a Board practice of long standing.

days after service of the complaint. Upon application the Board may extend the time within which the answer shall be filed. One copy of the answer shall be served on each party and Board's Attorney, and the original with proof of due service and two (2) copies shall be filed with the Board

Section 30. Answer; Verification: The answer shall be verified by the party filing it.

Section 31. Answer; Denials: The answer shall contain a specific denial of each allegation of the complaint controverted by the party filing the answer, or of any knowledge or information thereof sufficient to form a belief. An allegation in the complaint not specifically denied in the answer, unless the party asserts that it is without knowledge or information thereof sufficient to form a belief, shall be deemed admitted and may be so found by the Board.

Section 32. Answer; Defense; New Matter: The answer shall contain a concise statement of the facts constituting the grounds of defense. Allegations of new matter in the answer shall be deemed denied without the necessity of a reply.[19]

Section 33. Answer; Amendment: In the discretion of the Board or the Trial Examiner, an answer may be amended upon motion of the party filing it, upon due notice to all parties and Board's Attorney, at any time before the issuance of the final decision and order.

Section 34. Answer; Failure to File: If the party or parties against whom the complaint is issued fails to file an answer in the manner and within the time herein provided, it may be limited to cross-examination of witnesses called by the Board's Attorney or Trial Examiner and shall have such other rights as the Trial Examiner may deem proper.[20]

Section 35. Pleadings; Construction: All pleadings shall be liberally construed.

Article IV—General Provisions Relating to All Proceedings

Joinder

Section 36. Parties; Non-Joinder and Misjoinder: No proceeding will be dismissed because of non-joinder or misjoinder of parties. Upon motion of any party or Board's Attorney, parties may be added, dropped or substituted at any stage of the proceedings, upon such terms as may be deemed proper.[21]

---

[19]The second sentence of this section was added in 1940.

[20]The 1937 Rules placed no specific restrictions on the rights of respondents who failed to file an answer to the complaint. In 1940 this section was changed to read: "The respondent, however, in the event of such failure, shall have the right to appear at such hearings, and cross-examine all witnesses, but shall not have the right to interpose or seek to establish any affirmative defenses." This section was again amended in 1943 to read as the above. The 1943 amendment gives the Trial Examiner discretion as to what the respondent may be allowed to do.

[21]This section was added in 1940. In addition to the wording of the section as it now reads, the 1940 amendment stated that: "Such motions must be made at or

Section 37. Joinder of Parties; Relief: All persons alleged to have engaged in any unfair labor practices may be joined as parties, whether jointly, severally, or in the alternative, and a decision may be rendered against one or more of them, upon all of the evidence without regard to the party by or against whom such evidence has been introduced.[22]

Motions

Section 38. Motions During Hearing: All motions made during a hearing, except as otherwise provided, shall be made orally at the hearing and shall be decided by the Trial Examiner. All such motions and the rulings and orders thereon shall be part of the record of the proceeding.

Section 39. Motions Before or After Hearing: All motions, other than those made during a hearing, shall be made in writing to the Board, shall briefly state the relief sought and shall be accompanied by affidavits setting forth the grounds for such motion. The moving party shall serve copies of all motion papers on all other parties and in a proceeding under Section 706 on Board's Attorney, and shall within three (3) days thereafter file the original and three (3) copies thereof with proof of service with the Board. Answering affidavits, if any, must be served on all parties, and in a proceeding under Section 706 on Board's Attorney, and the original thereof together with three (3) copies and proof of service shall be filed with the Board within three (3) days after service of the moving papers unless the Board directs otherwise. All such motions shall be decided by the Board upon the papers filed with it, unless the Board decides to hear oral argument or take testimony thereon, in which case the Board shall notify the parties of such fact and of the time and place for such argument or for the taking of such testimony.

Waiver

Section 40. Objections; Waiver: An objection not duly urged before the Board or its Trial Examiner shall be deemed waived unless the failure to urge such objection shall be excused by the Board because of extraordinary circumstances.[23]

Intervention

Section 41. Procedure; Contents; Filing; Service: A person, employer or labor organization desiring to intervene in any proceeding shall file with the Board a verified written application and three (3) copies thereof, setting forth the facts upon which such person, employer or organization claims an interest in the proceeding. Such application must be served on all parties, and in a proceeding under Section 706 on Board's Attorney. Applications must be filed with the Board with proof of service at least two (2) days before the first hearing. Failure to serve or file such application, as above provided,

---

prior to the first hearing in any such proceeding, unless good and sufficient cause is shown why it could not have been made at such time. Failure to so move shall be deemed a waiver of all objections to the non-joinder or misjoinder of all parties." This sentence was deleted in 1943.

[22]Added in 1940.
[23]Added in 1940.

shall be deemed sufficient cause for the denial thereof, unless good and sufficient reason exists why it was not served or filed as herein provided. The Trial Examiner shall rule upon all such applications and may permit intervention to such an extent and upon such terms as he shall determine may effectuate the policies of the Act.[24]

Consolidation or Severance

Section 42. Consolidation; Severance: Two or more proceedings under Sections 705 and 706 of the Act, or either, may be consolidated by the Board. Such proceedings may be severed by the Board or Trial Examiner in its or his discretion.[25]

Witnesses and Subpoenas

Section 43. Witnesses; Examination; Record; Depositions: Witnesses at all hearings shall be examined orally under oath or affirmation, and a record of the proceeding shall be made and kept by the Board. If any witness resides outside the State or through illness or other cause is unable to testify before the Board or its Member, agent or agency conducting the hearing or investigation, his or her testimony or deposition may be taken within or without this State, in such form as may be directed. All applications for taking such testimony or deposition must be made by motion.

Section 44. Subpoenas; Application For: A party or Board's Attorney may apply to a Member of the Board for the issuance of subpoenas or subpoenas duces tecum. Such application shall be timely. It shall specify the name of the witness or the documents or things the production of which is desired, with such particularity as will enable such documents to be identified for purposes of production, the return date desired, and the general nature of the facts to be proved by the witness or the documents or things sought to be produced. The original and two copies of such application shall be filed with the Board and need not be served on any other party or on Board's Attorney. The Board may grant or deny such application in whole or in part and may make such subpoena returnable at any time.

Section 45. Subpoenas; Issuance; Production of Books, etc.: A Member of the Board may issue subpoenas at any time, requiring persons, parties or witnesses to attend and be examined or give testimony, and to produce any document or thing that relates to any matter under investigation or any question before the Board, Trial Examiner, Labor Relations Examiner, agent or agency conducting a hearing or investigation.

Section 46. Subpoenas; Parties; Failure to Obey or Testify: If a party refuses or fails, without reasonable excuse (a) to obey any subpoena or subpoenas duces tecum, or (b) to answer any question which has been ruled pertinent or proper, the Trial Examiner may strike from the record the

[24]The 1937 Rules provided for the Board to pass on such petitions for intervention. The 1940 amendments changed this to the Trial Examiner.

[25]Added in 1940. Although the 1937 Rules made no mention of this practice, it was part of the Board's procedure from the beginning.

pleading and/or all testimony offered in behalf of such party at the hearing, or may strike those portions of the testimony which are related to the question which the party has refused to answer, or to the matter called for in the subpoena. When the party so refusing or failing to obey a subpoena, or to answer any question which has been ruled pertinent and proper, is the person or labor organization making the charge, then the Trial Examiner shall have the same power to strike all or part of the evidence presented by the Board's Attorney at the hearing. The Trial Examiner may preclude the reintroduction of any testimony so stricken.

If a party fails or refuses, without reasonable excuse, to obey any subpoena duces tecum, the Trial Examiner may preclude such party from introducing any proof concerning such documents or things, or from introducing them in evidence.

If a party is a corporation or a labor organization, this section shall apply to failures and refusals of its officers or agents.[26]

Section 47. Witness Fees: Witness fees and mileage shall be paid by the party at whose instance the witnesses appear, or by the Board if the witnesses appear at the Board's instance. The person taking a deposition shall be paid by the party at whose instance the deposition is taken, or by the Board if the deposition is taken at its instance.

Hearings

Section 48. Hearings; Conduct: Hearings shall be conducted by a Trial Examiner designated by the Board. At any time, a Trial Examiner may be designated to take the place of the Trial Examiner previously designated to conduct the hearing. All hearings shall be open to the public.

Section 49. Hearings; Powers and Duties of Trial Examiner: During the course of any hearing, the Trial Examiner, in addition to the other powers specifically conferred upon him, and subject to the limitations imposed upon him by these Rules and Regulations, shall have full authority to control the conduct and procedure of the hearing and the record thereof, to admit or exclude testimony or other evidence, and to rule upon all motions and objections. It shall be the duty of the Trial Examiner to see that a full inquiry is made into all the facts in issue and to obtain a complete record of all facts necessary for a fair determination of the issues. The Trial Examiner shall have the right to call and examine witnesses, to direct the production of papers or other matter present in the hearing room, and to introduce documentary or other evidence, except as may otherwise be limited herein.[27]

---

[26]Added in 1940.

[27]The powers and duties of the Trial Examiner have been elaborated upon since the 1937 Rules. The original Rules and Regulations stated that: "It shall be the duty of the Trial Examiner to inquire fully into the facts as to whether one respondent has engaged in or is engaging in an unfair labor practice as set forth in the complaint or amended complaint. Counsel for the Board and the Trial Examiner shall have power to call, examine, and cross-examine witnesses and to introduce into the record documentary or other evidence."

Section 50. Hearings; Rights of Parties: In any hearing all parties and Board's Attorney shall have the right to call, examine and cross-examine witnesses, and to introduce documentary or other evidence, subject to the rulings of the Trial Examiner, except as otherwise provided in these Rules and Regulations.

Section 51. Hearings; Stipulations: At a hearing, stipulations may be introduced in evidence with respect to any issue, where such stipulation has been joined in by all parties and the Board's Attorney.

Section 52. Hearings; Continuation of: Subject to the Board's approval, the Trial Examiner may continue a hearing from day to day or adjourn it to a later date or to a different place by announcement thereof at the hearing or by other appropriate notice.[28]

Section 53. Hearings; Contemptuous Conduct: The Trial Examiner may exclude from the hearing room or from further participation in the proceeding any person who engages in contemptuous conduct before him.[29]

Section 54. Hearings; Oral Argument or Briefs; Unfair Labor Practice Cases: In a proceeding under Section 706, the Trial Examiner may permit the parties and Board's Attorney to argue orally before him at the close of the hearing or to file briefs or written statements with him. The time for oral argument or filing briefs or memoranda shall be fixed by the Trial Examiner. Argument shall not be included in the stenographic report unless the Trial Examiner shall so direct.

Section 55. Hearings; Oral Argument or Briefs; Representation Cases: At the close of hearings in a proceeding under Section 705, the Trial Examiner shall permit the parties to file briefs or written statements, which shall be addressed and submitted to the Board. The time for filing such briefs or written statements shall be fixed by the Trial Examiner. An original and three (3) copies, with proof of service, must be filed. Requests for oral argument before the Board must be submitted to the Trial Examiner at the close of the hearing. The granting or denial of permission to argue orally before the Board shall be within the discretion of the Board. Argument shall not be included in the stenographic report unless the Board shall so direct.[30]

Section 56. Hearings; Variance Between Pleadings and Proof: A variance between an allegation in a petition under Section 705 or a pleading in a proceeding under Section 706, and the proof, is not material unless it is so substantial as prejudicially to mislead the Board or any party or Board's

[28]The 1937 Rules gave the Trial Examiner discretion to continue hearings. This was made subject to the approval of the Board in 1940.

[29]The 1940 amendments to the General Rules and Regulations spelled out in particular the contemptuous conduct of attorneys. This part of the section was deleted by the 1941 amendments to the Rules.

[30]It should be noted that whereas the opportunity to present oral arguments after the hearings is a matter of Board discretion in representation cases, it is a matter of right in unfair labor practice cases. [See Sec. 60(c)].

Attorney. If a variance is not material, the Trial Examiner may admit such proof and the facts may be found accordingly.[31]

Section 57. Hearings; Motions; Objections: Motions made during a hearing and objections with respect to the conduct of a hearing, including objections to the introduction of evidence, shall be stated orally and shall be included in the stenographic report of the hearing. Argument shall not be included in the stenographic report unless the Trial Examiner shall so direct.

Section 58. Hearings; Reopening:
    (a) Motions for leave to reopen a hearing because of newly discovered evidence shall be timely made.
    (b) The Board may, in its discretion or on its own motion, reopen a hearing and take further testimony at any time.[32]

Section 59. Hearings; Evidence as to Transactions Had at Informal Conferences: No testimony or evidence shall be given or received at any hearing concerning transactions had or statements or communications made during the conduct or course of any informal conference called and held by the Board, or any of its Members or agents, concerning charges or petitions previously filed with the Board, unless at the hearing all parties and Board's Attorney shall expressly waive this provision. This provision shall not apply to the giving or receipt of evidence concerning a consent comparison pursuant to Section 16 hereof.[33]

Section 60. Trial Examiner's Intermediate Report; Recommended Findings of Fact, Conclusions of Law and Order; Exceptions; Oral Argument:
    (a) After the close of a hearing in an unfair labor practice proceeding and the filing of the record with the Board, the Trial Examiner shall issue his Intermediate Report and the Board shall cause it to be served on all parties to the proceeding and the Board's Attorney. The Intermediate Report shall contain, but need not be limited to:
        (1) A statement of the case and the preliminary procedure before the Board;
        (2) Such discussion of the evidence and credibility of the witnesses as the Trial Examiner may deem necessary and proper;
        (3) Recommended findings of fact;
        (4) Recommended conclusions of law;
        (5) Recommended order.
    (b) Within seven (7) days after service of the Intermediate Report, a party or Board's Attorney may file with the Board written exceptions thereto or to any other part of the record, including rulings

---

[31]Added in 1940.

[32]This section added in 1940.

[33]Although this section was not added until 1940 it had always been a Board policy to keep the informal conference "off the record". The word "petitions" (concerning charges or petitions previously filed...) was added in 1951 so as to clearly indicate that the section applied to the informal conferences held in representation cases as well as unfair labor practice cases.

upon all motions or objections made at the hearing. Exceptions shall specify the errors assigned and contain a concise statement of the grounds on which the exceptions are taken. A copy of such exceptions shall be served upon all other parties and Board's Attorney and an original and three (3) copies thereof, with proof of service, must be filed with the Board.

(c) A request for oral argument may be filed with the exceptions. Upon such request, or upon its own motion, the Board shall issue a notice to all parties and to Board's Attorney, informing them of the time and place set for oral argument. Argument shall not be included in the stenographic report unless the Board shall so direct. The parties and Board's Attorney shall have the right to file briefs not later than seven (7) days after the filing of exceptions. Such briefs shall be served on all other parties and Board's Attorney at or before the time of filing. Answering briefs may be served and filed within seven (7) days thereafter. An original and three (3) copies, with proof of service, must be filed. The Board in its discretion may extend for good cause shown the time to serve and file exceptions or briefs.

Section 61. Proposed Findings of Fact, Conclusions of Law and Order; Exceptions; Oral Argument:

(a) The Board, in its discretion, at any time after the close of a hearing under Section 706 of the Act, and the filing of the record with the Board, may direct that the record of all proceedings theretofore held be submitted directly to the Board, for purpose of the issuance by the Board of Proposed Findings of Fact, Conclusions of Law and Order, instead of the issuance by the Trial Examiner of his Intermediate Report. Such Proposed Findings of Fact, Conclusions of Law and Order shall contain, but need not be limited to:

(1) A statement of the case and the preliminary procedure before the Board;

(2) Proposed findings of fact;

(3) Proposed conclusions of law;

(4) Proposed order.

(b) The provisions of Section 60 hereof relating to exceptions, oral argument and briefs, shall apply to Proposed Findings of Fact, Conclusions of Law and Order hereunder.[34]

Section 62. Exceptions; Failure to File; Waiver: If any party or Board's Attorney shall fail to file exceptions, he shall be deemed to have agreed to the Recommended Findings of Fact, Conclusions of Law and Order contained in the Trial Examiner's Intermediate Report or in the Board's Proposed Findings of Fact, Conclusions of Law and Order, or to so much

---

[34]The practice of having the Trial Examiner issue an Intermediate Report began in late 1939. Originally, there was no intermediate step between the end of the hearing and the issuance of a final decision. Between the original procedure and the 1939 Intermediate Report procedure, the Board used the Proposed Findings of Fact, Conclusions of Law and Order procedure. This procedure is now rarely used, except when a Board member presides as Trial Examiner.

thereof to which exceptions have not been taken, and the Board may proceed to issue its Final Decision and Order.

Whether or not exceptions are filed, the Board may redetermine the whole or any part of the Recommended or Proposed Findings, Conclusions or Order.

Section 63. Waiver of Intermediate Report and Proposed Findings: If all parties and Board's Attorney, the Trial Examiner consenting, shall waive the issuance of the Trial Examiner's Intermediate Report, or Proposed Findings of Fact, Conclusions of Law and Order, the Board may proceed on the entire record before it to issue its Final Decision and Order.

If all parties to the proceeding and Board's Attorney shall waive the issuance of any part of the Trial Examiner's Intermediate Report, the Trial Examiner consenting, or of the Proposed Findings of Fact, Conclusions of Law and Order, the Trial Examiner or the Board may issue such portions thereof as have not been waived, and all proceedings may be taken thereafter as though a full Intermediate Report or full Proposed Findings, Conclusions and Order had been issued under Section 60 or Section 61 hereof.

Section 64. Record in Proceedings Under Section 706:

(a) The record in proceedings under Section 706 shall consist of the charge or amended charge, the pleadings, notices of hearing, notices of argument, motions, orders, stipulations, stenographic minutes, exhibits, depositions, Trial Examiner's Intermediate Report (or the Board's Proposed Findings of Fact, Conclusions of Law and Order), exceptions and the Final Decision and Order.

(b) If a proceeding under Section 706 is predicated in whole or in part upon a prior proceeding under Section 705, the record of such prior proceeding shall be deemed a part of the record in the proceeding under Section 706 for all purposes.

Section 65. Record in Proceedings Under Section 705: The record in proceedings under Section 705 shall consist of the petition or amended petition, notices of hearing, notices of argument, motions, orders, stipulations, stenographic minutes, exhibits, depositions, Decision and Direction of Election, Report on Secret Ballot, objections thereto, and Certification Dismissal or Decision.

Section 66. Public Record: The record as defined in Sections 64 and 65 shall constitute the public record of the case and shall be made available for inspection or copying under such conditions as the Board may prescribe.

Practice Before the Board

Section 67. Practice Before the Board: Any person who has been employed by the Board shall not be permitted to appear as attorney or representative for any party until the expiration of six (6) months from the termination of his employment with the Board, nor shall he at any time be permitted to appear in any case which was pending before the Board during the period of his employment.[35]

---

[35]Sections 62–67 were added in 1940.

APPENDIX D

Article V—Designation, Powers and Duties of Board's Agents

Section 68. Trial Examiners; Powers and Duties: All Trial Examiners now or hereafter in the employ of the Board, in addition to all powers hereinabove conferred upon them, are hereby designated by the Board as its agents:

(a) To conduct and be in full charge and control of any and all hearings;

(b) In connection with such hearings, to have access to and the right to copy evidence, to administer oaths and affirmations, to examine witnesses, to receive evidence, and in connection therewith, to do any and all things necessary and proper to effectuate the policies of the Act and these Rules and Regulations.

Section 69. Attorneys; Powers and Duties: All attorneys now or hereafter in the employ of the Board, in addition to all powers hereinabove conferred upon them, are hereby designated by the Board as its agents:

(a) To conduct any inquiry necessary to the functions of the Board;

(b) To investigate concerning the representation of employees;

(c) To represent the Board at hearings;

(d) To appear for and represent the Board in any case in Court;

(e) To have access to and the right to copy evidence, to apply to the Board for subpoenas and subpoenas dues tecum, to administer oaths and affirmations and to examine witnesses;

(f) To engage in any effort to obtain voluntary adjustments and compliance with the terms and provisions of the Act, following the authorization of a complaint.[36]

Section 70. Labor Relations Examiners and Labor Elections Supervisor; Powers and Duties: All Labor Relations Examiners and the Labor Elections Supervisor now or hereafter in the employ of the Board, in addition to all powers hereinabove conferred upon them, are hereby designated by the Board as its agents:

(a) To conduct any inquiry necessary to the functions of the Board;

(b) To investigate concerning representation of employees;

(c) To have access to and the right to copy evidence, to apply to the Board for subpoenas and subpoenas duces tecum, to administer oaths and affirmations and to examine witnesses;

(d) To engage in any effort to obtain voluntary adjustments and compliance with the terms and provisions of the Act.[37]

Section 71. General: The foregoing designations are not to be construed to limit the power of the Board to make such special designations of agents as may be necessary to effectuate the purposes of the Act, nor shall the foregoing designations be construed as limiting the power of the Board at any time to confer upon its agent or agents additional duties.

---

[36]Part (f) of this section was added in 1943. This addition corresponds to the 1940 amendment to Section 702(8) of the New York State Labor Relations Act. The addition simply put into the record a standard Board procedure.

[37]See n. 36 *supra.*

207

Article VI—Service of Papers

Section 72. Method; Proof: Complaints, orders and other process and papers of the Board, its Members, agent or agency, may be served personally, by registered mail, by telegraph, or by leaving a copy at the principal office or place of business of the person to be served. The verified return by the server, setting forth the manner of such service, or the return post-office receipt or telegraph receipt therefor, when registered and mailed or telegraphed as aforesaid, shall constitute proof of service.

Section 73. Service by a Party: Service of papers by a party may be made personally or by mail. When service is made by mail, a return post-office receipt, or affidavit of service by mail, shall constitute proof of service.

Section 74. Service upon Attorney: If a party appears by attorney, all papers other than the complaint and notice of original hearing may be served as hereinabove provided upon such attorney, with the same force and effect as though served upon the party.[38]

Article VII—Certification and Signature of Documents

Section 75. Executive Secretary; Certification of Papers; Notices and Reports: The Executive Secretary of the Board, or, in the event of his absence or disability, the Acting Executive Secretary of the Board, or such other person as may be designated, is authorized to certify copies of all papers and documents which are a part of any of the files or records of the Board, to sign and issue all notices or reports of the Board and to assign any Trial Examiner previously designated by the Board.

Section 76. Associate General Counsel; Issuance of Complaints: The Associate General Counsel of the Board, or, in the event of his absence or disability, the Acting Associate General Counsel of the Board, or such other person as may be designated, is authorized to sign and issue all complaints and notices of hearing in connection therewith authorized to be issued by the Board.

Article VIII—Construction, Amendment and Application of Rules

Section 77. Construction: These Rules and Regulations shall be liberally construed and shall not be deemed to limit the powers conferred on the Board by the Act.

Section 78. Amendments: Any Rule or Regulation may be amended or rescinded by the Board at any time, but such amendment or rescission shall not be effective until published by filing with the Secretary of State.

Section 79. Application: These Rules and Regulations and any Amendments thereto shall govern all proceedings filed with the Board on and after May 1, 1951. They shall also govern all proceedings then pending, except to the extent that in the judgment of the Board their application to such pending proceedings would not be feasible or would work injustice, in which event the General Rules and Regulations effective on February 1, 1943, as amended, shall apply.

---

[38]Added in 1943.

208

Table of Cases

Index

Discriminatory discharge, 4, 5, 8, 36, 52, 60–63 *passim,* 124–125
Dismissal of complaint, *see* Complaint
Dismissal of petition, *see* Petitions, Representation cases
Doyle-Newstein bill, *see* New York State Labor Relations Act
Dues, *see* Union dues
"Dummy unions," *see* "Paper locals"

E

Economic strike, *see* Strike
Elections, consent, 14, 72, 87–90, 90n; multiple union, 102; notice of, 73–74, 100–101, 102, 103; pre-hearing, 97n; postelection objections, 105–108; representation, 12, 13, 14, 19, 73–74, 86, 97, 99–108, 112, 122, 127, 133, 147–148; runoff, 12–13, 105, 105n; secret ballot, 83, 85–86, 87, 101, 103, 106–107, 152; voting, 11–12, 73–74
Election petition, 96
Employees, definition of, 128–129
Employer-employee relationships, 85, 130; family relationship, 85, 128–129
Enforcement proceedings, 118–120
"Exploratory expedition," 69

F

Federal Constitution, Supremacy and Commerce clauses, 129, 131
Federal Railway Labor Act, 128, 129
Final order, 115, 116, 120
Final report, 42

G

General Rules and Regulations, Section 8, 81; Section 9, 82; Section 11, 81; Section 12, 82; Section 17, 105–107; Section 19, 112; Section 24, 36–37; Section 25, 36, 43; Section 29, 48; Section 34, 49; Section 38, 65–66; Section 39, 66; Section 41, 67; Section 43, 68–69; Section 44, 69; Section 46, 69, 70–71; Section 49, 51–52, 66; Section 52, 68; Section 53, 54; Section 55, 98; Section 56, 68; Section 59, 41–42; Section 60, 56
Geographic regions, 24–25; Central Region (Albany), 23, 25, 29, 42, 43, 72, 145; Southern Office (New York City), 23, 25, 42; Western Office (Buffalo), 23, 25, 29, 42, 43, 72, 145
Grievances, discussion of, 7, 8

214

H

Hearing, conduct of, 52–53, 66; formal, 29, 50–54, 73, 91; motions, 65–67; "notice of hearing," 29, 46, 73, 93–95; posthearing objections, 52, 66; *see also* Posthearing procedure; reopening of, 65; unfair labor practice, 96; witnesses, 68–71
Hepton, Estelle, 128n
Hospital, nonprofit making, 128, 128n

I

"Independent" unions, *see* Labor organizations
Industrial Commissioner, *see* Personnel
Industrial relations, stability, 6–7, 111–112, 113, 114
Informal investigation, *see* Unfair Labor Practice case; *see also* Representation case
Interlocutory determination, 116, 120
"Intermediate Report," 29–30, 55–57, 61, 98, 161–168
Interstate commerce, *see* Jurisdiction
Intervening union, 86
Intervention, Application to intervene, 67, 67n

J

Judicial review, *see* courts
Jurisdiction, 21–22, 36n, 117, 121, 122, 127, 128–143, 148; advisory opinion procedure, 142; agreement of 1937, 130–131, 134; agreement of 1947, 135; cession of, 135–137; conflict, 129, 130; interstate, 33–36, 82n, 129, 130, 130n, 131, 136n, 137–142 *passim;* limitations, 128; N.L.R.B., 122, 128–143; "no man's land," 36, 134–135, 139–143, 148; of courts, 118; standards of 1950, 137–138; Taft-Hartley Act, 135–136; union, 81

K

Kramer, Board Chairman, 16–17, 17n, 18

L

Labor Elections Supervisor, 105
Labor-management relations, *see* Industrial relations
Labor-Management Relations Act, *see* Taft-Hartley Act
Labor-Management Reporting and Disclosure Act, *see* Landrum-Griffin Act
Labor organizations, 67–68n, 75, 77–78, 80, 83, 121–122; definition of, 16–17;